AVRO LANCASTER

Avro Lancaster

Ken Delve

The Crowood Press

First published in 1999 by
The Crowood Press Ltd
Ramsbury, Marlborough
Wiltshire SN8 2HR

British Library Cataloguing in Publication Data

A catalogue record for this book
is available from the British Library.

ISBN 1 86126 222 1

Frontispiece: With the war over, Lancaster bombers flew trips around Germany – known as 'Cook's Tours' – many were surprised at the level of devastation. Ken Delve Collection.

Designed by Sam Hemphill @ Focus Publishing, Sevenoaks, Kent

Printed and bound in Great Britain by Bookcraft Ltd, Midsomer Norton, Somerset.

Contents

Acknowledgements

A book of this nature owes a debt of thanks to a wide range of people and I duly acknowledge the help of all those ex-Lancaster men, aircrew and groundcrew, who have provided me with material. Extensive use has been made of official records and in this regard I am indebted to the staff of the Air Historical Branch (AHB) for their invaluable help and guidance. Much of the photographic material used in this book has come from my own archives, collected over many years from a variety of sources, but I have also received much help from Peter Green and Andy Thomas, as well as from the FlyPast archive.

My thanks also to those authors who have allowed me to use extracts from their published works. Thanks, too, to Luke for his help in typing up appendices and sorting out photographs.

Preface

The Avro Lancaster has gone down in aviation history as one of the truly great aircraft. The Lancaster joined RAF's Bomber Command in early 1942, at a critical period in the Second World War, and over the next two years it came to dominate Bomber Command with its superior performance and bomb-carrying capability. Bomber Command lost 3,500 Lancasters on operations; there were an average of seven crew in each aircraft, that is to say, a total of almost 25,000 aircrew, a high proportion of whom were killed.

This history aims to cover the Lancaster story in chronological order, with some aspects included in detailed appendices rather than in the main text. Where bomber numbers are given for raids, the total number of bombers is invariably followed by a figure stating the number of Lancasters on the raid. (Lancaster mission summaries are covered in Appendix II.) The statistics used for this are extracted from *Bomber Command War Diaries* by Martin Middlebrook and Chris Everitt (Viking, 1985, recently re-issued in paperback by Midland Counties). This volume remains one of the most valuable sources of data for the study of Bomber Command 1939-45.

Where raids appear to have been undertaken solely by Lancasters, they usually included a small number of Mosquitoes acting as target markers, although the latter are not included in the statistics.

TL D
TL E
TL R
TW870

CHAPTER ONE

Lancaster – The Operational Record

When war broke out, in September 1939, the RAF's offensive element, Bomber Command, was equipped with a variety of twin-engined aircraft, most of which carried an average 4,000lb bomb load and were designed to attack their targets in daylight. Within a matter of months, the vulnerability of these bombers to enemy fighters meant that Bomber Command had to transfer the bulk of its operations to the cover of night. Over the next two years, the Command waged its war, with limited success, against German industrial cities.

While types such as the Wellington, Hampden, Stirling and Halifax played significant parts in the bomber war, it was the Avro Lancaster that, from late 1942, came to embody the offensive striking power of RAF Bomber Command. Ken Delve Collection

Early 1942 brought two significant developments – the entry into service of the Avro Lancaster and the appointment of Arthur Harris as Commander-in-Chief of Bomber Command. Significant expansion plans, and the adoption of four-engined types such as the Lancaster, Halifax and Stirling, were already in place when Harris took over in February; Bomber Command strength stood at 54 squadrons with a bomb lift of 510 tons. By the end of the war the position had dramatically altered; strength stood at 105 squadrons with a dramatic increase in bomb lift to 5,264 tons. Of the operational squadrons, 62 were equipped with Lancasters. While the Vickers Wellington had shouldered the bulk of the campaign for the first three years, and other types such as the Halifax had key roles to play, it was the Lancaster that came to symbolize the striking power of Bomber Command.

In his post-war 'Despatch on War Operations', Sir Arthur Harris paid tribute to the Lancaster:

> The Lancaster... coming into operation for the first time on March 10/11, 1942, soon proved immensely superior to all other types in the Command. The advantage which it enjoyed in speed, height and range enabled it to attack with success targets which other types could attempt only with serious risk or even certainty of heavy casualties. Their high performance was a tremendous asset, but as yet their numbers were totally inadequate to deliver the concentrated attacks necessary to saturate defended objectives.

Bomber Command's pre-war strategy centred on daylight attacks against key German industrial targets as part of the Western Air (WA) plan. However, in the early months of the war, the bombers were restricted to attacks on shipping, as overland targets were prohibited. It was not until May 1940 that political authorization was given for attacks on targets in Germany, and by then the bombers had turned to the relative protection of night operations, having suffered prohibitive losses in

The Lancaster prototype, BT308, first flew in January 1941; it is seen here during a visit to 44 Squadron at Waddington. Ken Delve Collection

late 1939. Wellingtons, Whitleys and Hampdens attacked a range of industrial targets, most of them located in built-up areas. One particular area to be targeted was the heavily industrialized Ruhr, and this was soon termed 'Happy Valley' by the aircrews, with typical irony. Despite early hopes that the bombers would be able to hit small targets by night, it was obvious by 1941 that a great deal of the effort was being wasted; all too few bombs were falling anywhere near their targets. Indeed, 1941 became something of a critical year for Bomber Command. Its detractors were determined to demonstrate that the considerable resources being put into the bomber war could be better used elsewhere.

The first of the four-engined 'heavies' entered service in 1941 – the Short Stirling flew its first operation on 10/11 February, when aircraft of 7 Squadron took part in an attack on oil storage tanks at Rotterdam. The following month, the Handley Page Halifax was employed by 35 Squadron in attacking Le Havre. Other than an increase in bomb load (an important factor), the new types brought few significant improvements as they were still constrained by the same accuracy problems. The Butt Report of 8 August 1941 contained the unwelcome statistic that only one in three bombers was dropping its load within 5 miles (8km) of the target.

Attempts were made to improve this situation, including the introduction of navigation aids such as TR1335-Gee (first used on 11/12 August), and the bomber offensive continued; regardless of its shortcomings, it was, essentially, the only means of striking at Germany. It must be remembered that 1941 was another year in which Britain suffered a number of military reverses and in which the homeland was still under attack from the Luftwaffe. The bomber offensive against German cities continued into 1942, in the face of increasing loss rates; by now, the Germans had developed a night-fighter defence that had not existed in early 1940.

Bomber Command also carried out attacks on other targets, and for much of 1941 a fair degree of its effort was expended in support of the campaign against German warships and U-boats.

As 1942 opened, the majority of Bomber Command's effort was still being expended on the anti-naval campaign, with attacks on U-boat construction sites. The Battle of the Atlantic was at a crucial phase and it was essential to the war effort that convoy losses be reduced. Part of the anti-naval campaign involved mine-laying and Bomber Command aircraft had begun to play an increasing part in this role. The planners termed it 'gardening', with aircraft planting 'vegetables' in designated areas. On 3/4 March, Bomber Command sent 235 aircraft to attack the Renault factory at Billancourt near Paris, employing a new flare-marking tactic in an effort to improve bombing accuracy. The attack was considered to be a major success.

The night of 3/4 March 1942 was also significant from the point of view of the story of the Avro Lancaster, as it marked the aircraft's first operational outing. Four aircraft from 44 Squadron were tasked to lay mines off the German coast. Each aircraft dropped four mines (two Assembly 22s, one Ordinary and one PDM) from 600ft – L7546 (Sqn Ldr Nettleton) and L7568 (Flt Lt Sandford) at 'Yams' (the Heligoland Approaches), and L7549 (W/O Crum) and L7547 (W/O Lamb) at 'Rosemary' (Heligoland). The mission was uneventful; the Squadron Operational Record Book (ORB) entry for Nettleton's aircraft simply recorded the following:

> Height 600ft, time 2020, heading 272 degrees magnetic, speed 180mph. Rear gunner saw splash of four mines dropping.

On 8 March, the Squadron sent seven aircraft to Lossiemouth to stand by for operations against German shipping, but nothing came of this.

Two days later, the Squadron sent two aircraft on the Lancaster's first bombing mission, as part of a force of 126 aircraft attacking Essen. The first of the Lancs over the target was L7536 (Fg Off Ball), at 2148 hours:

> Height 18,000ft, bombs 14 SBCs each 90x 4lbs, dropped in area believed to SE of blitz area. 16 bundles of Nickles G.1 dropped over target area. At this height not worried much by searchlights and flak activities, but on leaving target area flak very accurate both for height and direction.

The other aircraft on the raid – Wellingtons, Hampdens, Manchesters and Stirlings – had to struggle along at lower altitudes, attracting far more attention from the German flak gunners. This aspect of the superior performance of the Lancaster was viewed later as a significant factor in the lower loss rate of the type.

Despite a few early teething troubles, it was obvious that the Lancaster was a winner. By 1942, the aircraft was in mass production. FlyPast Collection

Powered by four Rolls-Royce Merlin XXs, the second prototype, DG595, flew in May 1941. FlyPast Collection

CHAPTER TWO

Origins and Development

The Manchester

The Avro Lancaster's origins can be traced back to the Avro submission to meet Specification P13/36 of September 1936, a design that incorporated a number of advanced features. Two prototypes of the Avro Type 679 (later named the Manchester) were ordered and the first of these twin-engined bombers, L7246, flew on 25 July 1939. It was evident that a number of significant development problems had to be overcome, particularly in relation to the aircraft's lateral stability and the heaviness of its controls, but the initial A&AEE reports were generally favourable, and the bomber's performance figures looked reasonable. However, by the time the production version was under way, the gross weight had risen and the performance figures were rather less impressive.

When the Avro 679 Manchester was put forward to meet Specification P13/36, its only competitor was the HP 56, which was subsequently abandoned in favour of the four-engined HP 57 (later to become the Halifax). For its day, the Manchester was of an advanced design and its aerodynamics and twin 1845hp Rolls-Royce Vulture engines promised much. Following Prototype L7246's first flight, on 25 July 1939, production began in the same month with an initial order for 200 aircraft.

The first operational unit to receive Manchesters, in early November 1940, was 207 Squadron, based at Waddington; the Squadron flew its first operational sorties with the type on 24/25 February, when six aircraft attacked shipping at Brest. Other squadrons soon re-equipped until, eventually, twelve squadrons (9, 44, 49, 50, 57, 61, 83, 97, 106, 207, 408 and 420) operated the type.

It is generally accepted that the Manchester was rushed into service before it was truly ready, and problems with the Vulture engines were the most serious failing. A detailed analysis of the Manchester is beyond the scope of this book, but reference to the aircraft and its poor operational record is very much part of the Lancaster story; indeed, some commentators have stated that if the Manchester had been even a partial success, then the Lancaster might never have been adopted. This, however, is an oversimplification of the situation. In fact, in 1941, a decision had been taken to make Bomber Command an all four-engined bomber force at the earliest opportunity; the twin-engined bombers, including the Manchester, were therefore already 'doomed'.

The Manchester was not the complete failure that many accounts have suggested; indeed, towards the end of its career, many of its engine problems had been overcome. Despite the early indications of problems with the type, Manchester squadrons continued to form as Bomber Command attempted to expand its striking power and to replace medium bombers with heavy bombers. Nevertheless, loss rates for the Manchester were soon giving cause for serious concern, as was its poor serviceability; there was little option, however, for the

Manchester L7247 still with the central fin – an attempt to overcome lateral stability problems. FlyPast Collection

An 83 Squadron Manchester (its nose art translates as 'All through the night') and crew; loss rates for the twin-engined Manchester began to give cause for concern within months of its introduction. Ken Delve Collection

Command and the type continued to enter service, even after the first Lancasters had appeared.

The comment made by Francis K. Mason in his book *The Avro Lancaster* (Aston, 1989) appropriately sums up the importance of the Manchester to the Lancaster story:

> As it was, the success of the Lancaster, almost from the moment it entered service, can certainly be attributed to a great extent to the perseverance and sacrifices made by those two indefatigable Manchester squadrons – 97 and 207.

A 'Four-Engined Manchester'

As early as June 1940, Roy Chadwick and the Avro team had been looking at other developments, including a four-engined version to be powered by a variety of engine options. Chadwick had despaired of a solution to the problems with the Vulture engines and was pressing for four Merlins for the 'new' bomber design. There is some confusion as to developments in the spring and early summer of 1940 in respect of Type 680 development; some commentators felt that progress on the project was accelerated following Air Ministry concern over the performance prospects of what, at the time, was seen as the main four-engined bomber – the Handley Page Halifax.

By February 1940, Avro had a draft proposal for their Type 680 and were holding informal discussions with the Air Ministry's Deputy Director of Scientific Research, William Farren. These talks revealed that Spec B1/39 would call for a four-engined bomber with a max all up weight (auw) of 50,000lb and a bomb load of 10,000lb – close to the figures that Chadwick and his team were proposing for their new bomber. When the spec was issued, in March, it called for a performance that included 2,500-mile (4,000-km) range with a 9,000lb bomb load, plus a defensive armament of four turrets armed with 20mm guns; this latter requirement is fascinating in view of the often heated debate in various Air Ministry circles regarding the pros and cons of 0.303in (and 0.5in) guns against 20mm guns. As will be seen later in this history, the armament debate was one that would surface at regular intervals (and Bomber Command ended the war still primarily equipped with 0.303in guns).

Avro put forward their Type 680/681/682 proposals in response to the specification. Although Handley Page put forward their HP60A and Bristol their Type 157 (prototypes of both were ordered, but later cancelled), the Avro proposal was well ahead of the field in that it was already quite close to the stated specification – and a great deal of work had already been done. Despite Air Ministry interest, progress was slow, as Avro were fully occupied with Manchester development and production. Chadwick was, however, convinced of the potential of the new type; estimates indicated 300mph (480kph) at 18,000ft, and an auw of 58,000lb (with up to six 2,000lb bombs).

According to some historians, the most effective prod to Avro in respect of accelerating work on the new bomber was the Ministry of Aircraft Production (MAP) statement that Avro and Metrovick should switch to Halifax production once the existing Manchester production was completed. This was not well received! Dobson suggested that the new four-engined variant already under development would be far more suitable, especially as it had 70 per cent commonality of components with the Manchester.

According to the Air Historical Branch's account of this period:

> It would be idle to pretend that the project met with any enthusiasm at MAP. The Manchester was thought to be incapable of further development, and Mr Dobson's and Mr Chadwick's optimistic promises were thought to be ill-founded. Above all, the redesigned Halifax showed such promise and was ably advertised by its makers, that another similar aircraft appeared unnecessary. In an official interview with Mr Dobson, Mr Hennesey who, under Lord Beaverbrook, took charge of new projects, went so far as to refuse Avro the raw materials necessary for the construction of the first prototype. According to Mr Dobson's recollection, Mr Hennesey's final reply was "go and dig for it". And dig they did. Out of the crevices and interstices of the distributive system for light alloys they scrapped enough material to build a prototype. At the same time the inside views of the Ministry were neither so final nor so unanimous as Mr Henessey's official attitude implied.

In July 1940, the Air Ministry had agreed to the production of two prototypes of what was still referred to as the 'four-engined Manchester'; some 70 per cent of the airframe components would be adopted from the earlier aircraft – for example, the same basic 95ft wing would be used, but with wing-tip extensions. By September, the Merlin XX was considered the most appropriate engine and the type was considered likely to produce performance figures similar to those of the Handley Page Halifax.

In a note dated 4 September, William Farren had informed the Director of Technical Services that:

> The broad consensus is that the aeroplane should form a satisfactory development from the Manchester I, and that it should be put into production in order to utilize the tools and organization in being for the production of the Manchester I. This is the best way of obtaining the greatest number of aeroplanes in a given time, since it is the only way of using the complete Manchester production organization, which will otherwise have to be turned over to a different aeroplane when production of Vulture engines ceases. ...a full investigation has now been made of the prospects of the Manchester with four Merlin XXs. The position is briefly as follows. The wing span can be increased to about 100ft and the aircraft then becomes very similar to a Halifax. The maximum weight which the structure seems likely to be able to carry is about 50,000lbs... the bomb load:range capacity at a cruising speed of about 295mph, which is roughly the same as that of the Halifax with the Merlin Xs, will be nearly up to that of the Halifax (e.g., 6,000lbs at 1,500 miles), and about 1,500lb better than the Manchester as it stands.
>
> The Merlin XXs will, of course, improve the performance at altitude, making it possible to cruise at considerably higher speeds with some reduction in range. We may have to make some alterations to the tail, on account of the bigger wings, but I doubt it. I think we can get away with what we have here. I suggest that this justifies carrying on with the prototypes on which Avro have already done a good deal of work. I should like your agreement so that I may put in [an] order.

A handwritten note was added to the memo: 'Please initiate contract action for one prototype.'

The main cause of problems with the Manchester was its Vulture engines, which were underpowered and unreliable; however, the basic airframe showed promise. Ken Delve Collection

The Type 683 Manchester III was progressing slowly but at least it was progressing; engine runs on BT308 took place at the end of December, and the aircraft made its first flight on 9 January 1941, with Capt H. A. Brown at the controls. The prototype made nine flights over a two-week period and overall Brown was impressed with the aircraft; his sole major criticism concerned the degree of lateral instability.

A new tail unit – of 39ft span and somewhat taller, giving a greater area – was already under development. The Manchester had also had problems with lateral stability and had undergone various tail-unit modifications, and much of this experience was fed through to the new project.

By the time the prototype had undergone its initial Boscombe Down trials, still with the original tail design, the type had been named 'Lancaster', and a production contract for 200 aircraft had been issued.

The first operational unit was 44 Squadron at Waddington, the unit flying its first mission, a mine-laying sortie, on March 3/4, 1942; Lancaster I R5556 later went to 1661 Conversion Unit. Ken Delve Collection

BT308 had arrived at Boscombe Down on 27 January and, after a period of intensive evaluation, a generally favourable report was issued. In late February, BT308 was fitted with four Merlin XXs and a new tail unit before returning to Boscombe Down for performance trials. The result was an impressive 310 TAS (True Air Speed) at 21,000ft using [3,0000 rpm] (with FS and +8.5 boost). Over the next few months, the aircraft was at Boscombe a number of times for various handling and evaluation trials.

The second prototype, DG595, flew on 13 May; this aircraft was to the 60,000lb auw production standard and incorporated a number of changes effected in the light of experience gained with the first aircraft. The third, and final, prototype, DT810, was given four Bristol Hercules VI engines, as the Lancaster II prototype, and flew on 26 November 1941. The fitting of the Hercules engine was primarily as an 'insurance' against possible problems with the availability of Merlins. The first production Lancaster, R7527, flew on 31 October at Woodford; in the previous month, BT308 had gone to Waddington,

Prototype DG595 shows the basic lines of the Lancaster, which, in essence, changed little throughout the production run; note the early variant mid-upper turret and the ventral position. FlyPast Collection

The long slender fuselage of the Lancaster was to prove incredibly adaptable, considering the bomb load that it was able to carry. Ken Delve Collection

Fuel capacity

One of the important characteristics of the 'heavies' was their range. The Lancaster was given a high fuel capacity with six primary fuel tanks. There were three in each wing: No. 1 (inner, between the fuselage and the inner engines), No. 2 (centre, between the engines) and No. 3 (outer, outboard of the outer engine). The capacities were as follows:

No. 1: 580 gallons each, total 1160
No. 2: 383 gallons each, total 766
No. 3: 114 gallons each, total 228
Total: 2,154 gallons

attached for initial training purposes to the first Lancaster unit – 44 Squadron, commanded by Wg Cdr Learoyd VC.

Provision was also made on some aircraft for one or two 400-gallon fuel tanks in the bomb bay, which were connected to feed either or both No. 1 tanks. The Pilot's Notes state that 'when the maximum bomb load is carried, the No. 2 tanks should be filled first, and the remainder of the fuel put in the No. 1 tanks. This is on account of strength considerations of the aircraft structure.' The Pilot's Notes for the main Lancaster variants (I, III, X) also explain the operation of the fuel system, as follows:

Fuel cocks

The pilot controls four master engine cocks. On Lancaster I aircraft, the master engine cocks also control the slow-running cut-outs. The flight engineer controls two tank selector cocks which select No. 1 or No. 2 tank on each side. (No. 3 tank replenishes No. 2). A cross-feed cock (marked *Balance cock*) connects the port and starboard supply systems, and is on the floor just forward of the front spar, with the handle visible through a hole in the spar cover.

When the 400-gallon tanks are fitted in the bomb cells they each have an *On-Off* cock situated behind the front spar in the centre of the fuselage.

Vapour vent system

(Lancaster III and X aircraft only) – A vent pipe from each carburettor is connected to the No. 2 tank on the same side of the aircraft, and allows vapour and a small quantity of fuel to return to the tank. This carburettor is designed to work full of fuel, and it therefore requires the vent to carry away any petrol vapour and dissolved air. It also assists in re-establishing the flow of fuel to the carburettors when the pipe-lines and pump have been run dry due to a tank emptying.

Electric fuel booster pumps

(i) Originally, on Lancaster I aircraft, immersed pumps were fitted in all tanks; Mod.594 (temporary) removed the immersed pumps from No.1 tanks and fitted stack pipes in their places.

A later Mod.512 put back the immersed pumps in No.1 and No. 2 tanks and incorporated suction by-pass lines to allow fuel to be drawn from the tanks when the pumps are not in use. In aircraft incorporating Mod.539, including all Lancaster III aircraft, a Pulsometer FB Mk. I pump is fitted in each tank and by-pass lines are incorporated at No. 1 and No. 2 tanks. On Lancaster X aircraft, Thomson pumps, similar to the Pulsometer pumps, and by-pass lines are fitted.

No. 3 tank is used to replenish No. 2 tank by switching on the No. 3 tank pump. When the 400-gallon tanks are fitted in the bomb cells they each have a similar pump fitted to transfer their contents to the No. 1 tanks.

(ii) The main use of the electric fuel pumps in No. 1 and No. 2 tanks is to maintain fuel pressure at altitudes of approximately 17,000 ft. and over in temperate climates, but they are also used for raising the fuel pressure before starting and to assist in re-starting an engine during flight. If one engine fails during take-off and the electric fuel pump is not *on*, air may be drawn back into the main fuel system before the master engine cock of the failed engine can be closed, thus causing the failure of the other engine on the same side; therefore at take-off the pumps in Nos. 1 and 2 tanks must be switched on; this is also a precaution against fuel failure during take-off as an immediate supply is available by changing over the tank selector cock. The pump in each tank in use should also be switched on at any time when a drop in fuel pressure is indicated or when it is necessary to run all engines from one tank by opening the cross-feed cock.

Fuel contents gauges

On Lancasters I and III, the switch on the flight engineer's panel must be set *on* before the fuel contents gauges will indicate. On Lancaster X there is no fuel contents gauge switch; the gauges will indicate whenever electrical power is available.

Fuel pressure indicators

Fuel pressure warning lights show when the fuel pressure at the carburettor falls below 6lb./sq.in. on Lancaster I aircraft, and 10lb./sq.in. on Lancaster III aircraft. They are switched off by the fuel contents gauges switch, and this switch must therefore, always be on in flight. On Lancaster X, fuel pressure gauges are fitted on the flight engineer's panel. They will indicate whenever battery power is available.'

The fuel system proved to be very reliable and there are few recorded instances of major problems – other than the danger of fuel tanks catching fire when hit by flak or cannon shells, with resultant danger to the wing main spar.

Air Publication 2026A gives the following handling details for the fuel system:

Management of fuel system

(i) Testing electric fuel booster pumps: Before starting the engines each booster pump should be tested by ammeter (most aircraft have a permanent ammeter fitted on the flight engineer's panel while some early aircraft may have an ammeter test socket into which the ammeter must

Although NX612 was a late production Mk VII, the basic lines of the aircraft are the same as those of the main Mk I and MK III series. Ken Delve Collection

be plugged); to do this, the switch for each pump should in turn be set to the up (test) position, after ensuring that the idle cut-off switches are in the *Idle Cut-Off* position and air pressure is greater than 130lb./sq.in. (on Lancaster III and X aircraft); the ammeter reading should be perfectly steady and should be between 4 and 7 amps for a Pulsometer FB Mark I pump, between 3 and 5 amps for a Thomson pump, or between 2 and 4 amps for an immersed pump. Aircraft with Pulsometer pumps may be recognized by the small blisters on the underside of the wings.

(ii) Use of tanks:

(a) Starting, warm-up and take-off – No. 2 tanks should be used first because the carburettor vents return to these tanks, also because the contents of No. 1 tanks only can be jettisoned.

The electric fuel booster pumps in Nos. 1 and 2 tanks must be switched on for take-off, so that if for any reason the fuel supply from No. 2 tanks should fail, fuel pressure will be available immediately on turning the tank selectors to No. 1 tanks.

(b) In flight: After climbing to 2,000 feet, switch off booster pumps. Continue running on No. 2 tanks until 200 gallons remains in each, then change over to No. 1 tanks. Switch on No. 3 booster pumps to transfer their fuel to No. 2 tanks. Switch off the pumps when No. 3 tanks are empty. If overload fuel tanks are carried, continue to fly on No.1 tanks until enough fuel has been used from them to enable the contents of the fuselage tanks to be transferred to them. Then change over to No.2 tanks; turn on both long range fuel cocks (behind front spar) and switch on overload tank pump switches and fuel contents gauge. Transfer of fuel from long range tanks takes approximately 1 hour. Watch No. 1 fuel contents gauges and turn off each long range cock as soon as its respective No.1 tank is filled. Turn off pumps when both No. 1 tanks are filled.

When over enemy territory, keep contents of Nos. 1 and 2 tanks approximately the same by running on each alternately for about half-an-hour.

(iii) Use of cross-feed cock: The cock should be closed at all times, unless it is necessary in an emergency to feed fuel from the tanks in one wing to the engines in the other wing. If the cross-feed cock is open for this purpose, only one tank should be turned on to feed all working engines, and the pump in this tank should be switched on.

(iv) Changing fuel tanks on Lancaster III and X aircraft: If the engine cuts owing to exhaustion of fuel in one tank, back-firing may occur on turning on to another tank. For when the tank empties, the fuel pressure drops, and when the pressure falls to 4lb./sq.in. fuel injection ceases. When the new tank is turned on, the carburettor restarts and delivers the fuel already in it, but this supply is followed by vapour from the fuel pipe-lines, causing weak mixture and back-firing until fuel is delivered from the new tank.

When an engine cuts due to exhaustion of one tank:

(a) Close the throttle and change over to another tank.

(b) Idle the engine till it runs smoothly and open up slowly.

(c) The use of the booster pump in the tank turned on will help to restart the engine.

Lancasters of 207 Squadron, the unit re-equipped from Manchesters in March 1942 at Bottesford. Ken Delve Collection

The First Lancaster Squadron

Lancaster BT308 arrived at Waddington on 15 September to act as a crew trainer for 44 Squadron. The Squadron had been operating Hampdens since February 1939 and had taken part in a wide range of Bomber Command operations in the first three years of the war. Wg Cdr R. A. B. Learoyd VC was the first pilot to convert to the type, followed by Sqn Ldr John Nettleton, one of the Flight Commanders. The Squadron was instructed to have eight crews operational by 31 January 1942, even though the first three aircraft did not arrive until late December 1941. Training sorties were flown with a weapon load of four mines but in January the Squadron was also called on to help convert crews of 97 Squadron at Coningsby. (BT308 had flown to Coningsby on 10 January and was soon joined by a number of production aircraft.)

Once the initial missions had been flown without any real problems, 44 Squadron became a fully active part of Main Force, and other squadrons re-equipped. The second Lancaster unit, 97 Squadron, received its first aircraft on 14 January, and on the same day the two Flight Commanders flew dual instruction sorties. Further aircraft were collected from Woodford over the next few weeks, and by mid-March the Squadron had 16 Lancasters on strength. On 2 February, they had formed a Conversion Flight, with responsibility to convert crews for 97 and 106 Squadrons, using two Lancasters and two dual-control Manchesters. Operating from Woodhall Spa, 97 Squadron flew their first Lancaster operation on 20 March – a mine-laying sortie by six aircraft, five of which were successful, laying 30 mines in the Nectarine (Frisian Islands) areas. W/O Harrison (R5490) crash-landed at Abingdon and Fg Off Rodley (L7570) clipped a rooftop in Boston with his wing tip and had to crash-land at Frieston.

The introduction of the Lancaster was not free from problems. The minutes of the Air Council Meeting for 21 January 1942 stated the following:

> An enquiry by AMSO as to the trouble with the Lancaster; AM Linnell stated that there had been skin wrinkling trouble in the main planes. It was not a serious defect likely to lead to the collapse of the plane. The modifications, which involved removing the outboard engines, were now being done before the aircraft went to the squadrons. The flow to the squadrons would be delayed for 14 days. Modification retrospectively and on the line would be completed by the middle of March.

The 97 Squadron ORB for March recorded a signal from Group to the effect that:

> Lancasters are to be inspected for failure of flush rivets attaching wing-tip skin to rib attachment to mainplane, and wrinkling of skin on top surfaces. Aircraft defective are to be grounded, those not defective my be flown for practice only, with light load inboard tanks, remainder of tanks empty.

The Bomber Command ORB also recorded the problem on 29 March:

> The wing-tip mod has now been approved and ten Lancasters are expected to be ready for operations by April 3. Thereafter, 20 per week will be modified. At the same time, 120 engines will have to be changed on account of defective clutch mechanisms of the two-speed blower. The two jobs will be co-ordinated so that the period

Based at Skellingthorpe, 50 Squadron was another ex-Manchester unit, re-equipping in mid-1942; R5689 was destroyed on 19 September 1942. Ken Delve Collection

during which the aircraft will be out of action will be reduced to a minimum.

However, two days later, the ORB stated:

One of the modified Lancasters has now been tested, but wing tip trouble still persists. It would appear that a further modification will be necessary.

No further mention is made of this problem.

The First Raids

Targets in the industrial Ruhr – including complexes such as the Krupps works at Essen – had been high on Bomber Command's target list since 1940, although, for a variety of reasons, little damage had been inflicted. The major problem with the bombing was accuracy, and in this respect the advent of the Lancaster made no real difference to Bomber Command's efforts.

Attempts were made to improve navigation and bombing accuracy through the introduction of electronic aids such as Gee. The concept of TR.1335 (Gee) was simple: the aircraft received signals from a number of ground stations on a cathode ray tube; these gave, in effect, a grid of lines and, thus, a fix of the aircraft's position. Initial trials were flown by 1418 Flight, and operational trials by the Wellingtons of 115 Squadron in July 1941. By August 1942, the Germans were jamming Gee signals, but the system still remained of great importance – if only to help the bombers find their airfields on the way home.

Essen remained the primary target during March 1942, and was attacked by the bombers a number of times. Although they were using the new Gee navigation/bombing aid in an attempt to improve accuracy, at this stage, they saw few positive results.

Lancasters took part in the Essen raid of 10/11 March; this was the first attack by the type on a land target in Germany, although there was only a 'token' contribution of two aircraft. The bulk of the bombers comprised Wellington, and this was to remain the case for at least another year. The first operational loss of a Lancaster occurred on 24/25 March, when an aircraft of 44 Squadron (F/Sgt Lyster Warren) failed to return from a mining sortie.

The next major attack on Essen was on 25/26 March. This time, seven Lancasters (out of 254 bombers) took part. The bombers were back over Essen the following night but the Lancs were not involved.

March was also notable for two other features. First, certain bomber types were facing increasing loss rates. (The Manchester had a particularly bad period, losing, for example, five out of twenty aircraft that took part in the 26/27 March attack on Cologne. There was an increased urgency to replace such types as soon as possible and the logical choice was the Lancaster, with its already obvious superior all-round performance and capability.) Second, at the instigation of its new dynamic Commander-in-Chief, Air Marshal Arthur Harris, the Command used another new tactic when it launched a

June 1942 – the Merlins of a Lancaster are being serviced; all too often the contribution of the groundcrew is ignored in RAF histories. Ken Delve Collection

A well-known, but none the less effective, posed shot of the seven crewmen from a 44 Squadron Lancaster; five are expressing interest in the map, while the other two are idly chatting! Ken Delve Collection

massive incendiary raid against the city of Lübeck on the night of 28/29 March. This highly effective attack was reported in the British press as follows:

> Over 200 aircraft of Bomber Command tonight launched a shattering raid on the Baltic port of Lübeck, a shipbuilding and industrial centre. Hundreds of tons of incendiaries and high explosive were dropped, and about half of the built-up area has been destroyed by fire.

The damage was certainly extensive. There were no Lancasters among the 234 bombers that took part in the raid, but it is worthy of note in that the use of incendiaries became of increasing importance. The Lancaster dropped a massive tonnage of these weapons.

Conversion

At the end of March, the Command had 54 Lancasters on strength in three squadrons – 44, 97 and 207 Squadrons (the latter having finally given up its Manchesters in March).

Conversion to type was carried out by a Conversion Flight within each squadron; if more than one unit was co-located, as with 97 and 106 Squadrons, then the Conversion Flights were combined for convenience. This was fairly standard policy at this period of the Lancaster's introduction to service, the Conversion Flight usually having two or three aircraft on strength. However, the increasing pace of bomber re-equipment (not just Lancasters) meant that, from April onwards, the Conversion Flights were, in theory at least, included within the overall squadron strength.

Reorganization and New Tasks

Air Marshal Arthur Harris addressed a great many questions – from crew composition and training to tactics and reorganization – in his first months at the head of Bomber Command. He was also determined to 'fight his corner' in the arguments between Commands and Services, regarding the allocation of aircraft and other resources. Almost immediately, he was having to stand up to a Coastal Command/Admiralty plot to seize bomber squadrons for employment in the maritime war. Although he lost the argument, and had to give up six squadrons, he was able to protect what he saw as his most promising resource – his growing number of Lancaster squadrons. The Bomber Command spring campaign was to have two main tasks:

> 1. To destroy the enemy ports, ships and the mainspring of his great offensive against our ocean convoys.
>
> 2. To inflict the maximum damage on German and German-controlled war industries… in the course of such operations it is now part of our policy to create havoc to those German towns and cities which house the workers on whose efforts the Nazi war machine is dependent.

While aiming points would invariably be specific individual installations, it was now recognized that the inevitable damage to surrounding areas could also be useful, in that this was where the workers from the factories were often located. Arguably, this tactic was simply an excuse for what amounted to unrestricted 'terror bombing' of cities; in a controversial broadcast to the German people, Harris explained the Bomber Command plan in some detail, including the attacks on war workers, and stated that, town by town, city by city, Germany would be destroyed. By 1944, his words had come true.

Defects

The ORB for 44 Squadron contains the following interesting note for 1 April:

> Units must be warned that the Lancaster is intended only for manoeuvring appropriate to a heavy bomber; its ease of manoeuvring must not be abused.

This was an extract from an engineering signal issued in response to comments on aircraft skin wrinkling, following on from the problems originally noted in January. The modifications carried out in order to cure the skin wrinkling had obviously not been a complete success. The implications of the 44 Squadron note are that crews were being 'overly aggressive' in the way they manoeuvred the aircraft – this can be seen as a sure sign of the pilots' confidence in the Lancaster. The availability of Lancasters was under threat again by April:

> A defect in a bad batch of Crewe-built Merlin XX engines had necessitated the examination of 2,000 of this type in service. It was hoped to have 40 guaranteed engines available for the Lancasters by the end of the week. There had been trouble with the Lancaster last week; owing to weakness on the wing tips, all of this type had been grounded for operations but were continuing flying at light loads for training. The modification was not a long job. Two wing tips for 20 aircraft would be available by the end of the week. There would be a short hold-up of production of unmodified aircraft.

(Air Council Meeting 1 April 1942) (See also previous Bomber Command ORB comment).

CHAPTER THREE

Early Lancaster Raids

Armourers from 50 Squadron prepare 1,000lb bombs for another night raid. Ken Delve Collection

The Augsburg Raid

The Plan

As part of a series of attacks against specific high value industrial targets, a daring low-level daylight attack against the MAN diesel-engine factory at Augsburg in southern Germany was proposed. The Avro Lancaster was chosen to carry out this bold plan, which was to be the first of many special operations that helped to create the Lancaster legend.

The choice of squadrons was relatively simple, as only two units – 44 Squadron at Waddington and 97 Squadron at Woodhall Spa – were fully operational on the type. Sqn Ldr John Nettleton, a 23-year old South African, was chosen to lead the mission. The factory site was no bigger than a football pitch, so pinpoint accuracy would be essential; this was why they would need to attack in the daytime. The idea was to hit the target shortly before dusk, so that, although the attack would be made using daylight, the bombers could fly back over Germany under cover of night. The route was planned so that the two squadrons would fly 2 miles (3.5km) apart, in two sections of three.

The Raid

Just after 1500 hours on 17 April, the twelve Lancasters took off and set course. As they crossed the enemy coast, diversionary raids were made by fighter-escorted Bostons to try and keep the defences occupied. The ruse certainly brought the Luftwaffe fighters up, but it also almost led to disaster, as one group of fighters returning to base spotted the low-flying Lancasters and gave chase. In a 30-minute combat, all three Lancasters in Nettleton's second section were shot down. The fighters then turned on the lead section and the No 3 aircraft was soon downed; both the other aircraft were also hit, but the fighters then had to break off and return to

L7578 of 44 Squadron was used by Sqn Ldr John Nettleton and crew during training for the daring daylight raid on Augsburg. Ken Delve Collection

Lancasters of 83 Squadron taxi out; OL-H (R5620) was lost on the thousand-bomber raid against Bremen, on 25/26 June 1942. Ken Delve Collection

base. Nettleton and his sole remaining colleague pressed on to the target, where Fg Off Garwell was hit by flak and crashed just after releasing his bombs. Nettleton, the sole survivor from the 44 Squadron flight, made his lonely way home.

The six aircraft from 97 Squadron reached the target unscathed and made their attacks, each section losing one aircraft to the intense light flak. Seven of the twelve aircraft had been shot down and, of the 85 men who had taken part in the raid, 49 were missing; it was later revealed that 12 had survived to become PoWs.

A number of bombs hit the target and production was reduced for a few weeks, although the exact extent of the damage has never been determined. John Nettleton was awarded the Victoria Cross for his leadership and, despite the losses, the raid was considered a success.

Records

The 44 Squadron ORB entry against Nettleton's aircraft records reads as follows:

> Primary target attacked – MAN Diesel Engine Factory at Augsburg. Time 1955 hours. Height 50ft. Bombs 4x1,000lbs dropped in target area. Bombs seen to burst by rear gunner, and Captain on turning aircraft. Two of F/O Garwell's bombs seen to fall slightly south of target and two in other sections of area. Pilot states – set course for Selsey Bill at low level and whole trip done at low level until it became too dark on return. After setting course from Selsey Bill it was noticed that grooves appeared in the main-planes about 2 or 3 inches wide just outboard of the inboard engines on both sides. Ten minutes after crossing the coast [French] fighters were encountered and attacked the formation in the vicinity of Berney. On reaching the target light flak was intense and accurate, but heavy flak most inaccurate. F/O Garwell in 'A' of 44 Sqn

7 April 1942 – Sqn Ldr John Nettleton VC (No 44 Squadron)

John Dering Nettleton was commissioned into the RAF as a pilot in December 1938 and flew tours with 207 Squadron, 98 Squadron. and 185 Squadron. In June 1941, he was posted to No 44 Squadron at Waddington – the first Lancaster squadron – as a Flight Commander. His citation reads as follows:

Squadron Leader Nettleton was the leader of one of two formations of six Lancasters detailed to deliver a low-level attack in daylight on the diesel engine factory at Augsburg in southern Germany on April 17, 1942. The enterprise was daring, the target of high military importance. To reach it and get back, some 1,000 miles had to be flown over hostile territory. Soon after crossing into enemy territory his formation was engaged by 25 to 30 fighters. A running fight ensued. His rear guns were out of action. One by one the aircraft of his formation were shot down until in the end only his and one other remained. The fighters were shaken off but the target was still far distant. There was formidable resistance to be faced. With great spirit and almost defenceless, he held his two remaining aircraft on their perilous course and after a long and arduous flight, mostly at only 50 feet above the ground, he brought them to Augsburg. Here anti-aircraft fire of great intensity and accuracy was encountered. The two aircraft came low over the rooftops. Though fired at from point-blank range, they stayed the course to drop their bombs true on the target. The second aircraft, hit by flak, burst into flames and crash-landed. The leading aircraft, though riddled with holes, flew safely back to base, the only one of the six to return. Squadron Leader Nettleton, who has successfully undertaken many other hazardous operations, displayed unflinching determination as well as leadership and valour of the highest order.

Nettleton subsequently served with 1661 HCU before returning to 44 Squadron as its OC in January 1943; he failed to return from a raid against Turin on the night of 12/13 July, 1943.

> was hit and caught on fire. He made what appeared a successful forced landing and it is thought that all the crew would most probably have been safe. During the fighter attack the rear guns seized after firing approx 800 rounds. The return journey was uneventful. Three aircraft including 'H' (Capt. Sgt Rhodes) of 44 Sqn were seen to crash and another on fire. Time off 1512. Time in 0050 at Squires Gate.

There is a typical remark in the ORB records for 97 Squadron, relating to Fg Off Deverill's aircraft:

> Target attacked in formation, no cloud, from 400ft, bombs were dropped on target area. No 3 [W/O Mycock] seen to catch fire in the air and crash. Very heavy flak and light predicted flak and SA tracer. Aircraft caught fire on starboard side of fuselage and in bomb bay but was extinguished by efforts of W/Op and mid-upper gunner. Both mid and rear turrets unserviceable from target. Port outer engine was unserviceable and feathered on leaving target but restarted before reaching coast. Formated again on 'U' [Flt Lt Penman] for protection and landed base.

Harris later had this to say: 'The carefully planned attack on the MAN works at Augsburg in which seven out of 12 Lancasters were lost, showed the impracticability of daylight operations against Germany in anything but small numbers and on rare occasion, without long-range fighter cover.'

Despite this clear conclusion, further daylight attacks were mounted during the year.

The Augsburg Crews

44 Squadron
R5508 Sqn Ldr J Nettleton
L7536 Sgt G T Rhodes 7K
L7548 W/O H V Crum 7 pow
L7565 W/O J Beckett 7K
R5506 Flt Lt R R Sandford 7K
R5510 Fg Off R J Garwell 3K, 4 pow

97 Squadron
L7573 Sqn Ldr J S Sherwood 6K,1 pow
R5513 W/O T J Mycock 7K
R5537 Fg Off Hallows
R5488 Fg Off Rodley
R5496 Flt Lt Penman
L7575 Fg Off Deverill

Continuing Sorties

Losses in May

The Augsburg raid had cost 44 Squadron dearly and losses continued to mount in May; the unit lost four aircraft on the 8/9 May attack on Warnemunde, including the CO, Wg Cdr Lynch-Blosse. (All four aircraft were carrying eight crewmen and there was only one survivor, Sgt T Moore, who was taken prisoner.) Considering there were only 21 Lancasters (out of 193 bombers) on this attack, it was a horrendous loss.

Daylight raid assessment photo showing damage to the MAN diesel works. Andy Thomas Collection

Having operated Manchesters since November 1940, No 207 Squadron, based at Bottesford, received its first Lancasters in March 1942, flying its first operation on 24/25 April (Rostock). Lancaster R5499 (Sqn Ldr Beauchamp) of 207 Squadron was on its way to a mine-laying sortie in the Baltic on the night of 22/23 May when it ran into trouble (as reported in Bomber Command Quarterly Review No 1):

> Owing to the northern lights and bright moonlight it was necessary to fly as low as possible. Shortly after reaching Denmark the port engine seized up whilst at a very low altitude. In order to avoid dropping mines on Denmark, course was maintained until a suitable area was found where the mines could be jettisoned safely and the then the aircraft headed for base.
>
> Whilst over the sea the aircraft was caught in searchlights and subjected to considerable light flak. The windscreen had become badly obscured by oil which had leaked from the front turret, and in taking evasive action the aircraft hit the sea. It bounced three times and then ascended to about 50ft. There was very considerable vibration and the aircraft was turned towards land and preparations were made for ditching. Owing to excessive vibration it was necessary for the starboard inner airscrew to be feathered.
>
> It was then found that height could be maintained, and even gained, on the combination of starboard outer and port inner engines and course was set for base. Due to the skill of the pilot, the navigator, and wireless operator, the coast was crossed dead on track and base was eventually reached safely after crossing the North Sea at an average height of 700ft and at times in extremely poor weather conditions, with considerable interference from German stations to hinder the wireless operator. Owing to the fine airmanship and combined skill of these three members of the crew, this valuable aircraft was enabled to reach base under what at times seemed almost impossible conditions.

The aircraft landed at 0417.

(The *Bomber Command Quarterly Review*, published at the instigation of Harris, appeared from mid-1942 to the end of the war. It contained a summary of the Command's operations during the relevant period, along with various 'flying stories'. As a Secret publication, circulation was limited and few at squadron level were aware of its existence.)

Sqn Ldr John Nettleton (left) led the attack on the MAN diesel works at Augsburg. His was the only one of six aircraft from 44 Squadron to make it back (although the 96 Squadron section fared better). Nettleton is seen here, wearing his Victoria Cross ribbon, with the other 44 Squadron Flight Commander, Sqn Ldr R G Whitehead. (Andy Thomas Collection)

Success over Cologne

Bomber Command still had its detractors and Harris was determined to show what could be achieved if his Command was given adequate striking power. The Command continued to attack industrial cities in May, with mixed fortunes. Hamburg, Stuttgart, Warnemunde and Mannheim were all subjected to heavy raids; Stuttgart was hit on three consecutive nights between 5 May and 7 May (although the number of Lancasters taking part was quite small). The night of 30/31 May saw 1,047 bombers attack Cologne. The total losses of 41 aircraft included a single Lancaster (R5561 of 61 Squadron).

The gathering of this huge armada was a major achievement with operational squadrons and OTUs (Operational Training Units) pulling out all the stops to put up the maximum number of aircraft. No 5 Group contributed 73 Lancasters to the total effort. By late May, No 5 Group had seven Lancaster squadrons on strength (44, 61, 97 and 207 Squadrons being operational, with 50, 83 and 106 in the process of re-equipping). The Bomber Command records show 109 Squadron with a strength of one Lancaster among its primarily Wellington (soon to be Mosquito) composition; the Squadron was attached to No 26 (Signals) Group at this time.

The success of the raid on Cologne was Goering's first serious loss of prestige; in the eyes of Hitler, he, and the Luftwaffe, never fully recovered from this failure. Within a year, the Lancaster was to become, to the German leaders and people (and to the British public), the most significant Allied bomber, which came night after night, raining destruction on Germany. (As with the Spitfire/Hurricane comparison in the Battle of Britain, this was actually a rather inaccurate over-simplification, but it was very much the opinion at the time.)

A letter from the Air Ministry to HQ Bomber Command, dated 26 May, referred to production of 100 'armoured Lancaster aircraft'. Harris did not seem to be well disposed to this:

> [The production] is to begin about September 1942 and deliveries... may be expected in November. Since the armour would be unnecessary except during daylight operations, it is essential that the requirement should be cancelled, unless most of the armour could be attached and detached easily and quickly, in this case the idea would become more acceptable and even attractive. (Bomber Command ORB May 1942)

By bomber standards, the Lancaster had a fairly hefty self-defence capability with eight 0.303 in guns in three turrets; the subject of guns and turrets was to plague Bomber Command throughout the war. Andy Thomas Collection

June and July

Two more 'thousand-bomber' attacks were made: 956 aircraft (including 74 Lancasters) hit Essen on 1/2 June, and 1,067 aircraft (96 Lancasters) attacked Bremen on 25/26 June. For the Bremen raid, No 5 Group called for a maximum effort from its Lancaster units to try to achieve 100 aircraft. They actually achieved 96 Lancasters, and the only loss was 83 Squadron's R5620, which crashed at Winkesett with the loss of its seven crew. Industrial targets in the Ruhr, especially Essen, were the favoured targets in June. The worst night for the Lancs was 8/9 June over Essen, when three out of the thirteen aircraft, in a 170-bomber force, were lost.

It was impossible to keep the bomber concentration together any longer; it was having a detrimental effect on training, with the OTUs having to put a major effort into this operational scenario. The training system was in need of reorganization and expansion, as Bomber Command began to put in place its long-cherished plan for a front-line strength of 4,000 heavy bombers.

The combat record of the Command's aircraft was analysed by the Operational Research Section and by July concern was being expressed over both the Manchester and the Halifax; the latter was the subject of the following report, which looked at the experience levels of pilots in No 4 Group:

> There is no reasonable doubt that pilots on their first two operations have a casualty rate well above the average and that those who had survived 20 sorties had a rate well below the average. This must be aircraft-related as the Lancaster does not suffer the same problem. New pilots are a bit nervous of the aircraft, the aircraft having gained a bad name for instability in manoeuvres. It thus may happen that a new pilot is reluctant when he meets defences to manoeuvre his machine sufficiently in combat or that in a sudden emergency he puts the machine into an attitude in which he has had no previous experience of controlling it.

By implication, Lancaster pilots did not experience such reluctance and were quite happy to throw their aircraft around; indeed, in early 1942, they had been specifically warned against doing so.

On 20 July, the Bomber Development Unit formed at Gransden Lodge by expanding 1418 (b) Flight; the unit included two Lancasters, but this type was soon on the increase as the BDU took on more and more tasks.

The rear turret with its four guns was perhaps the most important – and vulnerable – position; it was cold, remote and uncomfortable, but the gunner had to stay alert, on the lookout for German fighters. Ken Delve Collection

An eighth Lancaster squadron formed in July, when 49 Squadron at Scampton received its first Lancs to replace its Manchesters. They flew their first op with the new type at the end of the month. Ten major raids were mounted in July, with an average of 300 bombers, of which the Lancaster contribution was around 10-20 per cent. Many of the targets were associated with the maritime war as part of the Battle of the Atlantic – the Danzig raid being a prime example. An attack on the Vulkan U-boat yard at Vegesack, 19/20 July, was foiled by cloud cover, the 99 bomber force (28 Lancasters) dropped on Gee but no damage was caused to the target. The heaviest raid of the month was the night of 31 July when 630 aircraft (113

A hive of activity, crews of 83 Squadron plan a sortie, June 1942. Ken Delve Collection

While night-fighters were the most serious threat to Bomber Command operations in terms of losses, a high proportion of aircraft were damaged by flak; this 429 Squadron Lanc had a 'significant hole' put in its starboard wing. Andy Thomas Collection

Lancasters – the first outing by over 100 Lancs) attacked Düsseldorf. Just under 500 bombers claimed to have attacked the target and the city suffered heavy damage. Bomber losses were also heavy, although only two Lancasters were lost.

Attacks on U-Boats

U-Boats at Sea

In June, the Lancaster had scored its first U-boat kill; a 44 Squadron detachment was operating from Nutts Corner and on 16 June Flt Lt T. Barlow's crew in L7568 …

The first operational sortie by this detachment was made on 12 June; the following day, R5603 flew a sortie of 11+ hours. The crew for each of these sorties included two aircrew from 220 Squadron, who were able to offer maritime expertise. This particular detachment returned to Waddington at the end of the month. In the middle of the following month, 61 Squadron sent a detachment to St Eval to fly maritime patrols over the Bay of Biscay. The first such patrol was flown on 17 July by four aircraft; the Lancaster was flown by Flt Lt P. R. Casement (R5724) and achieved immediate success, sinking a U-boat. The report stated that he:

> Sighted a U-boat on the surface and dropped stick of depth charges across it. Discovering that it was unable to dive he climbed to 700ft and dropped his anti-ship bombs from that height. Meanwhile, his gunners picked off several members of the U-boat crew who were trying to man the guns. The U-boat slid stern first under the water and confirmatory photographs of the success were obtained. (61 Squadron ORB)

The Coastal Command Review (No 4) gave details of this attack:

> The U-751 had been found and attacked by Whitley H/502, damage being caused by depth charges and bombs. As a result of H/502's excellent attack this U-boat was so disabled that F/61 was able to finish it off 2 hours later. This Lancaster flying at 1,500ft sighted an oil patch several hundred yards long and about 100 yards wide, 6-8 miles away. The pilot altered course to investigate and at 1422 hours a track was sighted about 4 miles off. A moment later the conning tower of a U-boat was seen moving very slowly. The pilot immediately climbed into cloud, altering course to get on the U-boat's starboard beam. The Lancaster broke cloud at 2,000ft a little later and found the U-boat one mile away on the port beam. The final run was made at an angle of 45 degrees to the U-boat's course and ten 250lb depth charges were released from 100ft (set at 25ft, spaced at 35ft). The stick straddled the U-boat half-way between the bows and the conning tower. When the foam and spray had settled, the U-boat had stopped so the Lancaster climbed to 800ft and approached to make a bombing attack… at 1430 hours two 210lb anti-submarine bombs were released… the U-boat was now very low in the water, the Lancaster circled and made a further attack with two bombs, which overshot by 20 yards. At 1444 hours the crew abandoned

ship; a minute later the bow lifted slightly and the U-boat foundered stern first.'

U-751 was Type VIIC, on its seventh war patrol.

The next sighting was not made until 10 August, when two submarines were seen and attacked, by Sgt Joslin and F/Sgt Dobson, but with no apparent result.

On 19 August, there was a series of attacks on a blockade runner off the Spanish coast. Seven sorties were flown and two aircraft were lost. According to 61 Squadron ORB, Sqn Ldr Weston (R5543)

Sighted a 12,000-ton vessel, the SS Corunna, just outside territorial waters. This fired on him; several photos taken later confirmed its identity as a blockade runner. Sqn Ldr Weston resumed search for the tanker, which was sighted shortly afterwards along the coast towards the west, making a level attack at 3,000ft, bombs were dropped but overshot the starboard quarter by 60 yards due to an inaccurate groundspeed setting on the bombsight.

Further sorties were made the following day, by 61 Squadron and 50 Squadron Lancasters, but with no success; R5543 failed to return. Over the period of the detachment, 61 Squadron flew 96 patrols, lost three aircraft and claimed one U-boat sunk; the detachment returned to Swinderby on 22 August.

It was rare for Lancasters to play such a direct part in the maritime war and, although such anti-submarine patrols were flown from time to time, the basic premise of Bomber Command was to attack the U-boats while they were under construction.

On 11 July, a force of 44 Lancasters was tasked to make a dusk attack on the U-boat construction works at Danzig. It would involve a 1,500-mile (2,400-km) round trip, the first half of which would be in daylight. Careful routing was planned to avoid known flak and fighter defences, the formation splitting up over Denmark in order to make individual approaches to the target, taking advantage of any cloud cover. Most aircraft carried either a single 4,000lb bomb or four 1,000lb bombs. It was a long, tiring sortie – some aircraft were airborne for over 11 hours – but the attack was fairly successful. Only two Lancasters were lost, both shot down by flak over the target.

Incendiaries being loaded into a Lancaster, June 1942; a high proportion of Bomber Command's tonnage comprised incendiary bombs. Ken Delve Collection

CHAPTER FOUR

Autumn 1942

Creation of the Pathfinder Force

The on-going problem of bombing accuracy had troubled bomber leaders for some time and, on 11 August 1942, the Pathfinder Force (PFF) was officially formed under the command of Gp Capt. Don Bennett. This was one of the key turning points in the development of Bomber Command's offensive capability. Discussions had been taking place since the spring regarding the creation of a specialist target-marking force. Air Marshal Arthur Harris was initially against the move, wary of creating an elite that would drain the bomber Groups of their most experienced leaders and crews. The need, however, to improve bombing accuracy, and the development of new navigation aids, finally prompted the move and the PFF was established.

The initial strength of five squadrons included two Lancaster units – 83 Squadron and 109 Squadron, the latter essentially a Mosquito unit, but with a number of Lancs for Oboe trials. The first PFF operation was flown on 18/19 August, with 31 Pathfinder aircraft as part of a 118-bomber force attacking Flensburg. It was not a good start; met winds were inaccurate and a number of the PFF aircraft bombed targets miles away from the right location, including Denmark. It was a similar story over Frankfurt on 24/25 August, although some damage was caused. Three nights later, the PFF led over 200 bombers to Kassel on a more successful attack, although only three Lancasters were involved. That same night, a small force of Lancasters from 106 Squadron undertook a special mission to Gdynia (*see below*).

New Tactics

The first significant success for the Pathfinders came on 28/29 August, when 159 bombers, led by PFF aircraft, attacked Nuremberg. The Pathfinders dropped a new marker, called 'Red Blob Fire', and the results seemed reasonable, although 23 bombers failed to return (including four Lancasters).

Bomber Command was slowly becoming more effective, but so were the German defences, especially the night-fighters. Loss rates were to cause concern for the rest of the year (although the Lancaster invariably suffered the lowest percentage losses on Main Force raids). Lancaster losses, however, were not light and some squadrons seemed to be suffering quite badly – 9 Squadron, for example, flew its first Lancaster mission on 10/11 September (Düsseldorf), having re-equipped in August from Wellingtons. Six aircraft were lost in the first four attacks.

Eighty-nine Lancasters had been part of the 479-bomber force on the Düsseldorf attack, the target being well marked by PFF aircraft with the first use of 'Pink Pansy' markers (modified 4,000lb bombs), leading to heavy damage in the city. Five Lancasters were among the 33 aircraft lost. The provision of special marking aids such as this and the development of more suitable tactics led to a rapid (but not universal) improvement in the overall effectiveness of both the PFF and Bomber Command. The Bremen attack of 4/5 September involved a new tactic using three 'waves' of Pathfinder aircraft: 'illuminators' to drop flares; 'visual markers' to drop coloured flares/markers (soon to be specially designed 'TI's, or 'target indicators'); and 'backers up', to drop incendiaries on the markers. The Main Force bombers would then bomb the incendiary/marker area.

The Command continued to develop new tactics to counter the defences; these tactics included a tight stream of aircraft to compress the time spent over the target, spoof or decoy raids to confuse and dilute the night-fighter effort, the adoption of electronic equipment to confuse the enemy, and at the same time the development of improved marking techniques. (The details of this are beyond the scope of this book, as indeed is an overall appreciation of Bomber Command's war. A good account is contained in Delve and Jacobs, *The Six Year Offensive* (Arms & Armour Press, 1992)).

Lancaster III prototype W4114 with Merlin 28 engines; over 3000 Lancaster IIIs were built. FlyPast Collection

Another daring daylight raid was mounted on 17 October 1942, when 94 Lancasters attacked the Schneider factory at Le Creusot; here, F/Sgt Smith's 97 Squadron aircraft is seen flying at a low level over France. Ken Delve Collection

Special Missions

The Lancaster force continued to be tasked with special missions in addition to its contribution to Main Force. In July, the Air Staff had tasked Bomber Command with attacking selected key armament works in France; the first attack on one of these targets was made on 17 October, when Lancasters of No 5 Group attacked the Schneider armament and locomotive works at Le Creusot. The Lancaster squadrons flew low-level practice sorties around the UK as part of the build-up for this hazardous mission. On the afternoon of 17 October, 94 Lancasters, led by Wg Cdr L. C. Slee of 49 Squadron, took off on Operation Robinson, flew at a low level over the Channel and sped on into France; one crew member recorded the scene:

> At the height we were flying we disturbed the cattle in the fields and numbers of them stampeded. At one place we saw oxen bolt, dragging their plough after them. Many of the French peasants in the fields waved to us as we swept over.

The bombers met no opposition, much to their surprise, and only two aircraft from the main force received light damage from flak in the target area. Of six Lancasters briefed to attack a nearby power station, one was shot down by flak. The only other casualty was the Flight Engineer on a 207 Squadron Lancaster that had turned back early; it had the misfortune to be pounced upon by three Ar 196s, two of which were shot down. A total of 140 tons of bombs had been dropped on the target, and damage was assessed as moderate.

The 97 Squadron ORB records the following message from Harris:

> Congratulations to all concerned in yesterday's brilliantly executed and highly successful operation. In less than five minutes, at the cost of one aircraft missing to at least two enemy aircraft destroyed, you have deprived the enemy of one of his major sources of armament supply. The timing and navigation to within one minute and less than one mile over a source of 2,000 miles and the landing of nearly 100 aircraft in darkness under bad weather conditions on strange bases without bending a rivet evidences a standard of airmanship throughout your command which has yet to be surpassed.

Less than a week later, No 5 Group's Lancasters mounted a daylight raid on Milan in northern Italy. The force of 88 bombers flew individual routes across France to a rendezvous point at Lake Annecy before crossing the Alps. Once again, the daring tactic paid off and only one aircraft was lost over the target. Two others fell over France.

This was followed by a series of night raids in the autumn on the Italian cites of Turin, Genoa and Milan.

Re-equipment

Lancaster deliveries were accelerating and more squadrons had re-equipped by late October, to bring the average availability of 'serviceable aircraft with crews' to around 200. No 5 Group's nine Lancaster squadrons were still the main element, although four of No 1 Group's squadrons were now in the process of working up with Lancasters.

This statistic is somewhat at variance, however, with that given by Harris in his 'Despatch', where he wrote:

The Le Creusot attack was a success; this post-raid photo shows damage to one of the main buildings. Ken Delve Collection

> When, in the autumn of 1942, I was urged to attack Berlin in strength, I had about 70 or 80 Lancasters available. This force was obviously quite insufficient for the purpose. Moreover, the Lancasters then suffered from fuel installation troubles which made them unable to exploit their full altitude. By New Year of 1943 those troubles had been overcome and between 150 and 200 Lancasters were available. Such a force would be able to drop some 400 or 500 tons of bombs on Berlin, and I judged that little would be gained by adding the 100-odd Halifaxes or 50-odd Stirlings then available since they would be forced to operate between 14-18,000ft. At that height they would attract the whole weight of the flak defences, and could in any case contribute a little over half of the load carried by a Lancaster at that range.

An informal pre-mission snap of all eight of the crew of DV267 – quite unlike the posed crew shot shown on page 21; Lancaster III DV267 of 101 Squadron (SR-K) went missing in February 1944. FlyPast Collection

The point about bomb load is a valid one; what was important was not numbers of bombers over a target, but the weight of bombs that they could deliver. Harris included statistics of bomb loads in his analysis, as follows:

Bomber Command bomb lift:

Feb 1942	510 tons
Jan 1943	1146 tons
Jan 1944	3047 tons
Jan 1945	5264 tons
Apr 1945	6236 tons

The reference to the fuel problem concerns an air lock in the fuel system that could cause failure of the fuel pumps at heights over 12,000ft. Modifications were in hand but it would be near the end of the year before these could be fully incorporated, although the problem does not, in fact, seem to have had much operational impact.

On 24 October 1942, Lancasters of No 5 Group attacked Milan in daylight, losing three aircraft; here, crews of 9 and 44 Squadrons at Waddington celebrate the success of the mission. Frank Walshaw

More Effective Weapons

Having started the war with a poor selection of fairly ineffectual bombs, Bomber Command had put a great deal of effort into acquiring more effective weapons – of both blast and incendiary varieties. The German bombing of the UK had provided evidence of the effectiveness of various types of bombs and this information was put to good use in developing more effective weapons for Bomber Command; one of the standard weapons was the 1,000lb GP (General Purpose) bomb, which had entered production at the end of 1939. However, one of the problems with such weapons was its limited blast effect, so attention was turned towards developing higher-capacity (HC) bombs, for blast rather than penetration. In September 1940, a request for a 4,000lb 'mine bomb' had been issued and, by mid-1941, trials on this weapon were under way at the A&AEE. In April, production orders were issued for the 4,000lb HC bomb. The 'cookie' was to become a standard weapon in the Bomber Command armoury.

The main weapons dropped by the Lancasters in 1942 comprised 500lb, 1,000lb and 4,000lb bombs plus a range of incendiary types. A number of 'special weapons' were also under development; one of these was the so-called Capital Ship Bomb (CSB). In the early months of 1942, attention was focused on developing a weapon capable of destroying the heavily armoured German Capital ships; even the 2,000lb AP (Armour Piercing) bombs were considered inadequate for this task. Lord Cherwell, Scientific Adviser to the War Cabinet, promoted development of a special bomb to be based on the 'shaped charge'

Loading a 4,000lb HC bomb ('cookie') in the bomb bay of a 90 Squadron aircraft; note positioning of the various bombs. Ken Delve Collection

principle. A number of different designs were under experiment in 1942 and by March the favoured designs were based upon the 'plastic nose' and 'disc ring' variants. Trials indicated that the bomb would need a diameter of 45in and would weigh up to 5,000lb – the Lancaster was the only aircraft capable of carrying such a weapon.

From April 1942, the new bomb was under trials at Shoeburyness and developments continued into 1943. Such was Bomber Command's desire to destroy German shipping that work on the bomb continued even though early indications were not promising; furthermore, it was decided to employ a specially trained squadron to undertake the first attacks using the new weapon. No 106 Squadron, now led by Wg Cdr Guy Gibson, one of Bomber Command's most experienced and determined pilots, was selected for this role. In August, Gibson was ordered to have six 'expert' crews ready by the end of the month to attack the shipyards at Gender (where the Battlecruiser Graf Spee was under construction). The mission was flown on 27/28 August. Poor weather over the target caused problems to the attackers and, although Gibson opted to stay over the target in the hope of some improvement, this was a forlorn hope. The bombs, a number of the 38in diameter trials weapons, were dropped, but without result.

Although development continued, there was little confidence in the weapon, especially as the Lancaster could only carry one bomb like this; accuracy of delivery (which included impact angle) was therefore vital. Orders for the weapon were halted in July 1943 and in 1944 the remaining stock was scrapped.

Bomb development continued and Bomber Command was seen employing an 8,000lb blast bomb; the Halifax was the first aircraft to drop this weapon. The original intention (of January 1941) was that this bomb would be carried by a modified troop-carrying glider, thus ensuring that the proposed 48in diameter would pose no problem. When aircraft carriage of this weapon was considered it was obvious that such a diameter would be impossible, so a 38in weapon was devised. By the end of 1942, Bomber Command had dropped 28 of these bombs, but, in the absence of ballistic evaluation, this had been a largely pointless exercise.

As early as 1941, it had been decided that the weapon should be fitted to the Halifax and Lancaster; however, according to SD719 Armament report:

> The Lancaster was designed to carry only one large bomb (4,000lb) in its bomb load and in May 1941 it was decided to forego this bomb for the Lancaster because of the alterations necessary for its carriage. In September 1941, however, the Air Staff decided that the aircraft should be modified to carry the bomb as soon as possible without interfering with current production. Although A. V. Roe soon re-designed the Lancaster – new bomb doors giving a fuselage bulge were necessary – the preparation of assembly jigs, tools etc, and then fitting them into the production schedule was quite a different proposition; in fact, by May 1942, the most the firm could promise was one modification a week until the end of the year, when it would go into the assembly line proper. Later it was discovered that the introduction of these doors interfered with the installation of H2S and as this was regarded by Bomber Command to be of paramount importance, Air Staff decided in December to modify only 10 per cent of Lancasters to take the 8,000lb bomb.

The Lancasters of 106 Squadron were the first to be adapted to take this weapon, in September 1944, the bulged bomb bays making the modified aircraft quite distinctive.

Training

A decision taken in September 1942 to combine the various on-squadron Conversion Flights into separate training units led to the creation of a number of Heavy Conversion Units (HCUs) equipped with Manchesters and Lancasters; by 31 October, the situation was as follows:

1654 HCU – Wigsley (combination of 50 and 83 squadrons CFs)

1656 HCU – Breighton (103 and 460 squadrons)

1660 HCU – Swinderby (61, 97, 106, 207 squadrons)

1661 HCU – Skellingthorpe (9, 44, 49 squadrons)

All except 1656 (No 1 Group) were for No 5 Group; 1661 was initially only three-quarters size and 1656 was half size (the full-size units had a UE of 16 Manchesters and 16 Lancasters), but by the end of the year these had both expanded to full size. Almost before the ink was dry on the plan, the UE was changed to 12 Lancasters plus 20 Manchesters or Halifaxes.

The Strategic Bombing Offensive

At the November War Cabinet Chiefs of Staff Committee there was wide-ranging discussion on the status of, and future potential for, the Strategic Bombing Offensive. It was considered that, 'a heavy bomber force rising from 4,000 to 6,000 heavy bombers in 1944 could shatter the industrial and economic structure of Germany to a point where an Anglo-American force of reasonable strength could enter the Continent from the West'. This force of 6,000 bombers would have a bomb lift of 90,000 tons per mission and 58 German towns were ear-marked for destruction. Harris and Bomber Command had come a long way in 1942 for such a positive forward-looking statement to be made by the War Cabinet. The heavy bomber force would comprise the Lancaster and the Halifax, with the former taking the major role.

At an Air Council Meeting on 3 November the following statement was made:

> The 50 squadron plan had been approved by the Chiefs of Staff. The following policy would be recommended to the Cabinet:
>
> i) to introduce the B3/42 at Weybridge and Chester, leaving Blackpool for the present Wellington;
>
> ii) to concentrate everything on reducing the period required for introducing the B3/42;
>
> iii) to set the Avro organization on to designing a replacement for the Lancaster, which would almost certainly be an aircraft with six engines;
>
> iv) to switch present production of Stirlings as soon as possible to Lancasters.
>
> The above would be subject to the difference in man hours between the B3/42 and the Lancaster not proving on further examination to be excessive.

The demise of the Stirling was already in the plan and, although the type continued in service to the end of the war, it was finally phased out of Main Force in 1944. However, the six-engined replacement for the Lancaster appears to have gone nowhere; the follow-on to the Lancaster did appear in due course – the four-engined Avro Lincoln.

The last two months of 1942 had been fairly quiet for Bomber Command, the majority of the Main Force attacks being made against Italian targets. Turin, with its diverse industries, was hit a number of times. One such attack took place on 28/29 November, when 228 bombers (117 Lancasters -- it was usual at this stage for the bomber force to include 100-plus Lancasters) attacked the city, two of the 106 Squadron aircraft dropping 8,000lb bombs; this was the first time this weapon had been used over Italy.

The 4,000lb HC bomb was one of Bomber Command's main weapons in the fight against German cities; Lancaster L7540 carries 83 Squadron codes (OL) on top of 44 Squadron codes (KM). Ken Delve Collection

Lancaster II DS604 of 61 Squadron. FlyPast Collection

Crew of 100 Squadron Lancaster; the Squadron re-formed with Lancasters in January 1943 as part of the re-equipment plan for No 1 Group. Ken Delve Collection

CHAPTER FIVE

1943 – The Storm Breaks

The Lancaster II

By February 1943, Bomber Command was fielding 17 Lancaster squadrons – two of them PFF (now called No 8 Group) units – out of a total strength of 65 front-line squadrons. The remainder were equipped with Wellingtons, Stirlings or Halifaxes. By the end of the year, the Lancaster total would increase to more than 30 squadrons.

A new Lancaster variant entered service in January, when 61 Squadron flew the first sorties with the Hercules-powered Lancaster II. The prototype Lancaster II, DT810, first flew on 26 November 1941, and Armstrong Whitworth was instructed to tool up for production of the Mark, with an order for one thousand aircraft. (In the end, only 300 were built.) The first production aircraft, DS609, first flew in September 1942. The first 27 aircraft were powered by Hercules VI engines and the remainder by the Hercules XVI. Other than the engines, there were no significant differences between the Mk I and the Mk II, and even their performance was very similar.

A third flight was formed on 61 Squadron to operate the Lancaster II, with six aircraft being delivered. The first operation by the Mark II took place on 11 January; the target was Essen. This target was attacked a number of times during the month, mostly by formations of between 20 and 60 Lancasters.

Strategy and Directives

The bombers had brought 1942 to an end with a series of attacks on German cities and it was the intention of Air Marshal Harris to continue these into 1943. On 14 January, he was issued with a new directive, giving U-boat bases in France as the top priority – but not at the expense of attacks on Berlin and other selected German cities.

Berlin was visited on the night of 16/17 January by a force of 201 bombers, primarily Lancasters from No 5 Group; this was the first operational employment of purpose-designed Target Indicators ('TI's). Berlin was attacked again the following night by 170 bombers, mainly Lancasters. During this raid, 22 aircraft were lost, including 19 Lancasters – a loss rate for the type of 11 per cent. That night, 9 and 12 Squadrons each lost four aircraft, as the fighters proved particularly effective.

The Allied leaders met at Casablanca to discuss the prosecution of the war. One of the items on the agenda was the Strategic Bombing Offensive (SBO). In due course, the Combined Chiefs of Staff issued a new directive, stating the following:

> Your primary objective will be the progressive destruction of and dislocation of the German military, industrial and economic system, and the undermining of the morale of the German people to a point where their capacity for armed resistance is fatally weakened.

Lancaster II DS685 of 115 Squadron; the aircraft was lost on the Hamburg raid of 2/3 August 1943.
ken Delve Collection

Groundcrew topping up the oxygen – one of many tasks that had to be done to prepare a Lancaster for its next operation. Ken Delve Collection

The directive gave five target categories for attack: submarine construction yards, aircraft industry, transportation, oil plants and 'others in the war industry'. It also gave added support to the concept of a 6,000-strong heavy bomber force.

By early February, the Command had a notional strength of 1,091 serviceable bombers, of which 642 were heavies – 119 Stirlings, 228 Halifaxes and 295 Lancasters. (The number of Lancasters was to increase rapidly in 1943.)

In addition to the other changes taking place, the first Bomber Command aircraft began to use another new blind-bombing device – H2S radar. Development of this system had started in October 1941 following a meeting at the TRE; trials with a 9cm set fitted to a Blenheim proved the concept was sound. Further trials with a Halifax evolved the standard arrangement of a 360-degree scanner with a PPI display for the operator, with later developments using a magnetron rather than a klystron. There were many problems to overcome but by mid-1942 the system showed great promise; it was supported by Don Bennett, who was keen to see it equipping his PFF aircraft. The system was first employed on the Halifax but in due course the majority of the Command's bombers were equipped with it.

A Plentiful Supply of Lancasters

In March 1943, Bomber Command launched a sustained offensive against targets in Germany. The first phase opened with an attack on Essen on 5/6 March, with 442 bombers being led by an Oboe-equipped Pathfinder force. The Lancasters were in the third wave, led by eight backer-up markers of 83 Squadron – two of their aircraft were equipped with H2S. The elusive industrial targets at Essen, so long virtually immune from severe damage, were hit hard. According to Harris:

> Years of endeavour, of experiment, and of training in new methods have at last provided the weapons and the force capable of destroying the heart of the enemy's armament industry.

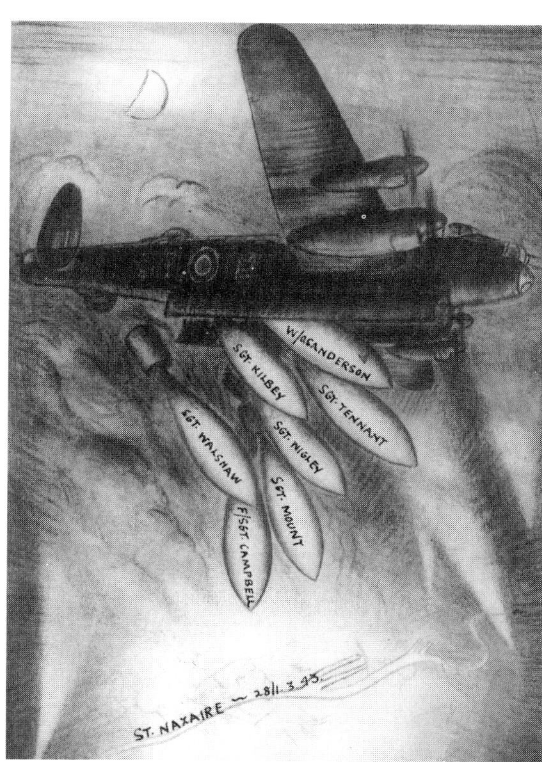

Aiming Point certificate awarded to a 44 Squadron crew (W4839) for the St Nazaire raid of 28 February/1 March 1943. Frank Walshaw

Thus began what has been called the Battle of the Ruhr – Bomber Command's attempt to cause critical damage to the German industrial heartland. In the period up to May, some 60 per cent of the Command's effort was expended against targets in the Ruhr.

The strike force now included 18 Lancaster squadrons, some of which were in the process of re-equipping with the Lancaster III. The basic design of the Lancaster required few changes, the only significant difference between the Mk III and the Mk I was its use of Packard Merlin 28 engines. Almost 3,000 of this variant were built, with the first example, W4114, leaving Avro in summer 1942; in October, this was under evaluation at the A&AEE.

German night-fighters continued to take their toll on the bomber streams and the ORS was continually looking at the statistics to see if any significant trends emerged. One report looked at the employment of the gun turrets in the bombers and concluded that almost 90 per cent of engagements were by the rear gunners. However, even then, they only fired a small percentage of the available ammunition; the Lancaster rear turret had 6,000 rounds for its guns but, on average, gunners only used between 235 and 1,000 rounds. It was suggested, therefore, that weight could be saved, and performance increased, if certain turrets were deleted and less ammunition was carried.

Despite loss rates that from time to time equalled those of other types, overall, fewer Lancasters were lost than had been anticipated; this, combined with deliveries of new aircraft, meant that there was a plentiful supply of the type. Crews were also freely available, as the HCUs were providing trained personnel at a faster rate than the squadrons could absorb them. There had been some concern as to the serviceability of the type, with a number of instances of low overall usage rates, but, while this was being investigated, the simple expedient of increasing the established strength of the squadrons eased the problem. By late spring the Lancaster units were contributing over 200 bombers to major attacks, with some squadrons putting up as many as 18 aircraft.

By May, the average 'contribution' had risen to over 300 aircraft, an indicator of the rapid nature of the re-equipment programme, an improvement in overall serviceability and the increase in UE per squadron to 26+2 aircraft.

Groundcrew

While historians have paid close attention to the training and availability of aircrew, all too often the groundcrew aspect has been ignored – yet, without the efforts of ground personnel, very few aircraft would have stayed serviceable for long! One of the reasons behind the low utilization rates had been a shortage of certain ground trades, especially engine fitters. This was partly remedied by increasing the numbers of such tradesmen on squadron strength. The engine problem itself was being investigated at Group level, but no common cause was evident. As an interim

Snow clearing was a case of 'all hands to the pumps'; squadrons prided themselves on exceeding the 'called-for' number of aircraft each day, keeping the aircraft serviceable and the airfield open. Ken Delve Collection

Engines being checked, fuel tanks replenished; the ubiquitous RAF bikes in the foreground make this an atmospheric shot. Ken Delve Collection

measure, squadrons were instructed to send any aircraft with over 300 hours to the manufacturer when it was next due a major servicing – in return, they would receive a brand-new Lancaster III.

Also in short supply were armourers, a group of tradesmen who were both essential and over-worked. It was, for example, not infrequent for bomb-load changes to be called for at very short notice. Occasionally, there were tragedies. On 15 March, a 4,000lb bomb was being loaded into 57 Squadron's W4834 at Scampton; it exploded, with devastating results. Three aircraft of 57 Squadron (W4834, ED306, ED594) were destroyed, along with three from 50 Squadron (W4112, W4196, W4823); varying degrees of damage were also caused to five other aircraft. This was not the only time such an accident happened and, sadly, once or twice there were casualties among the groundcrew.

March 1943

During March, the Command flew major raids against Nuremberg (8/9), Munich (9/10), Stuttgart (11/12), Essen (5/6, 12/13), Duisburg (26/27) and Berlin (27/28, 29/30) as well as two significant attacks on St Nazaire (22/23, 28/29). The second Berlin attack saw Main Force send 329 bombers (162 Lancasters) to the German capital; 11 of the Lancasters failed to return. One of the aircraft to fall to flak this night was W4858 of 12 Squadron, flown by Sgt Pinkerton. The crew baled out and Pinkerton evaded capture and made it back to England; his K report (report on loss of aircraft on operations, compiled from his debrief) gave the following details:

> This aircraft arrived over the target 5 minutes ahead of time, before the flares had gone down. It was held by a Master searchlight, which suddenly exposed on the aircraft. Then a very large cone, estimated to be about 40 searchlights, picked it up. The aircraft at this time was at 19,000ft. Flak began coming up about 1 minute after the aircraft had been coned, and the pilot believes that he was hit, probably in the wings. He then jettisoned his bombs. He lost height in his attempt to get out of the searchlights and finally escaped from them at about 3,000ft. The four engines were running well and there was no damage evident in the aircraft, but the aircraft would not climb above 15,000ft. The pilot found he could not get the rear gunner

This 97 Squadron aircraft was destroyed when the photo flashes exploded. Ken Delve Collection

on the intercom and sent the W/Op to investigate. After quarter of an hour the W/Op returned saying that the rear gunner's microphone was u/s.
The flight engineer gave the W/Op his helmet to take to the rear gunner; after quarter of an hour the flight engineer complained of lack of oxygen (15,000ft) and about 10 mins later became unconscious. They now ran into more searchlights and flak, possibly at Bremen. The pilot altered course to 191 degrees in order to escape from this defended area. He also lost height to 3,000ft to try and get the flight engineer round.

The navigator and mid-upper gunner went back to look for the W/Op and found him apparently dead with a broken neck near the step. 40 mins after leaving the area believed to be Bremen the pilot discovered he was still on course 191 degrees and at once changed course to due west. After a while both starboard engines cut due to lack of petrol, but the navigator turned on other tanks and they started up.

About 2 hours after leaving Berlin the starboard inner engine failed, not due to lack of petrol, and the propeller was feathered. The flight engineer now calculated that they had petrol for 1 hour's flying. After a time they crossed a flak belt, which they believed to be at the Dutch coast. The flight engineer now calculated that they had only 20 gallons left and just afterwards the starboard outer engine cut for lack of petrol. They were still at 3,000ft. The pilot gave the order to bale out and they baled out. The pilot landed 3km from Rotterdam. The aircraft was a complete wreck. When they baled out they had been flying for 7 to 8 hours. The pilot believed he should have had petrol for about 10 hours and he suggests that the flak hit over Berlin may have caused him to lose some petrol.

Without the pilot's report, the cause of this Lancaster loss would not have been known. The same applies to a great many Bomber Command aircraft losses.

April 1943

The Battle of the Ruhr continued into April with attacks on Essen, Duisburg, Frankfurt and Stuttgart. The Essen raid of 3/4 April was the first Main Force op to include over 200 Lancasters – of the 348 bombers taking part, 225 were Lancs. Nine Lancasters and 12 Halifaxes were lost. Severe problems could sometimes arise from minor incidents; this was the case with Lancaster 'P' of 467 Squadron on the night of 14/15 April. Stuttgart had been attacked by 462 bombers (98 Lancasters), with a loss rate of around 5 per cent. Lancaster 'P' was crossing the French coast at 500ft when it was fired at:

W/O Sanderson and 44 Squadron crew (ED331) happy to be back from the Berlin op of 1/2 March 1943; note the pigeon peeking out of its box (held by Sgt Frank Walshaw). Frank Walshaw

A single bullet fired from the ground entered the leading edge of the mainplane inboard of the starboard inner engine. For so insignificant a missile (the hole in the wing was only half an inch across) an unusual amount of trouble resulted from what was probably a chance in a million.

The first indication that things were amiss was the failure of the gyro instruments: the supply line from the vacuum pump had been severed. The pilot switched over to the port vacuum pump and while doing so noticed sparks coming from the exhaust of the starboard inner engine. The Flight Engineer reported that the coolant temperature was rising rapidly, indicating loss of coolant from this motor. The propeller was feathered and the supply of petrol switched off. Then the pilot attempted to open up the starboard outer engine, but unfortunately the bullet had partially severed the throttle control; with the additional load the control fractured completely. As no power could be obtained from this engine, its propeller had to be feathered also, and the Lancaster swung off course.

At first the pilot tried to fly with the aircraft banked but lost height rapidly – an uncomfortable experience at 500ft. Then, by applying full aileron and rudder trim, he held the aircraft level and used as much rudder as was necessary to fly straight. Having regained control in this way the pilot ordered the crew to jettison ammunition, flares, flame-floats and other impedimenta but not the guns, and then climbed to between 1,000 and 1,200ft for the journey home. It took 45 minutes to reach the Sussex coast. From that point the pilot flew at 150ft and made for the nearest landing ground, ready to put his aircraft down on the beach if necessary. In the vicinity of the airfield it was found that the undercarriage hydraulics were inoperative and, as the emergency airline to the starboard wheel was also out of action, only the port wheel came down. In spite of this the Lancaster made a successful landing with only the port and tail wheel, a minimum amount of injury being caused to the starboard side of the aircraft. The engineer's log shows that the boost and revs during the last part of the journey were +7lbs and 2,700 per minute, respectively, which could have been maintained a long time without straining or overheating the engines. Full boost and revs were only used when coming on to land, the approach being quite normal otherwise. The aircraft was perfectly manageable at speeds above 135 IAS.

This report was published in the Bomber Command Quarterly Review (No 4), but the lessons that it contained did not reach bomber crews in general. Few at squadron level were allowed to see this Secret document.

In May, the Bomber Development Unit at Feltwell carried out an investigation into the provision of a 'downward search position for night bombers', a trial fit being installed on Lancaster R5568:

A request was made by No 8 Group for the provision of a clear view aperture through which an efficient rearward and downward search can be maintained on operations. All the necessary materials were obtained locally from existing stores or from local salvage. It is recommended that in the absence of anything better as an immediate measure, this blister be fitted as a retrospective modification to all Lancaster aircraft. (BDU Report).

Later in the year, the BDU would be tasked with trials on an 'under defence position in night bombers' as part of the continued attempts to improve the self-defence of the increasingly vulnerable bombers. Little seems to have come of either of these good ideas.

Other targets hit in April included Kiel, La Spezia, Stettin and Pilsen. The Pilsen mission was aimed at the Skoda armament works and involved 327 bombers (197 Lancasters). The same target was attacked again by 156 Lancasters and 12 Halifaxes on 13/14 May, with equally little success. Lancaster III ED667 of 57 Squadron was shot down by a fighter:

The aircraft took off from Scampton at 2137 hours to attack Pilsen, carrying one 4,000lb HC bomb and five 1,000lb bombs. After leaving England the engine temperatures were a little high and the aircraft was climbing badly with the result that the Dutch coast was crossed at 17,000ft instead of 20,000ft as intended. Apart from running a little warm, the engines appeared to be functioning perfectly.

Just after turning into the second leg of the track and about 5 miles before crossing the coast of the Dutch mainland, the pilot noticed a white flare shot up behind the Lancaster, to about the height at which it was flying. This was reported by the rear gunner. It was a very dark night with no cloud and after crossing the Dutch islands the pilot (as was his normal custom) flew on a weaving course of about 15 to 20 degrees each side of his track but, two or three minutes after midnight, just before crossing the German border, he flew straight and level to check his DR compass.

When he had been flying straight and level for about 2 minutes the pilot suddenly saw white tracer passing the nose of the aircraft from dead astern about 30 degrees below level and heard shells hitting the aircraft. He believes that the enemy aircraft may have been following the Lancaster unseen all the way from the point at which the white light was seen. As soon as the aircraft was hit the pilot pulled back the stick to make a starboard peel-off, but almost immediately he felt the rudder bar suddenly go completely free and the rudder became serviceable. He accordingly side-slipped out of the peel-off down to about 16,000ft and then noticed that the aircraft was on fire and flames were coming from the underside of the fuselage and the bottom of the mainplanes below the inboard fuel tanks.

The fighter fired only one burst and was not seen at all by any of the crew. The pilot ordered the bomb aimer to jettison the bombs at once, and this he did but the fire continued just as fiercely as before. He then ordered the crew to abandon the aircraft. During this time the aircraft became very nose-heavy and the pilot had to keep turning back the elevators. The aileron control alone remained unaffected. The intercom also gradually became unserviceable. The flight engineer handed the pilot his parachute and he saw the bomber and flight engineer go past him and bale out.

The navigator shouted something in the pilot's ear but he was unable to catch what he said, and as the aircraft was becoming more and more out of control he waved to the navigator to get out at once. The navigator and W/Op then baled out. Meanwhile the pilot had to keep turning back the elevator control and he notice that the mid-upper gunner standing behind him without his parachute. He shouted to him to get his parachute and get out, but by this time he had turned back the elevators as far as possible and the aircraft suddenly went into a steep dive and the stick was useless. The fire had spread rapidly and the inside of the aircraft was filling with smoke and flames, it was also blazing up round all the engines, which, however, continued to run satisfactorily. The IAS was then 250 and rising and about 2 minutes after the Lancaster had been hit the pilot was forced to abandon the aircraft, which was then at about 10,000ft.

Lancaster I ED825 was one of a number of aircraft modified as Lancaster I (Special) to carry Barnes Wallis's special 'bouncing bomb' to attack German dams. FlyPast Collection

Plt Off. J B Haye (a Dutchman) landed in Holland and evaded capture with the help of local people. Two of the crew were killed, and the others were taken prisoner.

The Dams Raid

The first part of May had been generally quiet for Bomber Command, including almost ten days with no major operation. Towards the end of May, the pace increased, with a return to Ruhr targets by bomber forces that now included more than 300 Lancasters. However, the most significant attack in May was made by 617 squadron against the Dams.

The mounting bracket for the 'bouncing bomb' is clearly visible in this shot of 617 Squadron's ED817; the aircraft survived the war and was finally struck-off-charge in September 1946. FlyPast Collection

The best-known incident of 1943, and the one that helped assure the Lancaster's place in history, was Operation Chastise – the Dams Raid. The concept of causing industrial disruption by attacking certain critical dams had been in the British bombing plans for some time – as far back as the pre-war Western Air plans. However, the plan only became practicable with the advent of a suitable weapon. The weapon, and the impetus for the raid, came from one of Britain's most brilliant designers, Dr Barnes Wallis. After both theoretical and practical investigations, he concluded that the only way to cause critical damage to such structures was to explode a weapon against the inside face of the dam – under water. The resultant shock wave would, in theory, cause structural failure of the dam. The bomb would require a special, and accurate, delivery technique, and a specialist squadron would have to be created.

Operation Chastise**, 16/17 May 1943, succeeded in breaching the Mohne and Eder (as here) dams, but at a cost of eight of the 19 Lancasters that took part.** Ken Delve Collection

The man chosen to lead the new unit was Wg Cdr Guy Gibson, a very experienced bomber captain who had just finished his tour as CO of 106 Squadron, which had itself been something of a specialist squadron. By early May, Gibson had brought together and trained the crews that he required, and the Lancasters had been modified to take the 'Upkeep' weapon (a mine rather than a bomb). It had not been easy – numerous problems had to be overcome with both the weapon and its delivery technique, but all of these had been solved by the May deadline date. (This was crucial, since the dams had to be attacked when the water level was still high.)

The attack plan was for 19 Lancasters in three waves to attack the Mohne and Sorpe dams. Gibson, leading nine aircraft, would attack the former while another five aircraft, would attack the latter. The last wave of five aircraft was to act as an airborne reserve. The first wave left at 1650 hours on 16 May. Few problems were encountered en route to the target, although one aircraft fell to flak and crashed near Dorsten. Gibson arrived over the Mohne just after midnight and made his run, scoring a good hit. Flt Lt Hopgood went in next, but his aircraft was hit by flak and he dropped late, the mine bouncing over the dam and the Lancasters crashing soon afterwards; only two of the crew survived. Gibson escorted the third aircraft, Flt Lt Mick Martin, in order to divide the anti-aircraft fire. Martin's mine went short. Sqn Ldr 'Dinghy' Young was next; he was escorted in by both Gibson and Martin, and made an accurate delivery. The fifth attack was made by Flt Lt Maltby; again, the mine was well placed. As the attackers watched, a crack appeared in the dam, followed by a large part of its centre crashing away, and water pouring through. Gibson took those Lancasters still carrying mines on to the Eder Dam, while the others were ordered to return to base.

The Eder Dam had no defences and so the Lancasters set up their attack pattern. Flt Lt Shannon's mine was accurate and caused a small breach. Sqn Ldr Maudslay placed his mine too long and his Lancaster was damaged by the explosion. The third attacker, Plt Off. Knight, put his mine in the right place and the Eder Dam collapsed outwards. Meanwhile, the second wave had suffered badly – two aircraft had been forced to turn back early with technical problems, and two others had been shot down en route, both probably victims of flak.

The sole remaining Lancaster, flown by Flt Lt McCarthy, pressed on to the Sorpe Dam and carried out an attack. The mine hit the dam – an earth dam, not a standard concrete structure – but caused little damage. The third wave also suffered two losses to flak, while a third aircraft had to abort the sortie. The remaining two pressed on. F/Sgt Brown attacked the Sorpe Dam and F/Sgt Townsend attacked the Ennepe Dam, both without result. Sadly, two more Lancasters – Sqn Ldr Young and Sqn Ldr Maudslay – were lost on the way home.

Although the results achieved by this attack have been the subject of hot debate over the years – some commentators claim that it achieved nothing, while others claim huge destruction and damage to morale – Operation Chastise was undoubtedly a great success. Two of the primary targets were breached, resulting in widespread damage from flooding. The German war industry had certainly suffered damage, albeit short-term, and the British had scored a major propaganda coup, an important factor at this stage of the war. Losses, however, had been high, with eight aircraft failing to return and 53 aircrew being killed. Wg Cdr Guy Gibson was awarded a Victoria Cross for his 'outstanding bravery and leadership during the raid'; five officer pilots were awarded DSOs, the two NCO pilots received CGMs, and other aircrew members received 15 DFCs and 12 DFMs.

Harris sent the following message:

> Please convey to all concerned my warmest congratulations on the brilliantly successful execution of last night's operation. To the air crews I would say that their keenness and thoroughness in training and their skill and determination in pressing home their attacks will for ever be an inspiration to the RAF. In this memorable operation they have won a major victory in the Battle of the Ruhr, the effect of which will last until the Boche is swept away in the flood of final disaster. (Bomber Command ORB)

No 617 Squadron had not yet finished its specialist role; its Lancasters were to feature in a number of other spectacular missions before the war was over.

The Allied Commanders Conference held in Washington in May led to another new directive (effective 3 June) This brought into effect the Combined Bomber Offensive (code-named Pointblank), with the US 8th Air Force attacking strategic targets by day and Bomber Command covering the night period.

16/17 May 1943 – Wg Cdr Guy Gibson VC DSO DFC (No 617 Squadron)

Guy Penrose Gibson was commissioned into the RAF as a pilot in 1937, his first posting being to 83 Squadron, equipped with Hinds and then Hampdens, based at Scampton. Gibson took part in operations from the very first day of the war and had completed his first tour by September 1940. After a short tour as an instructor with Nos 14 and 16 OTUs, he was posted to 29 Squadron based at Digby, flying Beaufighters as a night-fighter pilot until December 1941. He flew 100 operational sorties and was credited with three enemy aircraft destroyed.

Following a short period as an instructor with 51 OTU at Cranfield, Gibson returned to operational flying in April 1942 as Officer Commanding 106 Squadron at Coningsby, equipped with the Manchester and then the Lancaster. Having completed his tour of operations with No 106 Squadron, he was asked to form and lead a special bomber squadron and thus became OC of 617 Squadron, leading the Dams Raid on the night of 16/17 May 1943. His citation reads as follows:

> Under his inspiring leadership, this squadron has now executed one of the most devastating attacks of the war – the breaching of the Mohne and Eder dams. The task was fraught with danger and difficulty. Gibson personally made the initial attack on the Mohne Dam. Descending to within a few feet of the water and taking the full brunt of the anti-aircraft defences, he delivered his attack with great accuracy. Afterwards he circled very low for 30 minutes, drawing the enemy fire on himself in order to leave as free a run as possible to the following aircraft which were attacking the dam in turn. Gibson then led the remainder of his force to the Eder Dam where, with complete disregard for his own safety, he repeated his tactics, and once more drew on himself the enemy fire so that the attack would be successfully developed. Wing Commander Gibson has completed 170 sorties. Throughout his operational career, prolonged exceptionally at his own request, he has shown leadership, determination and valour of the highest order.

Gibson was grounded shortly afterwards and took on various Staff appointments, although he 'escaped' from the office whenever he could to fly operational sorties. On the night of 19 September 1944, Gibson was flying a 627 Squadron Mosquito as Master Bomber against rail and industrial targets at Rheydt and Munchen-Gladbach. Eyewitnesses reported seeing his aircraft in flames – it crashed at Steenbergen in Holland.

Bombsights

Once it arrived in the target area it was essential for the bomber to be able to deliver its load on the target as accurately as possible. Various bombsights were evaluated for use in the Lancaster:

> In May, I requested the Air Ministry to consider increasing the height limitation of the Mk XIV bombsight from 20,000ft to 30,000ft as Lancaster aircraft were then carrying out operational attacks up to 22,000ft. The Air Ministry replied that the introduction of the Mk XIVA bombsight in the production line would make it possible to bomb up to 25,000ft. (Harris, 'Despatch on War Operations')

The SABS (Stabilised Automatic Bombsight) had been installed in aircraft of No 5 Group from early 1943, the Lancasters of 97 and 207 Squadrons being equipped with SABS Mk II. In May, Harris 'informed the Air Ministry that I proposed to discontinue the use of the SAB in Lancaster aircraft and to use the Mk XIV sight in its place'. The Air Ministry agreed to this proposal on 26 May, but at around the same time another variant of the SABS sight was under evaluation:

> Service trials on SABS Mk IIA by 617 Squadron revealed that given good maintenance and well-trained crews, a very high standard of accuracy could be obtained with this bombsight. As a

Fg Off Mathieson glances away from his crew station in this 50 Squadron aircraft. Ken Delve Collection

For his leadership of the Dams Raid, Wg Cdr Guy Gibson was awarded the Victoria Cross; this portrait is from his time as a pilot with 83 Squadron. Ken Delve Collection

Post-attack photo showing severe damage to the Zeppelin works at Friedrichshafen following the 'shuttle' mission of June 12/12 . Ken Delve Collection

result of the operational experiences of 617 Squadron, various modifications were incorporated in the SAB Mk IIA, and by the end of hostilities in Europe it was possible for a well-trained crew to obtain an average error of 80 yards from 20,000ft when using this bombsight. (Harris, 'Despatch on War Operations')

June and July 1943

June opened with another ten-day 'rest period', with the first significant attack taking place on 11/12 against Düsseldorf; Bochum was hit the following night. The Oberhausen raid of 14/15 June resulted in a high loss rate for the all-Lancaster Main Force – 17 of the 197 aircraft (8.4 per cent) failed to return. This was the highest figure for a while, as Lancaster losses had fallen to an average of 3-4 per cent.

Major attacks by formations of 800+ bombers were made on Dortmund, Düsseldorf, Cologne, Essen, Bochum, Wuppertal, Munster and Oberhausen. Among this series of attacks was one on 19/20 June, against the Schneider and Breuil steelworks at Le Creusot. This was a night low-level visual bombing attack, with only two Lancasters included in the 290-bomber force. Such precision attacks by night (as well as by day) would become an increasing feature of the Command's operations, and the Lancasters would, in due course, take the lead in these missions.

'Shuttle' Missions

The following night saw No 5 Group's Lancasters fly the first of the so-called 'Shuttle' missions, with aircraft taking off from England to attack a target in southern Germany before flying on to land at airfields in Allied-held North Africa. The force of 60 Lancasters was tasked, under Operation Bellicose, to attack the ex-Zeppelin works, now involved in the production of 'Wurzburg' early-warning radars, at Friedrichshafen on the shores of Lake Constance. This was part of Bomber Command's new directive, which called for attacks on the German aircraft industry, and the fighter industry in particular, as both day- and night-fighters were causing heavy losses to Allied bombers. One crew member recorded his view of the mission:

Approaching the French coast at 19,000ft, we encountered heavy cloud and electric storms up to 24,000ft. We therefore decided to come down below the front and lost height to 5,000ft. We were suddenly engaged by the defences of Caen or the outer defences of Le Havre – owing to technical difficulties with navigation instruments we were uncertain of our exact position. Four 4-gun heavy flak positions engaged us for about four minutes. During this time we altered course by about 30 degrees every 8 seconds, alternatively losing and gaining height by 1,000ft. The flak bursts were mainly 3-500ft behind and about the same distance above us. It was noticed that the rate of fire of the guns was extremely high! We flew on below cloud at 2,500-3,000ft across France and encountered no further opposition.

Three-quarters of an hour's flying time from Lake Constance it was necessary to feather the port-inner engine, which was emitting showers of sparks, so we continued on three engines until we sighted the lake. By that time we had increased height to 6,000ft. As the port-inner engine is essential for the Mk XIV bombsight, it was unfeathered and allowed to windmill, but shortly afterwards the engine caught fire. We were unable to feather it or extinguish the fire, which grew in intensity. The Captain then jettisoned the bombs, told the Deputy Leader to take over and gave the order to prepare to abandon the aircraft, first diving across the lake into Switzerland, and subsequently turning the aircraft towards Germany. We were about to bale out, expecting the petrol tanks to explode, when the engine seized and the fire went out. By this time we had descended to 4,000ft but were able to maintain height.

We stayed over Lake Constance for 13 minutes and had an excellent view of the attack. There were approximately 16-20 heavy flak guns and 18-20 light flak guns, and 25 searchlights, within a radius of 6-8 miles of the target. Several aircraft were coned but not for any length of time. As the defences were heavier than expected, the Deputy Leader gave the order for all aircraft to increase height by 5,000ft, so that the attack was actually delivered from 10,000ft to 15,000ft. Leaving the target area, we commenced to fly over the Alps. By skirting the peaks we eventually crossed, gradually gaining height to 14,000ft. The 600-mile flight over the Mediterranean was slow, as we had to fly at 140mph to prevent over-heating. Eventually, we sighted the Algerian coast and landed safely at Maison Blanche at 0752 – after a flight of 10 hours and 13 minutes.

The attack had been delivered by two waves of aircraft; the first following the PFF-laid TIs and the second using the technique of a 'timed run' from a visual point on the shore of the lake. The factories were hit and badly damaged. The attack had been 'directed' by Wg Cdr G. L. Gomm to keep the bombers

Lancaster X KB700. The Canadian-built Lancaster Xs (by Victory Aircraft) were delivered from early 1943; KB700 was delivered to 405 Squadron in October 1943. FlyPast Collection

on target – this use of a controlling aircraft, later to be designated as Master Bomber, would soon become standard for Bomber Command. None of the bombers was lost on this attack.

Three nights later, 23/24 June, the Lancasters returned to the UK, bombing La Spezia on the way.

Fg Off Henderson and his 460 Squadron crew on return from Mulheim June 22, 1943, their 23rd operation. Ken Delve Collection

Attack on Reggio nell'Emilia

Ten Main Force attacks were made in July, most of these against German cities such as Aachen, Essen and Cologne, although a number of attacks were also mounted over Italy. Lancaster III JA679 (Fg Off M. R. Head) of 9 Squadron was part of the force that was tasked to attack the Reggio nell'Emilia transformer station on 15/16 July. The Squadron ORB records that a message was received at 0405 that the aircraft had been hit by another aircraft and was trying to make it back to base. It was to prove a forlorn hope, according to the intelligence debrief, which stated that:

> The Lancaster took off from Bardney at 2215. There was a full moon and visibility was fairly good throughout the flight. After crossing the French coast, the pilot flew low on a moderately weaving course. The Lancaster carried AI and GL Boozer. Over France a large number of AI indications were received some of them lasting for several minutes. Frequent Monica indications were also received during a large part of the flight. At first the pilot took corkscrew action on receiving the indications, but as this had no apparent effect and no other aircraft were sighted except a single Lancaster which appeared to be on a parallel course about 3-400 yards away on the starboard beam, the pilot came to the conclusion that the instrument was unserviceable.
>
> The flight was accomplished without incident as far as the rendezvous point at the southern end of Lake Garda was reached about 5 minutes late. R/T communication was established with the leader of the formation and a further 5 minutes spent awaiting the arrival of another aircraft. This did not turn up so the remaining 5 set course together for the target.
>
> The crews had been briefed to make a time and distance run from the S tip of Lake Garda to a point on the main line west of Reggio where it ran parallel to the main road.

The crew were unable to make an accurate first run and turned to make a second attempt:

> A few seconds later, Fg Off Head glanced ahead and saw another Lancaster approx on the same level (1800ft). The other aircraft was only about 100 yards off when first seen and there appeared to be no time to avoid a collision by making a turn. Fg Off Head therefore pulled the control column hard back in the hope that he would pass over the other aircraft.
>
> The other pilot apparently sighted Fg Off Head's Lancaster at the same time and began to turn to port, but almost immediately a collision occurred. As far as Fg Off head can judge the starboard wing tip of the other Lancaster hit his port wing about midway along. He believes that the underside of the fuselage was struck by the top of the fuselage of the other aircraft, possibly its mid-upper turret. His own mid-upper gunner reported a large hole in the fuselage but did not specify its exact position and he also heard someone say that there was a lot of blood near the navigator's position. The other aircraft was seen to crash and burst into flames.
>
> Fg Off Head at once noticed that the spinner of the port inner propeller had come off and he immediately feathered this engine. The trimming controls of both the rudder and elevators were unserviceable and in order to fly straight and level it was necessary to keep the control column pressed right forward and the rudder hard over to starboard. After a short interval he noticed that the port outer engine was only revolving slowly and that the temperature had dropped right down. He then feathered this engine also.
>
> The rear gunner reported that he was jammed in his turret and Fg Off Head therefore decided that he would have to make a crash landing. He tried to jettison the bomb load but the bomb doors would not open. The bomb aimer therefore went aft and released them manually. Most of the load fell clear through the hole made by the collision, but two bombs could not be released. Meanwhile the navigator had also gone aft and managed to free the rear gunner.

The decision was then taken to try and reach the coast in order to ditch; however, the aircraft continued to lose height and eventually the crew were ordered to bale out. All escaped safely, except the flight

Incendiaries cascade from SR-B of 101 Squadron; note the large ABC aerials on top of the fuselage – the Squadron's primary role was RCM (Radio Countermeasures). Ken Delve Collection

engineer, whose parachute caught on the aircraft. The six survivors were all made prisoners of war.

Attacks on Hamburg

Hamburg was designated as a target to receive a concentrated series of attacks over a short period of time; under Operation *Gomorrah*, the first of these, on 24/25 July, was significant in that it saw the first operational use of 'Window'. This was another defensive aid, which employed small aluminium foil strips, to act as radar reflectors and so confuse the enemy's radar picture. It was an extremely successful tactic, which reduced bomber losses for a number of raids. The Germans soon developed tactics that rendered this simple and cheap countermeasure less useful, but they never fully negated it.

(The downside for Bomber Command was that the use of 'Window' forced the German night defences to undertake a major re-evaluation of their failing system. The modified system that was gradually developed gave far greater flexibility and freedom of action to the night-fighters – when a fighter had found the bomber stream, it was able to engage target after target. Multiple victories by night-fighter experten became increasingly common.)

The Main Force over Hamburg consisted of 791 bombers, including 354 Lancasters from 19 Squadrons (four of these being Pathfinder units), with 103 Squadron sending no less than 27 aircraft (although 3 of these returned early and 3 were lost). This series of four major attacks on Hamburg caused major destruction in the city and seriously disrupted its war industries. The last sortie, 2/3 August, had been an all-Lancaster mission, as the weather forecast was poor.

The anti-maritime campaign remained of great importance and mine-laying was seen as the one of the most effective ways for Bomber Command to contribute to this effort. By July 1943, a new mine, the Assembly 32, was being issued to units; when this was available in sufficient numbers, a major operation – Operation *Bobbery* – was to be executed on a single night to lay mines in areas between Danzig and Bordeaux. The Bomber Command element was to be 190 aircraft, including 31 Lancasters from No 5 Group.

Training

The training system expanded in early 1943 as Bomber Command's requirement for trained crews continued to accelerate. By January 1943, with the formation of 1662 HCU at Blyton, there were a total of eleven HCUs, most of which had variations on the standard 12-Lancaster/20-Halifax/Manchester establishment. The plan was to increase the total to 16 by November, seven of which would be for Lancaster crews, which would revert to the original 16-Lancaster/16-'other' establishment. May saw the formation of 1678 HCF

Oakington, June 11, 1943, home to 7 Squadron as part of the Pathfinder Force. Ken Delve Collection

The hangars of Waddington are visible in the distance but little remains of this burnt-out Lancaster.
Andy Thomas Collection

(Heavy Conversion Flight) at East Wretham and 1679 HCF at East Moor, both with only eight Lancasters, plus other types. Two more conversion units formed that summer; these were 1667 HCU at Lindholme in July, and 1668 at Balderton in August.

In mid-March, the Pathfinder Navigation Training Unit (PFF NTU) had formed at Upwood, in order to 'instruct aircrews of Pathfinder Force in PFF technique and in the use of special equipment used by the PFF squadrons' (AHB Narrative 'Flying Training'). The initial establishment included eight Lancasters plus four Stirlings and four Halifaxes. (By late 1944 it was an all-Lancaster unit.) All PFF crew attended the one-week (12-hour) course before joining their squadrons.

One of the new squadrons to form in this period was 426 Squadron, based at Linton-on-Ouse; by late July, the unit had 24 Lancaster IIs on strength and was undertaking an intensive training programme. The ORB entry for 1 August reflects this:

> The gunnery section continued for the fourth day their concentrated air to air gunnery programme. A total of five details were arranged with 18,500 rounds fired. The past four days training resulted in 119 gunners and bomb aimers firing as each detail allowed up to six gunners to fire and a total of 97,000 rounds of 0.303 were expended. The Squadron Gunnery Leader expressed keen appreciation of the help offered by the Target Towing Flight of RAF Leconfield who made available for four days, exclusive for Squadron use, towplanes and drogues. The training achieved has given the new gunners a great deal of confidence and should assist the crew confidence when operations begin.

A few days later, the bomb aimers were able to try out their new Mk XIV bombsights, and achieved an average error of 122 yards. On 11 August, the Squadron was declared operational, but the following day there was:

> Stand-down from ops again after a considerable discussion involving bomb loads and petrol consumption. The targets chosen were declared to be beyond present range of the Squadron carrying a paying bomb load, until more data on air miles per gallon is available. Crews were very disappointed as they were keen to get cracking even if the trip meant operating from an advanced base.

Two days later, Sqn Ldr Lashbrook from the RAF Handling Squadron at Hullavington was at Linton to discuss the problem.

Late Summer 1943

The Peenemunde Raid

Although the ORB does not record the outcome of the discussions about bomb loads and petrol consumption, 426 Squadron was able to send nine Lancasters to take part in the Peenemunde raid of 17 August. Sadly, they lost their CO, Wg Cdr L Crooks.

On 17/18 August, just under 600 bombers (324 Lancasters from 22 squadrons – the only squadron not taking part was 617 Squadron) undertook Operation *Hydra*, the attack on the German research site at Peenemunde. Gp Capt. John Searby of 83 Squadron acted as Master Bomber. Although 40 aircraft were lost (24 Lancasters), mainly from the last wave, which was caught by German night-fighters who had raced to the area, Operation *Hydra* was a major success.

Nine Lancasters from 426 Squadron took part in the operation (the Squadron having re-equipped from Wellingtons to Lancasters only in June/July); Flt Lt Shaw's report stated the following:

> Excellent visibility and green TI markers guided this aircraft to the target. Ruden Island turning point was plainly marked with green TIs. Bombing done with green TIs in bombsight while whole peninsula wall appeared ablaze and

> smoke was rising to 4,000ft. Bombed at 0036 hrs from 8,000ft.

Peenemunde was heavily damaged and the German rocket research programme was, without doubt, delayed by many months.

German Reactions

The series of Bomber Command attacks in summer 1943 had proved the potential accuracy and destructive capability of the RAF's main strike weapon. German leaders had mixed reactions. In late August, Milch said:

> [We] must decide on our priorities... only the [Me] 110 in sufficient numbers can give us the necessary relief at night... Germany is the real front line and the mass of fighters must go for home defence... the only chance to defeat the day and night bombers.

Jeschonnek (Chief of General Staff of the Luftwaffe) was of a different opinion:

> Every 4-engined bomber the Western Allies build makes me happy, for we will bring these down just as we brought down the 2-engined ones, and the destruction of a 4-engined bomber constitutes a much greater loss to the enemy.

Enemy Defences and Bomber Losses

The four-engined bomber continued to increase in numbers. Bomber Command's striking power also increased when Lancaster IIs were modified to carry an 8,000lb bomb.

Following the Allied Commanders' Quebec conference in August, a new directive was issued, giving the bombers new priorities in the air campaign for the planned invasion of Europe. Many of the existing industrial targets were still included but there was also to be increasing emphasis on lines of communication and enemy air assets.

During the summer, the loss rates of Stirlings and Halifaxes had once more raised questions at Bomber Command; the Stirlings on occasion had suffered a staggering 16 per cent loss rate. Earlier in the year, the ORS had been tasked to look at the 'trend of Lancaster losses' and had concluded the following:

> The rise in casualty rate to approx 4 per cent for the period December 1942 to January 1943 approximates to that of other types. This is probably because other types are improving and a general improvement in the defences. (ORS Report R69 dated 29 March, 1943)

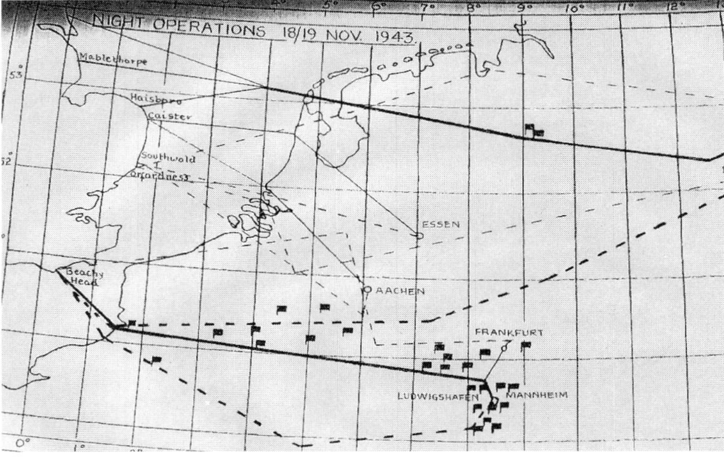

Operational Reserach Section graphic of the raids of November 18/19; the flags indicate aircraft losses. Ken Delve Collection

Lancs in dispersal at Tuddenham – a scene repeated at dozens of wartime airfields. Andy Thomas Collection

A large number of aircraft made it back to the UK only to crash-land; this Lanc has just missed the railway lines. Ken Delve Collection

Loss rates frequently varied throughout the bomber stream. ORS Report B163 looked at the 'enemy defensive tactics against the operation on Berlin' to see what lessons could be learned. In this attack, on 23/24 August, the RAF suffered 56 losses from its 727 bombers, in the greatest single night loss of the war to that date. Among the 134 Pathfinder aircraft were 83 Lancasters, five of which were lost. The first bombing wave over the target comprised 90 Lancasters in the period Z+2 to Z+8, and seven of these aircraft failed to return (7.8 per cent). No 1 Group's 30 aircraft lost four of their number. Thus, both of the early waves over the target suffered appreciable losses. Although loss rates were higher in some subsequent non-Lancaster waves (the Stirlings losing 16 of their 121 aircraft), the other Lancaster waves had far lower losses in the period Z+23 to the end of the raid at Z+42. The ORS Report concluded the following:

> The losses in the various sections of the attack seem to bear no relation to the probable window cover given to each wave of aircraft. The large scale employment of fighters over and near the target area, where the majority of losses to fighters were probably sustained in conditions where searchlights, fires, and to some extent, the moon, gave illumination. The evident determination to have fighters to protect Berlin at the earliest indication that an attack was heading for the city. The assistance given to fighters by track markers put down a long way before the target.

The dangers of the Berlin defences were soon to be brought home to Bomber Command over a sustained period.

On the night of 3/4 September, a force of 316 Lancasters carried out a moderately effective attack on Berlin – but at the cost of 22 aircraft; at 7 per cent, this was a high loss rate for the Lancaster element. No 106 Squadron lost two aircraft that night, including Lancaster III JA893 (Sqn Ldr D. Howroyd). The fate of this particular aircraft was mentioned in the Bomber Command Quarterly Review:

> The target was Berlin, while the bomb doors were still open, a Me 110 attacked without warning from directly astern. There was one definite hit by a cannon shell, and the rear gunner reported that he was severely wounded. Although the pilot carried out the appropriate combat manoeuvres during this and subsequent attacks, three further shell hits were experienced. All of the turrets were damaged, the fuselage hit at the fore end of the bomb-bays and near the IFF position, and the bomb aimer fatally wounded. Nevertheless, the mid-upper gunner continued to reply effectively to the attacks, and his claim to have destroyed the fighter was corroborated by the wireless operator in the astro hatch. As the intercom was severed during the combat the pilot was only aware that the attacks had suddenly ceased.'

The remainder of the story was given in the pilot's own words:

> I had my course already set on the DR compass and flew it for some way. In actual fact, this course was probably 060 degrees, as I did not realize that my DR compass was out of action. We were then at about 10,000ft, so I started to climb, and tried to find out the state of my crew. The bomb aimer [Fg Off T Saxby] was either dead or dying. The mid-upper gunner had passed out, owing to damaged oxygen supply, and I was under the impression that he was dead. I knew that the rear gunner [Sgt L Mckenzie] was badly injured. There was no intercom, or call lights and as we were by that time flying at over 20,000ft it was difficult to make contact by word of mouth. After about half-an-hour, when I had time to check my DR compass against the P4, I found that the former was out of action and remained stationary on changing course. Then, steering by P4 compass and Sperry gyro, we presently made landfall on the SE coast of Sweden. At the time we did not recognize it, and subsequently mistook Lake Vattern for the Kattegat – we were by then up to 27,000ft, having no means of defence other that height. Our course was 255 degrees until we obtained a fix 70 miles west of Denmark and changed course to 260 degrees. We then knew we had to ditch but hoped to get within 80 miles of the English coast. All this time the wireless operator was trying to get fixes. The flight engineer was acting as my runner and helping the navigator with the wounded. The former had previously said that he was all right but we found out later that he too was wounded. I discovered that my straps had been shot away, and the flight engineer managed to fix me up some makeshift ones from oxygen extension tubes. At 0450 hours he went aft, after I had given him 3 minutes warning of ditching. That was 5 hours after leaving Berlin.
>
> Ditching the aircraft presented no troubles, although only 10 degrees of flap could be obtained… I went back and got the pigeon, wireless and other equipment which might be of use. As soon as it was light, and a rather large

predatory-looking bird had left the area, I launched the pigeon. The rear gunner went into a coma and died at about 0600 hours. At about 0900 hours I was keeping watch while the crew were asleep and saw two specks on the horizon, which came straight towards us at about 500ft. They resolved into Hudsons, dropped smoke-floats and circled us. Emergency rations were dropped and at about 1100 hours an airborne lifeboat was dropped. At 1600 hours two Naval MLs appeared and we were taken aboard. (Bomber Command Quarterly Review No 6)

The same night, Fg Off Randall and his 460 Squadron crew in Lancaster III W4988 fell victim to a combination of flak and fighters:

> The flight was uneventful until the approach for bombing the target was made at a height of about 19,000ft when the Lancaster was held by one or two searchlights. The pilot immediately put the aircraft into a turn and dive, attaining a speed of about 300mph IAS, but the Lancaster was soon afterwards coned and fired on by heavy flak. Hits by fragments were registered several times during this time.
>
> When the aircraft was coned the pilot turned on all the cabin lights and found that this was of great assistance in seeing his instruments. He then made an approximate bombing run on the flares, and ordered the bomb aimer to jettison the bombs.
>
> As the searchlights appeared to be thinnest to the north it was decided to go out of the target that way; continuous weaving and a gentle dive were carried out as evasive action against predicted flak as the aircraft was still coned.
>
> After diving to about 14,000ft, the Lancaster was in such a position that the searchlights were pointing nearly vertically; suddenly the flak stopped and fighters came in to attack. It is believed that there were three fighters – two Ju 88s and a Me 109. The first attack came from dead astern and level, but although the tracer passed close to the Lancaster, the pilot believes no hits were made on it. The second attack came from about 45 degrees on the port quarter and slightly above, and in this attack the port engine was hit and set on fire. The pilot cut off the petrol and feathered the propeller and the flight engineer operated the fire extinguisher, with the result that the fire went out shortly afterwards. The pilot was about to trim the aircraft for three-engined flying after feathering the port outer engine but found that this was not necessary; there must therefore have been some unusual drag on the starboard side and the pilot thinks that the starboard undercarriage may have dropped, since the warning light showed red about 5 minutes later. In addition it was not possible to close the bomb doors.
>
> There were several more attacks, and at one stage there were probably two fighters attacking simultaneously from the port and starboard quarters as there were two streams of tracers intersecting in front of the aircraft. During the second or third attack the mid-upper turret was hit and badly damaged so that it was useless and the gunner whose microphone had been blown off his face, got out of his turret and went aft to the rear turret, where he found that the rear gunner had got out of the turret as his guns were unserviceable due to the barrels being buckled by cannon fire.
>
> Finally the starboard outer engine was hit and set on fire and the searchlights then doused and the fighters broke off their attack. The fire was extinguished by the same drill as was used for the port outer engine. The pilot was told later by the mid-upper gunner that at this time there was a fire above... the bomb doors and a considerable quantity of smoke in the fuselage. After feathering the two outer engines, the inboard engines were running at 2850 +9 but it was not possible to maintain height and the control of the aircraft was poor. The pilot tried to trim the aircraft but was unable to do so and the aircraft continued diving rapidly.
>
> Shortly after telling the crew to stand by to abandon the aircraft, the pilot noticed a sudden torrent of wind blowing up from the nose and going out through his perspex canopy which had been damaged.... The aircraft which was at about 7,000ft was still losing height and the pilot told the flight engineer to get 3000 +12 on the two remaining engines. However, as even then the aircraft continued to lose height the flight engineer pulled the cut-out when they were down to 5,000ft and got 3000 +14 from the engines. The pilot's idea was to get as far away from the target as possible before it was necessary to bale out.
>
> The port centre and starboard inner petrol tanks were badly holed in the engagement, because on leaving the target there were only 600 gallons left whereas on arrival there had been 1200 gallons. After pulling the cut-out, the loss of height was checked and, after jettisoning the bomb carriers, it was possible to climb slowly to 6,000ft. When it became apparent that the aircraft might be able to remain airborne for some little time it was decided to set course for Sweden... It was necessary to fly at an IAS of 105-110mph to maintain height, and to keep straight full port aileron and full weight on port rudder applied. The elevator control was forcing the control column back, so that considerable force was required to push it forward and keep the aircraft level as the trimmer was useless. Moreover, the control kept shuddering. (Report K56, Bomber Command ORS)

When they were over what they thought was Sweden – which was, in fact, Denmark – three of the crew baled out. By the time the remaining crew were able to bale out, they were indeed over Sweden – and being engaged by Swedish AA fire. When the aircraft crashed, it was the Swedish who claimed to have shot it down!

There is some record that the Lancaster IIs were taken off operations in September. Few details are available, but it is recorded that this decision was reversed in October.

As part of routine investigations into bomber losses, the ORS gave consideration to the effect of fire on them. The conclusion was that a great many aircraft were lost due to fires in the wings, with the petrol tanks burning or even exploding. On 11 September, the Air Staff agreed to the installation of a nitrogen system in the petrol tanks, 'to be fitted in the following order – Lancaster, Halifax, Stirling, Wellington... All production aircraft were, therefore, to have the system fitted pre-delivery'. The first Lancasters to be fitted were delivered to 617 Squadron in March of the following year.

The most effective way to reduce losses was to avoid the enemy defences. The growing scale of the RCM (radio countermeasures) war – window, ABC (*see below*) and other elements – as well as attempts to prevent the enemy guessing the true target, had all become important in the increasingly complex battle being fought over Germany.

One new tactic introduced in September was the 'spoof' raid, intended to confuse and divide the enemy night-fighter force. The first example was carried out by 21 Lancasters and eight Mosquitoes on the night of 22/23 on Oldenburg; the pattern of the attack was designed to simulate that of a Main Force raid, while the real Main Force attack by 711 aircraft was over Hannover.

Weather Factors

Bomber Command was well aware of the dangers involved in operating in bad weather. An unknown number of aircraft had been lost to weather-related causes –

not least to airframe icing. Various 'fixes' had been attempted, including a de-icing paste called 'Kilfrost', but a memo of October 1942 highlighted the problems with such material:

> On average it added 30lb weight and it took at least 15 minutes to apply to leading edges of mainplanes and control surfaces. (By late 1943 it was only being used on control surfaces).

According to ORS Memo M134, 'The Lancaster was shown to be in general less affected by icing than the other types of aircraft.'

The number of aircraft lost due to weather factors is one of the great unknowns of the bomber war. Icing in particular was a significant factor in a number of post-sortie debriefs where pilots had lost control of their aircraft in icing cloud. The Lancaster had an advantage over many of the earlier types in that it was often able to climb out of such cloud layers, although the climb to 20,000ft took over 40 minutes.

Technological Developments

ABC Operations

October was a hectic month for Bomber Command. Main Force operated on six nights in the first nine days, with 200-300 Lancasters forming part of the attacks on Hagen, Munich, Kassel, Frankfurt, Stuttgart and Hannover. The majority of these attacks achieved reasonable results for light losses.

Perhaps the most significant event in October was the participation in the Stuttgart raid (7/8 October) of the ABC-equipped Lancasters of 101 Squadron (commanded by Wg Cdr C. A. Carey-Foster, and based at Ludford Magna). Airborne Cigar (ARI 5558) was developed at the Telecommunications Research Establishment (TRE) as a means of disrupting the night-fighter R/T control frequencies in three main frequency bands: 30-33, 38.3-42.5, and 48-52 MHz. The aircraft system comprised three transmitters (with three aerials) and one receiver (with one aerial), a visual indicator for the Special Operator, plus various power units and modulators. The receiver swept the frequency band and displayed any received signal as a blip. The operator checked to see if this was a German signal and could then, if desired, tune one of the transmitters to jam the signal; search could then continue until all three transmitters were allocated.

The Air Historical Branch study 'Radio Countermeasures' summarized ABC operations as follows:

> Lancasters of No 101 Squadron were fitted with a panoramic receiver and three transmitters, and carried a specially trained German-speaking ABC operator in addition to the normal crew. The operator listened for German fighter control R/T traffic, in the nature of which he had already been trained by the use of gramophone recordings of actual enemy signals, and applied the jamming to any transmissions which he heard.
>
> Originally, the ABC operators received some assistance from the 'Y' Service control station at West Kingsdown, which passed them details of active frequencies by means of coded references. The 'Y' Service in this country was not able to pick up VHF traffic from the whole of the area over which the bombers operated. Hence, it was soon decided that the ABC operators should find and jam frequencies independently of any ground control. ABC aircraft were spaced at intervals along the bomber stream in order to give complete protection to all aircraft taking part in the raid, and each operator was normally expected to hear and jam VHF transmission in his own vicinity. In addition, they carried out their normal bombing functions, subject only to a limitation in the bomb load due to the extra weight of equipment and a special operator. This weight limitation was in the order of 1,000lbs.

The Squadron lost its first two ABC aircraft on the Hannover raid of 18/19 October, when both Fg Off Humphries (DV230) and Sgt R Daye (DV266) failed to return; only one of the 15 aircrew (Humphries carried a crew of eight) survived to be taken prisoner. This had been an all-Lancaster raid by 360 aircraft, and 19 aircraft had been lost. The tasking for the Squadron was so intense that it became one of the largest Lancaster operators, with over 40 aircraft on strength.

ABC ops were also later flown by other aircraft, including the Stirlings of 214 Squadron. In the second half of October there were a number of all-Lancaster raids, by 350-plus aircraft, although the majority of attacks were still by a Main Force now comprising almost 600 bombers. The offensive power of Bomber Command was expanding at a rapid pace and the Lancasters were beginning to take an increasingly significant role. Furthermore, more of the attacks were proving accurate and the destruction of German cities, with their associated industrial and communication facilities, increased dramatically.

More bombers on operations inevitably meant higher losses – 18 out of 360 Lancasters failed to return from the 18/19 October attack on Hannover, while 16 out of 358 Lancasters did not make it back from Leipzig two nights later.

Gunsights

On 13 October, the Air Fighting Development Unit issued its report into trials on the Mk IIC Gyro Gunsight. (Lancaster II DS719 of 408 Squadron had been flown by the AFDU from late August to late September.) The purpose of the report was to do the following:

> 1. Form an opinion upon the tactical value of the IIC GGS in an FN120 turret by day and night.
> 2. Consider the amount and method of training necessary to obtain satisfactory results from an average air gunner.

The report continued:

> Mk IIC GGS is a development of the MK IC but is a reflector instead of a prismatic sight and has two graticules – a fixed ring seen by the left eye and a moving graticule, controlled by gyros, by the right eye. The moving graticule is not a complete circle but comprises six diamonds radially disposed around a central spot.
>
> The Mk IIC can be used with exceptional accuracy against all fighter targets [by day]. The sight can also be used accurately throughout the standard combat manoeuvres. The sight is the complete answer to gunnery problems and if a reasonable standard of training can be achieved, adequately armed bombers should be perfectly capable of defending themselves against fighters in daylight operations. Good results can be obtained under moonlight conditions using Gyro Day techniques; the accuracy of the gunner's shooting will be increased if the maximum range setting is restricted to 400 yards. On dark nights the gunner's shooting must mainly depend on the type of attack made by the fighter. Under most circumstances the Mk IIC sight is an improvement on the GJ.3. (AFDU Report No 98)

Bomber Protection

Questions of bomber protection were also being addressed by the Bomber

Development Unit. The BDU, now at Newmarket, reported in November on its examination into the provision of an 'under defence position in night bombers', Halifaxes and Lancasters both being subjected to the same tests. The Lancaster trial installation was completed in late September and the aircraft were delivered to the BDU on 1 October. A series of day and night air firing trials were conducted over the Wash area; for the Lancaster, the general conclusions were as follows:

> [The Lancaster installation] is cleared subject to the following points:
> 1. ammo box to be raised 7in;
> 2. support for link chute must have proper anchorage;
> 3. gun-securing strap necessary for stowing gun;
> 4. adjustable back-stop necessary to limit travel of swinging arm and so ensure engagement of locking device;
> 5. electric plug point for reflector sight lead repositioned as liable to damage by gunner's heel;
> 6. guard rail fitted to protect rear turret ammo tracks from damage by crew passing and by gunner helping himself out of his seat.
>
> Field of view and fire from the Lancaster are good, being from 120 degrees forward of vertical to 31 degrees from horizontal aft of vision, and from 10 degrees forward of vertical to 39 degrees from horizontal aft for fire. (BDU Report dated 13 November 1943)

Despite these basically favourable comments, this was yet another 'good idea' that made little progress towards front-line employment.

No 100 Gp

The electronic war had become so complex and intense that on 23 November the RAF created No 100 Gp to specialize in RCM, although no Lancaster units joined this Group. The main RCM Lancaster unit, 101 Squadron, remained part of No 1 Group throughout the war.

Gee-H

The BDU conducted a number of trials in the latter part of 1944 to evaluate various aspects of ARI 5025 (Gee-H, or, more simply, 'G-H'). In Part 2 of Report 19 (dated 15 August 1943), the results of a Gee-H test using a Lancaster II with Llandow as the 'target' were summarized thus:

> 147 runs were made using Llandow as a target, the average error was 420 yards, but this can be reduced to 280 yards if the systematic error is allowed for. Thus 98 per cent of bombs would fall within a 1,300 yard circle. On the basis of these figures, it is considered that practise bombs may be dropped blind at Stormy Down range without interfering with the comfort of holiday makers at Porthcawl[!].

The bombing at Stormy Down's sea range took place in two phases by aircraft detached to Fairwood Common for the period 1-13 September and 7-13 October. The results were summarized in Part 3 of the Report (dated 18 November 1943):

> On the basis of the Part 2 results it was calculated that the likely error in bombing Ruhr targets would be 610 yards. The Ruhr is approaching maximum effective blind bombing range. Targets nearer to the transmitting stations would be bombed more accurately.
>
> Results of the bombing at Stormy Down showed that the technique of a Timed Run gave more accurate results and allowed greater freedom to the pilot in both height and groundspeed. 87 runs using this technique gave an average error of 335 yards.

Use of this bombing aid increased throughout 1944.

Lancaster I W4963 shows to good effect the H2S blister under the fuselage, plus various aerials at the base of the rear turret. Ken Delve Collection

The Hercules-powered Lancaster II served with a number of units; DS778 went to 408 Squadron in September 1943, and was lost on the night of 22/23 October. Ken Delve Collection

The End of 1943

November

November began quietly, with Main Force operating on only three nights in the first half of the month. One of these operations was significant: on the Düsseldorf raid of 3/4 November, Lancaster IIs made the first large-scale use of the new Gee-H aid. Some 38 Lancasters equipped with Gee-H were tasked to attack the Mannesmann steelworks in the northern part of the city. The failure rate of the equipment was high and a number of other aircraft were either shot down or had to return early. As a result, only 15 Gee-H aircraft claimed to have attacked the target, although German records show that it did suffer some damage. In an attack by 589 bombers (344 Lancasters), Main Force had carried out a reasonably effective raid, losing 18 aircraft (11 Lancasters).

This attack on Düsseldorf brought yet another VC to a Lancaster pilot. The recipient was Flt Lt Bill Reid of 61 Squadron.

A target that had been proving difficult to destroy was the Antheor viaduct. On 11/12 November, this was tasked as a 12,000lb bomb target and 617 sent ten aircraft on the long route to southern France. The searchlight defences made the attack difficult and no bombs hit the viaduct, although a few near misses were scored. The Lancasters flew on to North Africa. They returned home on the night of 16 November; ED375, flown by Flt Lt Youseman, crashed on take-off from Rabal.

The Battle of Berlin

November also saw the opening of what has been called the Battle of Berlin. The first raid took place on 18/19 November, when 400 Lancasters attacked the 'Big City', with a second force attacking Ludwigshaven to split the night-fighter force. A combination of poor weather and poor PFF marking led to a scattered raid – although losses were light. The night of 22/23 November saw the Command mount a maximum effort against Berlin; of the 765 bombers, 469 were Lancasters. Marking was accurate and Berlin was hit hard. An all-Lancaster force returned the following night, bombing through cloud.

A few nights later, on 26/27, another all-Lancaster attack, by 443 aircraft, marked the operational debut for another three Lanc squadrons (432, 463 and 550). Results were again good, but bomber losses were high, with 28 Lancasters falling to the defences. Further disaster struck when the bombers returned to England, to discover that virtually all bases south of Yorkshire were covered in thick fog. As many aircraft were short of fuel, they could not divert, but had to try to land at bases in the south – 14 Lancasters crashed or crash-landed, and a number of crewmen were killed.

The Bomber Command ORS Reports had this to say:

> Night Raid Report No 470, Berlin 18/19 Nov 1943. The first of four great November attacks on Berlin was delivered by a force of 440 Lancasters and four Mosquitoes. As on most subsequent occasions during this winter, the German capital was covered with a blanket of 10/10 cloud, but TIs could be seen cascading to the ground, and much of the effort undoubtedly fell on the city. Fighters were not very active and there is no evidence that they achieved any success; only nine Lancasters (2 per cent) were lost but a further 90 were damaged by flak. (Night Raid Report No 476, Berlin 26/27 November 1943)
>
> The fourth raid was delivered by 376 Lancasters and seven Mosquitoes from a cloudless sky, but primary blind-markers were scattered short of the target and all but one of the secondary markers had become u/s. There were few fighters but flak was intense. 28 bombers lost (6.2 per cent), 14 others wrecked beyond repair. Nine were lost over Berlin, two of these to fighters, nine were shot down on the outbound

route, 40 were damaged by flak and 11 damaged by fighters; there were three collisions.

One of the interesting features in these reports is the mention of 14 bombers 'wrecked beyond repair'; this aspect of the bombers' efforts is often ignored.

On 2/3 December, the Command suffered another dismal night over Berlin; a planned maximum effort was abandoned when the Yorkshire-based Halifax units were fogged in (only 15 Halifaxes joined the 425 Lancasters on this raid). Other bombers turned back because of bad weather over the North Sea, while those that made it to the target found the German night-fighters waiting. Results were poor, and losses were once again high, with 37 Lancs among the night's 40 casualties. Attacking Berlin was proving to be expensive and difficult.

One of the squadrons to suffer particularly badly was 625 Squadron, which lost five of its 25 bombers. W/O Sydney Ellis received the Conspicuous Gallantry Medal for his actions that night. The citation for W/O Sydney Ellis's CGM reads:

> One night in December 1943 W/O Ellis was the pilot of an aircraft detailed to attack Berlin. During the initial bomb run the aircraft was hit by AA fire, which injured the rear gunner [Sgt D. G. Wightman] and rendered his turret unserviceable. W/O Ellis maintained a steady run, however, and made his first attack. Just as the first bombs had been released the aircraft was raked by bullets from a fighter and the rear gunner sustained further injuries; the mid-upper gunner [Sgt W. G. Jones] was also wounded. Although the enemy delivered another long burst of fire, W/O Ellis continued his run and attacked the target exactly as planned. On leaving the target area it was discovered that much damage had been sustained. The intercom and hydraulic systems and the turrets were all unserviceable. The mainplane and the fuselage had been damaged, while the bomb doors could not be closed. In spite of this, W/O Ellis flew on and eventually reached an airfield in this country, landing his aircraft safely without the aid of flaps and in spite of punctured tyres. In harassing circumstances, this pilot displayed skill, courage and devotion to duty beyond praise.

The Bomber Command ORS Report (No 481) for the 2/3 December attack on Berlin makes interesting reading:

> 458 aircraft, mostly Lancasters, left to give Berlin its fifth heavy raid within a fortnight. Unexpected winds were encountered en route, which blew many aircraft off track and nullified the Pathfinders' efforts to make DR runs from Rathenow. Consequently, although there were gaps in the cloud covering the city, most of the bombing was scattered over a wide area of open country to the south. Forty bombers (8.7 per cent) were lost. Some 'Y' aircraft found their own winds from H2S fixing en route, but they differed so much from those forecast that the latter were used in preference.
>
> Defences. Ground – at the beginning of the attack, heavy flak was fired in a loose barrage up to 22,000ft around the marker flares, and was predicted at seen targets through gaps in the cloud. Searchlights were active in great numbers and took every opportunity the weather offered for illuminating our bombers. after the raid had been in progress half an hour, and soon after the appearance of fighter flares, the ceiling of the barrage was lowered and the flak decreased, although individual aircraft were heavily engaged when coned. Fighters – sightings of enemy aircraft were almost entirely confined to the target area and the last part of the outward route. Most of the types identified were twin-engined, with Ju 88s predominating. The running commentary began plotting our aircraft from the neighbourhood of the Zuider Zee, and

November 3/4, 1943 – Flt Lt William Reid VC (No 61 Squadron)

William Reid joined the RAFVR in April 1941 and was posted to 61 Squadron at Syerston in September 1943. On 3 December 1943, he was en route to Düsseldorf. His citation reads:

Shortly after crossing the Dutch coast, the pilot's windscreen was shattered by fire from a Me 110. Owing to a failure in the heating circuit, the rear gunner's hands were too cold for him to open fire immediately or to operate his microphone and so give warning of danger; but after a brief delay he managed to return the Messerschmitt's fire and it was driven off. During the fight with the Messerschmitt, Reid was wounded in the head, shoulders and hands. The elevator trimming tabs of the aircraft were damaged and it became difficult to control. The rear turret, too, was badly damaged and the communications system and compasses were put out of action. Reid ascertained that his crew were unscathed and, saying nothing about his own injuries, he continued his mission.

Soon afterwards, the Lancaster was attacked by a Focke-Wulf 190. This time, the enemy's fire raked the bomber from stem to stern. The rear gunner replied with his only serviceable gun, but the state of his turret made accurate aiming impossible. The navigator was killed and the wireless operator fatally injured. The mid-upper turret was hit and the oxygen system put out of action. Reid was again wounded and the flight engineer, though hit in the forearm, supplied him with oxygen from a portable supply.

Flight Lieutenant Reid refused to be turned from his objective and Düsseldorf was reached some 50 minutes later. He had memorized his course to the target and had continued in such a normal manner that the bomb aimer, who was cut off by the failure of the communications system, knew nothing of his captain's injuries or of the casualties to his comrades. Photographs show that when the bombs were released the aircraft was right over the centre of the target. Steering by the pole star and the moon, Reid then set course for home. He was growing weak from loss of blood. The emergency oxygen supply had given out. With the windscreen shattered, the cold was intense. He lapsed into semi-consciousness. The flight engineer, with some help from the bomb aimer, kept the Lancaster in the air despite heavy anti-aircraft fire over the Dutch coast.

The North Sea crossing was accomplished. An airfield was sighted. The captain revived, resumed control and made ready to land. Ground mist partially obscured the runway lights. The captain was also much bothered by blood from his head wound getting into his eyes. But he made a safe landing although the leg of the damaged undercarriage collapsed when the load came on.

Wounded in two attacks, without oxygen, suffering severely from cold, his navigator dead, his wireless operator fatally wounded, his aircraft crippled and defenceless, Flight Lieutenant Reid showed superb courage and leadership in penetrating a further 200 miles into enemy territory to attack one of the most strongly defended targets in Germany, every additional mile increasing the hazards of the long and perilous journey home. His tenacity and devotion to duty were beyond praise.

Bill Reid subsequently served with 617 Squadron, failing to return from a raid on 31 July 1944, when his Lancaster was struck by a bomb from another Lancaster. Only two of the crew managed to escape and both were taken prisoner. Bill Reid remained a PoW to the end of the war. In December 1998, he was the only surviving Bomber Command VC.

announced that Berlin was the main objective at 1947, 19 minutes before zero hour. Many illuminated targets were provided for the fighters over the capital. Corona warned the fighters of fog and told them to land, angering the commentators.

Aircraft missing 40
Aircraft damaged flak 53
Fighters 8
Flak/fighters 3
Non-enemy action 15

The casualty rate was above the average for recent raids on Berlin. The unexpected winds caused aircraft to stray from the route; cloud gaps over the target enabled searchlights to illuminate our bombers, and the enemy fighter force was in action over the target almost as soon as the attack began. 56 aircraft (12.4 per cent) were reported damaged by flak and 11 (2.3 per cent) by fighters; two aircraft were wrecked on landing, two collided over enemy territory but escaped serious injury.

Despite (or perhaps because of) the recent heavy loss rates, Harris issued an upbeat message. In a letter of 7 December, he outlined the recent achievements of his Command and concluded that, by April 1944, they could achieve 'a state of devastation in which surrender is inevitable'. This, however, he stated, would require priority in production for Lancasters, and equipment to make No 100 Group fully operational. As we now know, the Lancaster never made it to this Group.

Phase II of the Battle of Berlin began on 16/17 December, when just under 500 bombers (483 Lancasters) attacked Berlin. A combination of strong defences and bad weather on return to the UK meant that 54 aircraft (25 Lancasters) were lost. (The bad weather had also covered the Continent and reduced night-fighter operations to a minimum – otherwise, losses would no doubt have been even higher.) Of the 54 bombers lost, 30 crashed on return to the UK, the weather not having made the forecast improvement. No 97 Squadron lost eight aircraft – seven due to the bad weather back in England; only two crews, having neared the end of their fuel endurance, baled out. As Bill Chorley commented, in his excellent *RAF Bomber Command Losses of the Second World War, Volume Four* (1943), 'This had been the worst night in the wartime history of 97 Squadron and amounted to around one-sixth of the Squadron's losses for 1943.'

A maximum effort, 700+ aircraft (457 Lancasters), attacked Berlin on 29/30 December and this was followed two nights later by an all-Lancaster raid by 421 aircraft. The bomber tactics seemed to work quite well on the first night, with a non-direct approach path and a series of diversionary raids by Mosquitoes; they were also aided by bad weather, which grounded many fighters. However, these conditions did not prevail for the second attack, when the night-fighters were once again active and effective. Most of the 28 Lancasters that were lost fell victim to night-fighter attacks on the outbound route. This 6.7 per cent loss rate was one of the worst for some time.

Lancasters were over Berlin again the next night but, once again, the fighters proved effective – almost one-third of the Pathfinders were lost or returned to base early. This ended Phase II of the Battle of Berlin. The assessment was that the battle was proving harder than expected, partly because of the lower number of available aircraft (and, thus, bomb tonnage that could be dropped on the target), following the decision to withdraw the Halifax. This decision was reversed for the remaining two phases of the battle.

Flt Lt Bill Reid (centre) of 61 Squadron won the Victoria Cross for his actions during the Düsseldorf attack of 3/4 November 1943. Andy Thomas Collection

Other Targets

Other targets were also attacked around this time; for example, on the night of 20/21 December, a force of 650 bombers attacked Frankfurt. The Halifax element, 257 aircraft, lost 27 of their number, whilst the 390 Lancasters suffered 14 losses, many of these falling to fighter attacks on the route out to the target. Flt Lt Richard Starkey's 106 Squadron Lancaster was attacked and damaged:

Our third operation was to Frankfurt on December 20, 1943; the second had been to Berlin at the commencement of the Battle of Berlin, which opened in November. We took off for Frankfurt in aircraft JB534. My mid-upper gunner had been granted compassionate leave and his replacement was a sergeant whose crew had already completed their first tour, and he had to complete his by flying with other crews.

We had no trouble on the outward journey and flew at 21,000ft. The target was covered by a lot of cloud so the ground markers were hidden and I also remember that the Germans had lit a decoy fire south of the city.

About 10 miles north of the target on our return journey, we were fired upon by cannon and machine gun from what we presumed was a night-fighter. The rear gunner immediately instructed me to corkscrew, as enemy tracer came from the port quarter. I did so and after one complete corkscrew, resumed normal course. I could tell we had been hit around the port mainplane, and hoped there would be no flames. However, a further attack followed immediately and the aircraft was hit again. I corkscrewed again but no fighter was sighted by either gunner so we resumed course. The fighter was never seen and although the rear gunner attempted to open fire on three occasions, his guns failed to function. When we resumed course it was evident that the aircraft had been severely damaged, because it started to shudder violently and I had great difficulty controlling it. The vibration transferred to my body as I fought to maintain control. The rear gunner reported that the port fin tail plane rudder was extensively damaged, and a large part had disappeared. As for the mainplane we could not see any damage but we knew there was some.

Soon after the attack the navigator instructed me to change course, but on applying rudder and aileron, the aircraft began to bank steeply and I put her back on an even keel by using automatic pilot – manual controls were ineffective. The shuddering continued and I decided that this was due to damage to the port tailplane. I asked the navigator what the remaining headings would be according to his flight plan and log. He informed me that there would be slight turnings to starboard which meant that I would not have to apply port rudder. At this particular point we did not know that the aileron was just a skeleton, the covering having disappeared during the attack. I also decided that if we were to get back to base safely, it would necessitate a right-hand circuit.

We were lucky that the engines were intact, but the shuddering continued and after approximately two and three-quarter hours we approached base. The wireless operator informed the control tower of the condition of the aircraft and that it was essential to make a right-hand circuit and also that we must land immediately. Permission was given to circuit to the right at 800ft and other aircraft were ordered to maintain their height. On our approach down the funnel we began to drift to starboard and I dared not counteract this. I switched the landing light on and touched down on the grass, 50 yards to the right of the flare path.

When the aircraft was examined next morning, the full extent of the damage was revealed. There was severe damage to the port fin and rudder, more than 50 per cent was missing. The port side of the fuselage had been riddled with bullets which stopped just before the wireless operator's position. Material covering the port aileron had been ripped off and a cannon shell had exploded on the underside of the port mainplane creating a jagged hole approximately one foot in diameter. If the shell had exploded further forward, it would have hit the fuel tanks and the aircraft would have 'gone up'. Repairs had to be carried out on the airfield by workmen from Avro, and took approximately six weeks to complete. Aircraft JB534 was transferred to A Flight after the repairs were completed, only to crash near the village of Martin adjacent to the airfield, when returning from its first operation, killing all the crew except one.

SECRET (30) (57)

FUEL AND BOMB LOAD DATA

	LANCASTER I AND III *		HALIFAX II 1A		HALIFAX III	
Distance	Minimum Petrol	Maximum Bombs	Minimum Petrol	Maximum Bombs	Minimum Petrol	Ma B
300	560		625		655	
350	620		695		730	
400	680		765		805	
450	740	15375	835		880	
500	800	15055	905	12810	955	
550	860	14625	975	12325	1030	
600	920	14190	1045	11820	1110	1
650	980	13760	1115	11310	1185	1
700	1040	13330	1185	10805	1260	1
750	1100	12895	1260	10295	1335	1
800	1160	12465	1330	9690	1410	1
850	1220	12030	1400	9180	1490	1
900	1280	11600	1470	8675	1565	
950	1340	11165	1540	8165	1640	
1000	1400	10735	1610	7660	1715	
1050	1460	10305	1680	7150	1790	
1100	1520	9870	1750	6645	1865	
1150	1580	9440	1820	6135	1945	
1200	1640	9005	1890	5630	2020	
1250	1700	8575	1965	5120	2095	
1300	1760	8145	2035	4615	2175	
1350	1820	7710	2105	4105	2245	
1400	1880	7280	2175	3595	2320	
1450	1940	6845	2245	3085		
1500	2000	6415	2315	2575		
1550	2060	5983				
1600	2120	5550				

Fuel and bomb load data table as featured in a PFF instruction manual dated December 1943; in addition, the manual gave the operational air miles per gallon for the Lanc as 0.84 mile/gallon. Ken Delve Collection

Window was one of the major counter-measures employed at this time and in late 1943 the ORS re-examined the bomber wave plans:

> Window dropped in still air at 500ft/min and it is desirable therefore to arrange that each high-flying wave should be followed by a wave of aircraft flying 2-3,000ft lower so that window dropped by the earlier wave should be of benefit to the latter. Thus waves should, for preference, attack in the order Lancaster-Halifax-Stirling, although this gives problems of the slower aircraft straggling post target. The proposal was compromised so that the Halifax flew the first one or two waves, followed by the Lancaster as this gave a more uniform concentration over the target. The stream would also be more compact on leaving the target as the lower flying and slower types would be away from the target area before the fighters arrived. (AHB Narrative, 'ORS in Bomber Command')

1943 Summaries

The following summaries of Lancaster effort for 1943 are contained in the War Room Manual of Bomber Command Operations:

> The number of Lancaster squadrons had risen from 17 (272 aircraft) on December 31, 1942 to 35 (632 aircraft) by December 1943, the latter figure representing over 50 per cent of the total Bomber Command strength of 65 squadrons (1,192 aircraft). The Lancasters flew 28,142 sorties at an average rate of 112 sorties per month per 20 aircraft (the next best utilization was that for the Wellington at 99 sorties/month/20 aircraft). These sorties comprised 42.5 per cent of all day/night operations by Bomber Command but the bomb load dropped was nearer to 70 per cent of the total – 59,267 tons of High Explosive (70.77 per cent of total) and 100,517 tons of incendiary (63.85 per cent of total). Of the Main Force Lancasters despatched, 92 per cent claimed to have reached the target. Losses of 962 aircraft (7204 aircrew) were, at 3.4 per cent, the lowest of all the bomber types, although the Lancaster 'gardening' effort proved the most expensive with a loss rate of 3.89 per cent (for 590 sorties) dropping 2367 'X' type and 129 'Y' type. Perhaps the most significant statistic for the Lancaster is that of bomb lift – only 50 per cent of the bomber force but 70 per cent of the bomb tonnage. (Manual of Bomber Command Operations)

CHAPTER SIX

January to July 1944

Changes to the Training Establishment

In 1944, there was a major change in training policy. All Lancasters were withdrawn from the HCUs, in order to accelerate the replacement of Stirlings within No 3 Group. The HCUs attached to No 3 and No 5 Groups therefore received Stirlings, while No 1 Group received Halifaxes.

The policy of employing the maximum number of Lancasters at the front line meant that very few aircraft were available for training purposes. With all the other bomber types, crews went through an appropriate Heavy Conversion Unit. For the Lancaster crewmen, the initial parts of the training were the same as for their colleagues who ended up on the Halifax or Stirling.

It was, however, realized that some Lancaster conversion was required pre-squadron, so three new units – the Lancaster Finishing Schools (LFS) – were formed. These were No 1 LFS at Lindholme, No 3 LFS at Feltwell and No 5 LFS at Syerston (the numbers relating to the Group to which the unit belonged), although 1678 HCF and 1679 HCF also retained Lancasters. The initial intention was that each LFS would train 36 crews per fortnight; thus, the student pilot would have a four-week (40 hours' flying) HCU course, followed by a 10-day LFS course of 10 hours.

By mid-1944, the Lancaster pilot would have followed, in general terms, this routine:

Coming in to land, Lancaster II DS723 of 408 Squadron, the aircraft was lost on the November 27, 1943 attack on Berlin. Ken Delve Collection

	week	flying hours day	flying hours night
Training Unit	10	40	40
Aircrew School	2	nil	nil
Conversion Unit	4	20	20
Finishing School	2	5	5
Squadron	1	5	5
Total	19	70	70

An 'Aircrew Training Bulletin' of mid-1944 summarized the purpose of the LFSs:

> Here they receive a course of 10 hours' flying, consisting almost entirely of conversion to type. Engine handling is carefully taught, as in many cases Lancasters are equipped with different-type engines to those in the CUs and OTUs.

In mid-1944, John Gee, having flown a tour in Halifaxes, was sent to 1662 HCU at Blyton and then to the No 1 Group LFS at Hemswell, en route to a Flight Commander tour:

> I had my first taste of flying the Avro Lancaster. To get into the pilot's seat was a bit difficult as one had to clamber over the main wing spar centre section and then go through a small opening. This was not all that easy particularly if you were wearing full operational flying clothing and parachute harness. As soon as one got into the pilot's seat one could feel that there was something special about this aeroplane. All the controls were easily to hand and the perspex cover over the cockpit was slightly higher than the top of the fuselage, giving the pilot a commanding view. I was able to turn my head and see all round, even directly rearward over the two tail fins and the rear gun turret. There was none of that claustrophobic feeling that we got in the cockpit of some other aeroplanes.
>
> As soon as I took off on my first flight, I could feel the difference, it was so wonderfully balanced and light on the controls, it handled more like a fighter than a bomber. I immediately fell in love with it. Its peformance with one engine stopped was quite incredible. You could stop one engine and feather the propeller and, apart from a slight drop in speed, you would barely notice it. Any tendency to turn could be trimmed out on the rudder trim. There was no pressure required on the rudder to keep the aeroplane straight. Even with two engines stopped and feathered on one side it could be very nearly trimmed to fly straight without leg pressure [on the rudder]. It would even fly on one engine for a while in an unladen condition.
> (John Gee in *Wingspan*)

John Gee was posted to 153 Squadron at Scampton in October 1944. This unit had been a fighter squadron since its formation in 1941, but it re-formed in October 1944 at Kirmington by acquiring crews from 166 Squadron (which had been operating Lancasters at Kirmington since September 1943).

Bomb aimer Don Clay was with his crew at No 1 LFS in August:

> We were airborne on August 5, 1944 on a Familiarisation and Circuits and landing exercise that lasted 3 hours; a similar exercise took place two or three days later. The ground work consisted mainly of getting to know our various stations and equipment in the Lancaster as well as escape procedures for baling out and dinghy drill. As my operational position in the aircraft was in the nose to the rear of the front turret, I would be responsible for the two 0.303 Brownings – they were my 'babies' should the aircraft be attacked.
>
> The Lancaster's escape routine when baling out was from the front of the aircraft; in fact, in an emergency it was my job to pull the escape hatch into the aircraft so that the crew could, on an order from the skipper, exit – with parachutes on, of course. The rule was that six of the crew would escape in this way, and the rear gunner would rotate his turret and go out backwards. We were to have two more exercises at LFS before being posted to operational squadrons. The first was a fighter affiliation exercise in conjunction with a single-engined fighter – in our case a Spitfire and a Mustang. The aircraft would carry out mock attacks on us at about 15,000ft and from all angles and our skipper would be on an alert from the gunners who would give him instructions over the intercoms to what evasive action he should take. By the end of the exercise our 'lad' left us in no doubt that, given the correct gen by the gunners, no Jerry fighters would ever mark us down as a 'kill' – of course, predicted flak would be a totally different problem, one just prayed that no AA shell had our number on it.
>
> With our last exercise at LFS on August 9, we were sent home on leave for a week and told to report back to Hemswell before being posted to an operational squadron.
> (Don Clay, pers comm)

Fine airborne study of Lancaster X KB783; the aircraft was used by the A&AEE for trials with the Martin mid-upper turret before going on to serve with 428 and 419 Squadrons. It survived the war to return to Canada in June 1945. FlyPast Collection

Don and his crew arrived at Waltham to join 100 Squadron on 18 August.

The Battle of Berlin Continues

On the first night of 1944, Berlin was again the target. Of 421 Lancasters, 28 were lost (6.7 per cent), most falling to fighters en route to the target. It was a similar story the following night with 27 Lancs (out of 362) becoming casualties. The PFF suffered heavily; 156 Squadron, for example, lost five of its 14 participants. Only two other Main Force attacks were made in the first half of January – Stettin on 5/6 and Brunswick on 14/15. The Brunswick attack cost 38 of the 496 Lancasters (7.6 per cent), but caused little damage to the target. The German 'running commentary' tactic was proving difficult to counter; the bomber stream was usually picked up by night-fighters soon after coasting in, and was subjected to attack all the way to and from the target.

On 20/21 January, 769 bombers were tasked to attack Berlin; little had changed from the previous attacks – results were at best average and losses were high (22 of the 35 lost aircraft were Halifaxes, out of a despatched force of 264 aircraft). The next raid, on 27/28 January, saw 515 Lancasters en route to Berlin in the first operation to involve more than 500 Lancasters; they made a reasonably effective attack, but lost 33 of their number.

One of the night-fighter aces who found the bomber stream that night was Wilhelm Johnen; in the space of 30 minutes, he had claimed three Lancasters:

> The met reported a cloud ceiling of 150ft with solid cloud up to 13,000ft. From 3,000ft there was a danger of icing. The night was pitch black... a green flare was fired from the control tower, starting orders at last! Visibility was appalling and the green flarepath lights could hardly be seen through the thick rain-lashed perspex.

The Squadron Commander, Hpt Bar, crashed on take-off but Johnen was safely airborne, although having to struggle with icing as his Bf 110 climbed higher. The bombers' position was given away by British flares and Berlin's flak defences:

> I approached this square on a southerly course and spotted a couple of four-engined Lancasters directly above the target. After a short attack the first bomber exploded and fell in burning debris through the clouds. The second banked steeply to starboard, trying to escape. The Tommies fired at me with all their guns, framing my aircraft with gleaming tracers. I pressed home the attack; the tail unit grew even larger in my sights. Now was the time to shoot. The firepower of my guns was terrific. My armour-piercing shells riddled the well-protected wing tanks and the pilot's armoured cockpit; the tracers set fire to the petrol and the HE shells tore great holes in the wings.

A maximum effort went out on the night of 28/29 January, with 432 Lancs included in the 677-aircraft force. Berlin was hit again two nights later; with high bomber losses, this brought Phase III to a close.

Despite the loss rates, this series of four attacks was assessed as a success, with damage to Berlin having been significant. The final Phase of the Battle comprised only two raids: on 15/16 February and 24/25 March 1944. On the second of these, the overall loss rate was almost 10 per cent – the highest of the campaign so far. Since 18/19 November 1943, the Command had mounted 9,099 sorties against Berlin (7,249 by Lancasters), dropping 29,804 tons of bombs; overall losses were 501 aircraft, 380 of these being Lancasters.

Dealing with Enemy Defence

Jamming and Spoofing

Throughout 1943, and into 1944, the German night-fighters posed an increasing threat. According to Bomber Command ORB, to counter the 'appearance of night-fighter R/T in the 30-35 M/C band, modifications [were] made to a number of existing ABC transmitters, one in each of three aircraft of 101 Squadron, to produce some jamming effort in this band'. The active jamming of German control frequencies and radars was to increase dramatically in 1944, with new equipments being fitted to a greater number of Main Force aircraft for self-defence. Specialist jamming aircraft, such as 101 Squadron's ABC Lancasters, were split up throughout the bomber stream in order to give cover to as many bombers as possible. A great deal of jamming and spoofing was also carried out by groundstations in the UK.

Dropping Window

While the RCM campaign was having some effect, the individual protection of aircraft still relied on passive aids such as Monica and Fishpond, plus the dropping of window. In December 1943, the BDU was testing an automatic launching machine made by Fairey; its function was 'to convey bundles of window at a predetermined rate from a bulk storage and deliver them singly through a chute'. One of the problems with the operational use of window was the need for one or more crew members to spend a great deal of time dispensing the window bundles. The new machine was intended to relieve the aircrew of this duty while, at the same time, ensuring the correct dispersal of window. The BDU report concluded that the machine was too heavy and bulky for use in operational aircraft and would need extensive modifications.

Camouflage

One of the simplest ways of avoiding the attention of night-fighters (and searchlights) was effective camouflage. Various trials were carried out, including one conducted by the BDU using a Lancaster III. Its aim was:

> To see if the new scheme suggested by the RAE was better – flat undersurfaces painted shiny black, curved undersurfaces matt black, top surface a special pattern of light grey. One normal and one new-scheme Lancaster was used in searchlight trials and with air observation by an FIU fighter. The results were the same in all cases: the new scheme proved no more effective.

There were no significant changes to the camouflage used by the Lancasters during the war, until the creation of Tiger Force in mid-1945 for operations in the Far East.

AGLT

It was inevitable that a percentage of bombers were going to be engaged by flak or fighters. With flak, little could be done, other than using window to decoy radar predictors, and numerous memoranda were issued to the effect that evasion was pointless – turning away from one anticipated flak burst was likely to put the aircraft into the path of another burst, so it was better to maintain course, especially in the target area. With fighters, a great deal depended on the ability of the gunners to pick up the threat, and call for evasion while engaging the fighter. With visual acquisition being very limited at night, attention was turned to providing a radar system. This led to the Automatic Gun Laying Turret (AGLT) system, developed under the code name 'Village Inn'.

The first AGLT-equipped Lancaster, JA959, arrived at Newmarket on 24 October 1943 for the BDU to undertake trials. A radar scanner was fixed underneath the rear turret and the gunner was provided with a GGS, to which was added:

> A small cathode ray tube projecting an image in the form of a green spot in the line of sight of the gunner when he looks through the GGS. When the scanner picks up another aircraft, the green spot moves off in the direction of the other aircraft and sprouts wings the size of which is proportional to the range. When the scanner is pointing within 3 degrees of the following aircraft the green spot should be exactly superimposed on the aircraft, thus providing the gunner with a target at which to aim, with the aid of the moving graticule of the GGS. (BDU Report No 26)

Overall, the BDU was impressed with this prototype system, although various points were raised in the hope that they would be addressed when the second aircraft arrived. Among the conclusions were the following:

> AGL appears to be able to pick up another aircraft at about 1,400 yards range and to hold that aircraft till it is within 150 yards. The radar automatic ranging device appears most satisfactory and to be capable of setting more accurate range on the GGS than the gunner could by pedal action in daylight. The presentation of range to the gunner by size of wings on the green spot seems sufficiently accurate to enable the gunner to estimate approximately the correct range at which to open fire.

In mid-January, the BDU issued a Report (No 28) on its investigations into 'identification devices for use with AGLT'; one of the perceived problems with the use of blind-fire by the rear gunners was their reluctance to open fire until they could see that the aircraft in question was German – thus negating much of the value of the system. The BDU trial suggested that 'every AGLT aircraft is to be fitted with a telescope through which IR radiation can be discerned. Every friendly aircraft engaged on the same night operation is to have a source of IR light in the nose that can be coded if so desired'. The Report summarized the trial itself:

> The Admiralty Research Laboratory gave the BDU a selection of telescopes for trial... if the telescope is directed towards a sufficiently strong source of IR light, a corresponding green spot is viewed on the coated glass at the rear end of the telescope. The Z-type telescope designed for Bomber Command use appears to be the most suitable with a field of view of +/- 5 degrees and a useful range of at least 1,000 yards when viewing two 80 watt lamps; indeed, airborne tests gave a range of 2,000 yards – i.e. greater than the range of AGLT. This appears, therefore, to provide an efficient answer to the problem of identification for use with AGLT. (BDU Report No 28, 13 January 1944)

The first squadron to employ AGLT was 460 Squadron in mid-1944.

The superior performance of the Lancaster allowed it to operate on nights when the other bomber types were restricted. Harris later wrote:

> The most important consideration in regard to target marking was the low ceiling of the Stirling, Wellington and Halifax in that order, as compared with the Lancaster. For while the Oboe Mosquitoes could operate at great heights above the clouds, the number of Main Force aircraft able to bomb on sky markers was progressively reduced as the height of the cloud tops increased. The whole force could be employed provided the clouds were below 12,000ft but only Lancasters if the cloud tops were at 17,000ft. Thus to maintain the offensive in periods of cloudy weather I had sometimes to employ a smaller force of Lancasters that I would have liked. Mosquitoes, and sometimes a small force of Lancasters, would [also] be despatched to more distant targets as often as possible to compel the enemy to spread his defences.' (Harris, 'Despatch on War Operations')

The main danger to the lower-flying types came from flak rather than fighters. Flying higher brought its own problems – not least the colder air.

The rear turret was a key defensive point for the Lancaster, yet problems were frequently recorded in respect of the turret 'freezing up' and becoming unusable:

> To eliminate the turret-freezing troubles, a Lancaster III fitted with ducted heating in the rear turret has completed preliminary trials at Skellingthorpe. (Bomber Command ORB)

However, in the following month, the ORB was recording a:

> Lack of progress in providing a solution to the problem of turret heating, causing loss of many of our aircraft due to the gunners being below maximum efficiency through cold, or to the guns and firing gears freezing and failing to fire.

In early April, the RAE received a production version of the Gallay heater (a paraffin heater) for flight trials. The hope was that, should this prove to be successful, sufficient heaters would be available for 1,000 Lancasters (and 1,000 Halifaxes) by September 1944. An order had also been placed for 2,000 American Selas 10 hp heaters, for the Halifax, and a number of 20 hp Selas heaters for Lancaster rear turrets (the 10 hp version did not provide 'a satisfactory temperature rise in the tail gun station'. It was also anticipated that ducted heating from the engines would be available on production aircraft from September, to provide 20 hp of heat; however, if that engine was lost, then the ducted heating would also be lost. Additional tests were being conducted on fitting electrical gun heaters to the tail guns, and on the use of anti-freeze gun lubricants. The June entry in the ORB also dealt with this matter:

> Rear turret heating by the 'engine heat' method, which would give a very considerable improvement over existing conditions, would be provided in all Lancaster I and III aircraft coming off the production line after September 1944, and in all Lancaster IVs if present production arrangements stand. Retrospective fittings of this modification could not be made because of the work involved. Good supplies of Gallay Heaters for fitting to production Lancaster IIs and for retrospective fitting to Lancaster I, II and III were expected in late summer 1944.

February 1944

Berlin was not the only target attacked during this period and among the other missions was one on 20/21 February to Stuttgart. One of the 598 bombers (460 Lancasters) on this sortie was J-Jig of 100 Squadron; its pilot, F/Sgt Wadge, was awarded an immediate DFM following a harrowing sortie, the details of which were

Lancaster VI JB675, January 1944, was converted from a Lancaster III and used by Rolls-Royce before going to 635 Squadron at Downham Market. Ken Delve Collection

included in a history compiled by the Squadron:

> F/Sgt Wadge's crew was one of eleven Squadron crews sent to attack Stuttgart. This was successfully accomplished with Wadge's crew bombing at 0402 hrs from 22,000ft, and all continued well on the return journey until J-Jig was 65 miles NW of Saarbrucken. There, at 0450 hrs and 23,000ft, an unidentified but very fast-moving twin-engined aeroplane came in from the port beam. The mid-upper gunner was at that very moment rotating his turret from port to starboard so there was no warning of the intruder's approach before he collided with the top of the Lancaster. The Lancaster lurched violently and fell uncontrollablely for 3,000ft so F/Sgt Wadge ordered his crew to prepare to abandon aircraft, but then at around 19,000ft he managed to regain control and took stock of the situation. The engines were vibrating excessively, part of the port wing had been torn away and the upper part of the starboard rudder had been badly bent, but despite this alarming survey, F/Sgt Wadge found he could maintain heading by holding the control column to starboard and the rudder well to port, so he set off for the English coast 260 miles away. When he checked his crew over the intercom, all responded except the mid-upper gunner, so the W/Op was dispatched to check on him. He found that the mid-upper gunner had sustained facial injuries and as his intercom had been knocked out, he was about to abandon the aircraft – fortunately he was restrained in time.
>
> Then the W/Op went to the rear turret and found the rear gunner trapped inside jammed doors with his oxygen hose severed. After a struggle the W/OP, who was also without oxygen, managed to force the turret doors apart, but the rear gunner refused to leave his post and remained there without oxygen until the aircraft was about to land. The return journey was made at 19,000ft with the navigator successfully avoiding all heavily defended areas over which it would have been impossible to have taken evasive action. J-Jig landed at Ford at 0646 without R/T.
>
> Ground inspection of the aircraft revealed the following damage. Six feet of the port wing tip had been torn off, the mid-upper turret had been stoved in, the top 18 inches of the starboard fin and rudder had been bent out at right angles, two propeller blades from the port inner had been twisted at the tips, approximately 12 inches of one tip of the port outer propeller was missing and all the other blades were damaged. The navigator's perspex window had been smashed, all the aerials torn away, there were numerous holes in the fuselage – and assorted other damage.

The citation for F/Sgt Francis Wadge's DFM reads:

> One night in February 1944 this airman was captain and pilot of an aircraft detailed to attack Stuttgart. Soon after leaving the target the aircraft was heavily hit. Some six feet of the port wing was ripped away, both the port propellers were bent, the mid-upper turret was shattered and some other important parts of the bomber's structure were damaged. Considerable height was lost and F/S Wadge gave orders to prepare to abandon aircraft. He succeeded in regaining control, however, and promptly informed his crew that he intended to try and reach England. His efforts were successful and, in the face of great difficulties, F/S Wadge effected a masterly landing at an airfield near the coast. This airman displayed skill, courage and resolution of the highest order.

Four nights later, the crew returned early from a mission to Schweinfurt as Wadge was feeling unwell. He was told to coast out and jettison fuel but returned to report that the fuel jettison would not work; he was ordered to go out to sea and jettison the bombs – the aircraft was not heard from again.

The Stuttgart raid had involved 598 bombers (460 Lancasters) in a reasonably effective attack with light losses.

February had started slowly for Bomber Command. The first Main Force raid took place on 15/16 February, when a force of 891 bombers (561 Lancasters) attacked Berlin, causing significant damage to the German capital. Other targets hit by Main Force in February included Leipzig, Stuttgart, Schweinfurt and Augsburg. Early February also saw 617 Squadron mount another specialist raid, the first under their new CO, Wg Cdr Leonard Cheshire. Twelve Lancs attacked the Gnome & Rhone aero engine factory at Limoges; Cheshire made a number of low-level passes over the factory to warn the French workers to get out, on his fourth pass, he dropped his incendiaries to mark the target for his Squadron. The Lancasters dropped their 12,000lb bombs – ten of which hit the factory, causing severe damage. The hazardous low-level marking technique was one that Cheshire was to continue to develop, later employing a Mustang for the task.

March 1944

A Comprehensive Bombing Strategy

March saw the 'heavies' tasked against selected railway marshalling yards in France. In the first of a sequence of eight attacks, on 6/7 March, Trappes was hit. These raids were connected with the pre-Overlord strategic bombing plan and, although Bomber Command was still free to pursue its own strategic plan against German cities, it would, from May, become increasingly involved in pre-invasion targets. The first Lancaster participation came the following night when 304 bombers (56 Lancasters) made a very effective attack on the railyards at Le Mans.

Allied planners had decided on a comprehensive bombing strategy that included attacks on a wide range of lines-of-communication targets, as well as coastal defence and other military installations. As part of the overall deception, the general policy was to make two attacks on targets not connected with the invasion area for every one made in the intended landing area; the complex deception plan to convince the Germans that the Pas de Calais was the most likely invasion area appears to have worked. Le Mans was hit again a few nights later (13/14 June), while railyards at Amiens, Laon, Aulnoye, Courtrai and Vaires were also hit during March.

Precision Bombing

Lancasters took part in very few of these missions, although small forces of Lancasters did undertake a number of precision attacks in March. On 2/3 March, 617 Squadron made a successful attack on an aircraft factory at Albert, but they were foiled by bad weather in their attempt to attack the La Ricamerie needle-bearing factory at Lyons on 4/5 March. La Ricamerie was hit by the Squadron a week later (10/11), in a period when the specialist skills of this Squadron were becoming increasingly important:

> In particular, a raid on the Nadella needle-bearing factory at La Ricamerie near St Etienne on March 10/11 was an outstanding achievement in night precision bombing. The target, which covered an area of no more than 170 x 90 yards was almost completely destroyed by Lancasters of 617 Squadron. (AHB narrative)

The Michelin tyre factory at Clermont-Ferrand was attacked by 617 Squadron on 16/17 March and, before the month was out, the same Squadron had also attacked explosive factories at Bergerac and Angouleme, as well as a number of aero-engine factories. These latter series of raids were usually undertaken as part of a small force of 20 or so aircraft from No 5 Group. Indeed, this was the first month in which No 5 Group mounted a significant number of independent raids, including 10/11 March, when 44 Lancasters took advantage of a bright moonlit night to attack an aircraft factory at Marignane, near Marseilles. The following night, the Group sent out four small-scale raids (a total of 102 Lancs, including the previously mentioned 617 Squadron raid).

Although such small-scale precision bombing made a significant contribution, the German cities were very much still on Harris's list, and Stuttgart, Frankfurt, Berlin, Essen and Nuremburg were all attacked during March. The Stuttgart attack of 15/16 March was the first time that over 600 Lancasters had set out. A total of 863 bombers (617 Lancasters) attacked this target, while other bombers attacked Amiens. The Lancaster force lost 27 aircraft. Frankfurt was attacked on 18/19 and 22/23, each time by over 800 aircraft, with both raids causing heavy damage. An 800-plus bomber raid (577 Lancasters) on Berlin on 24/25 March proved to be the last Main Force trip to the German capital. This was the final phase of the Battle of Berlin.

The Raid on Nuremberg

An effective raid on Essen on 26/27 cost only nine of the 467 bombers. However, the Main Force attack on the night of 30/31 March was to prove a disaster for Bomber Command. The major industrial city and communications interchange of Nuremberg was chosen for an attack by 795 bombers (572 Lancasters); 95 aircraft (64 Lancasters) failed to make it back home.

The raid on Nuremberg started to go wrong from the moment the bomber stream penetrated German-held territory, and the night-fighters found the first of their prey. Les Bartlett was the bomb aimer in a 50 Squadron Lancaster out of Skellingthorpe:

> We altered course for Nuremberg and I looked down at the area over which we had just passed. It looked like a battlefield. There were kites burning on the deck all over the place – bombs going off where they had been jettisoned by bombers damaged in combat, and fires from their incendiaries across the whole area. Such a picture of aerial disaster I had never seen before and hoped never to see again.
>
> On the way into the target the winds became changeable and we almost ran into the defences of Schweinfurt – but we altered course in time. The defences of Nuremberg were nothing to speak of, a modest amount of heavy flak which did not prevent us doing a normal approach, and we were able to get the Target Indicators dropped by the Pathfinder Force in our bombsight and to score direct hits with our 4,000lb 'Cookie' and our 1,000lb bombs and incendiaries. We were able to get out of the target area, always a dodgy business, and set course for home. To reach the coast was a binding 2-hour stooge. The varying winds were leading us a dance. We found ourselves approaching Calais instead of being 80 miles further south, so we had a slight detour to avoid the defences. Once near the enemy coast, it was nose down for home at 300 kts. Even then we saw some poor blokes 'buy it' over the

Channel. What a relief it was to be flying over Lincoln Cathedral once more.

Richard Starkey was the pilot of a 106 Squadron aircraft on the same raid:

With only three weeks to go to the end of our tour, the raid on Nuremberg was to be the crew's 22nd trip – and I remember that after the afternoon briefing, some of the crews had doubts about the operation. We took off in Lancaster ND535 and climbed on course over the Norfolk coast towards Belgium. The moon was very bright and almost full. At our cruising height of 21,000ft the air temperature was very low and the bomber stream began to make condensation trails as we flew towards the long leg which ran south of the Ruhr, then east to a turning point NW of Nuremberg.

Flying conditions were ideal for fighter aircraft, the sky was absolutely clear with a nearly full moon – and the four-engined bombers were making condensation trails that could be seen for miles.

The fighters began their attack and, from the number of tracers being fired, it appeared that there were combats everywhere. It was not long before several aircraft were destroyed as they plunged to the ground. As we continued towards the target the ground below was covered with burning debris. We continuously operated the 'banking search', looking for enemy aircraft. This was achieved by turning steeply to port 15 degrees and the crew looked down to see if any fighters were preparing to attack from below and then banking to return to the original course.

We had been flying on the long leg for many miles when our luck changed; about 80 miles north west of Nuremberg, tracer bullets and cannon fire came from the port quarter hitting the port mainplane and flashing past my head outside the perspex covering the cockpit. I remembered when we were attacked North of Frankfurt in December and hoped we would not be set on fire. However, within three or four seconds the port outer engine and mainplane were on fire.

There was only one action to be taken – I gave the order to abandon aircraft. The engineer feathered the engine as he helped me with the controls, and the next few seconds I remember vividly. The bomb aimer acknowledged the order and said he was baling out. The navigator came to the cockpit to escape through the front hatch, the rear gunner also acknowledged the order but there was no reply from the mid-upper gunner and the wireless operator. I assumed they must have been killed by the burst of fire. The flight engineer handed me a parachute from the rack at his side, which housed two chutes. I managed to connect one of the hooks on the chute to the harness I was wearing. That is the last thing I remember because the aircraft exploded with a full bomb load (we had no time to jettison) and hundreds of gallons of high-octane fuel.

Many years later I was told an unopened parachute was found next to the body of the flight engineer, who had landed in a wood 6km from the aircraft. He must have been blown out like me, but I was lucky – my parachute had been opened, probably by the force of the explosion.

I had a feeling of being pushed upwards out of my seat. When I regained consciousness and realized what had happened, my first thought was, 'Where am I?' Then I heard the sound of engines as the Main Force passed overhead. I expected to feel the parachute supports in front of my face but could not find them – I thought I was coming down without a parachute! I desperately groped around and located the one hook attachment and hung on. By this time I did not know how quickly I was descending. I looked up and saw the canopy of the chute quite clearly in the bright moonlight. It was riddled in parts with a number of small burnt holes, some 1 inch in diameter, and I was afraid that my descent might be too fast for a safe landing. Although the moon was bright I could not see the ground, but there were several fires burning which I took to be wreckage from our aircraft. The fires did not help me to judge my altitude because I did not know the size of them. I had also lost my flying boots, no doubt when the parachute opened, and my nose was bleeding.

I hit the ground with an almighty wallop and rolled backwards down a steep hill. My neck and back were very painful and when I tried to stand my left leg collapsed; it was not long before the Germans picked me up and I eventually ended up as a PoW. Only one other member of my crew survived the explosion, the bomb aimer, Waliy Paris.

Richard Starkey's Lancaster had been shot down by Martin Becker, one of a number of rising night-fighter aces; it was one of eight bombers shot down by Becker that night.

The overall Lancaster loss rate, including five aircraft damaged beyond repair, was 12.1 per cent – by far the worst figure the type ever suffered. (The Halifax force that night suffered a 16.8 per cent loss rate.) Thirty-four Lancaster squadrons, including seven PFF units, had been involved in the attack, the largest single contribution being made by 101 Squadron, who sent 26 ABC aircraft on the raid; they lost six aircraft shot down, and one crashed.

Fortunately, this was the last major raid before the majority of Bomber Command's effort was switched to support of Overlord. The analysis of, and reflection on what had gone wrong began immediately. The weather – strong winds at variance with those forecast – had been partly to blame for scattering aircraft, and putting them over defensive zones that should have been avoided; the majority of losses, however, had been to night-fighters.

The post-war AHB narrative summarized the developments that came out of the Nuremberg disaster:

Nuremberg left no further room for doubt as to the impracticability of operating the whole force against a single target on any one night. The enemy was fully alive to existing bomber tactics and the only hope seemed to be in forcing him to split his fighters into such small groups as to render them comparatively harmless. What was now required was a system of multiple objectives which would both divide and confuse the night-fighter defences. (AHB narrative, 'The Bombing Offensive', Vol VI/VII)

Lancaster Production

The Bomber Command ORB for March 1944 records a memo sent by Sir Charles Portal, Chief of the Air Staff, in respect of Lancaster production:

A very careful study has been made of the problems involved in changing Halifax production over to Lancaster, but the jig and tool capacity of the country was not sufficient to permit changing the Halifax firms to Lancaster production at the same time as changing the Stirling and further that, even if it were practicable to make such a switch, there would be a prohibitive loss of bombing effort during the vital period between mid-1944 until probably late 1945… further, … after doing everything practicable to increase Lancaster production, including diversion of Halifax resources, deliveries will still be at a rate of four Halifaxes to seven Lancasters to the end of this year, although the proportion of Lancasters will continue to increase until the end of 1945.

There is every hope that the German Air Force would be so weakened by the fighting this year that the Halifax can be retained as a first-line bomber in 1945, but if this proves false, first-line bomber operations must be limited to Lancasters, deliveries of which will rise from 350 to 450 per month in 1945, and employ the Halifax for mining and other second-line targets, as well as for training.

As part of the continued development of the Lancaster, Rolls-Royce fitted the higher-power Merlin 85 or 87 to the Lancaster; the first two were DV170 and DV199. Seven others were similarly modified for service trials; one of them, ND479, crashed soon after the trials began. Two aircraft, JB713 and ND418, visited a number of Lancaster squadrons in order to get crew reaction to the new type. A few of the aircraft underwent service evaluation by selected squadrons, including operational flying, but, in the event, little further development took place and Bomber Command remained largely equipped with Lancaster III and, later, Xs.

April 1944

Independent Operations and RCM

On 1 April, Harris authorized attacks on two or more targets the same night. Although this tactic had been used previously, it now became a firm policy – albeit not one that was always adhered to. This new system, however, placed great strain on the resources of the Pathfinders and the decision was taken to 'hand' two of the Lancaster PFF squadrons (83 and 97 Squadrons) to No 5 Group for independent operations:

> The reasons for the selection of No 5 Group were that it was the largest operational group and could, if required, supply at least two effective forces for a combined attack on multiple objectives, and also because it already had much experience in the development of marking and bombing techniques during a recent series of precision of attacks in France. (AHB narrative, 'The Bombing Offensive', Vol VI/VII)

Communications problems led to the fitting of VHF sets in aircraft of 83 and 97 Squadrons for this Pathfinder work (with the ultimate desire to fit all Bomber Command heavies with such radios as soon as possible). The Groups had already carried out a number of independent ops in March.

Not everyone in Bomber Command was happy with the employment of the Pathfinder Force and, for some time, No 5 Group, under Air Marshal Ralph Cochrane, had been developing its own techniques. To a great extent, this had been prompted and led by distinguished bomber figures such as Guy Gibson and Leonard Cheshire. No 5 Group had been the first of the all-Lancaster Groups and, as such, had developed the tactical employment of the type on both special and Main Force operations. Harris later summed up the situation as it stood in mid-1944:

> No 5 Group operated largely as an independent unit and developed its own techniques, including the original Master Bomber concept, also offset skymarking continued to be developed e.g. '5 Gp Newhaven' using offset techniques 1-2,000 yards from the aiming point, any error in the Red TIs being cancelled by yellows from the Master Bomber. Other techniques developed, including 'sector bombing' with each aircraft given a heading and overshoot setting. This gave a good bomb distribution but needed very accurate low-level marking.

The RCM war was very much an important part of the overall Bomber Command attempt at reducing loss rates, especially among the PFF, which had been suffering heavily. According to the Command ORB for March 1944:

> It was decided that in view of the fact that PFF aircraft are normally outside the area of protection afforded by window and that Carpet II would give them individual cover against the Wurzburgs, the initial installation of the device would be made in aircraft of No 8 Group – starting with 156 Squadron.

It went on to say that:

> Boozer III will be fitted to Lancasters as a first priority, with a triple channel warning light on the instrument panel: yellow = enemy AI, bright red = enemy ground RDF (GL) for flak/searchlight, dim red = RDF(GCI).

The technique evolved for the pinpoint attacks was based upon visual marking of the aiming point with Red Spot fires, combined with R/T and W/T co-ordination and control by a Master Bomber. Before zero hour, illuminating aircraft dropped flares to allow the visual marker a clear view of the aiming point in order to drop his markers. These were assessed by the Master Bomber, who then called in other marker aircraft to back up the most accurately placed markers with further spot fires. This marking technique, with some minor variations, was used on all the operations by No 5 Group in April and into May.

No 5 Group continued to sharpen its independent role on targets in France, with 144 Lancasters hitting an aircraft factory at Toulouse on 5/6 April; the other independent raids in the first half of the month were as part of the increased weight of attacks on rail facilities. Such was the Command's confidence in 617 Squadron that Cochrane soon proposed using the unit as the lead pathfinder for the No 5 Group independent attacks. The target would be marked by a low-flying Mosquito of 617 Squadron and would then be bombed by the rest of 617, followed by the remainder of the bomber force.

The first independent deep penetration operation by the Group was flown on 22/23 April; the target was Brunswick, and the bombers were escorted by ten ABC Lancasters from 101 Squadron (No 1 Group). The raid was not a total success, as an early accidental release of sky markers meant that a number of aircraft bombed to the south of the target. Only four of the 238 Lancasters were lost.

Two nights later, the Group attacked Munich and this time the raid was considered to be successful. The first 617 Squadron-led attack took place on 18/19 April, the target being the Juvissy marshalling yards, in Paris. Exceptional accuracy was needed to avoid French casualties. The tactic was repeated two nights later when 247 Lancasters attacked La Chapelle, causing serious damage to the railyards.

By far the greatest effort in April was expended against such lines-of-communication targets, with up to four being hit in a single night. Lille, Villeneuve-St-Georges, Tours, Tergnier, Laon, Aulnoye, Ghent, Aachen, Rouen, Juvissy, Noisy-le-Sec, La Chapelle, Ottignies, Lens, Chambly, Somain and Acheres were all targeted in April. The accuracy on many of these attacks was amazing. Relatively few bombs fell outside the target area, although, sadly, French casualties were sometimes unavoidable.

Main Force Attacks

In an ineffective Main Force attack on Schweinfurt, on 26/27 April, Sgt Norman Jackson of 106 Squadron climbed on to the wing of his burning Lancaster to try and put out a fire that threatened to spread to the fuel tanks. The attempt failed, but Sgt Jackson was awarded the Victoria Cross for his incredibly brave action.

Bombing accuracy was a regular topic of discussion at Bomber Command HQ and the armament section of the ORB includes frequent reference to bombsight development; in early March, concern was being expressed over a bombsight for the Lancaster VI:

> The only suitable bombsight for the Lancaster VI is the Mk XIVA, which has been modified to be reasonably accurate up to 25,000ft. [We] are pressing for a new sight although there is the possibility of using SABS IIA as an interim measure.

The same summary went on to say that:

> The Air Ministry has agreed to store all FN64 mid-under turrets in Aircraft Equipment Depots rather than on squadrons.

This was intended to free up storage space at the front-line units, as it seemed unlikely that these turrets would see much use. A third point was also covered:

> An increased percentage of 30lb incendiaries in standard Lancaster bomb loads will increase maximum loads; the new twin adaptor for the centre bomb station can carry the Mk VB SBC but trials at Waterbeach showed that the bomb doors would not close – it therefore needs to be modified before the VB can be used. (Bomber Command ORB)

The night of 27/28 April saw a force of 322 Lancasters (plus one Mosquito) engaged on a hazardous attack on Friedrichshafen. The target was deep in southern Germany and would involve the bombers in a long flight over enemy territory. What is more, the attack was ordered in bright moonlight, in order to achieve better accuracy; these were exactly the same conditions that had prevailed only a few weeks before during the disastrous Nuremberg mission. The town was on the list of pre-invasion targets as it was the location for a number of important factories making engines and gearboxes for tanks. Careful routing, and the use of diversion and spoof raids proved successful, and few night-fighter intercepts were reported on the route out to the target. One aircraft that was engaged was from 35 Squadron:

> About 50 miles short of the target a twin-engined enemy fighter attacked the Lancaster, then at 17,000ft. The captain was the first to see the fighter, which came in rapidly from directly ahead, and nearly level with the bomber. The mid-upper gunner saw it also, but had no opportunity to open fire, and the captain 'corkscrewed' immediately. Although no bullets were heard striking the bomber, hits were evidently sustained in the starboard outer engine, as no power could be obtained from it, and flames came from the exhaust. After stopping the engine and feathering the propeller the flames died down at once without the use of the extinguisher. Then the Lancaster proceeded on three engines, bombed the target from 16,000ft and set course on the homeward route.
>
> A few minutes later the Lancaster was attacked again, this time there was no warning. The night was dark, and there were no searchlights, flak bursts or other signs of enemy activity. The wireless operator, who was standing in the astrodome, saw tracer coming from astern, and then a fire broke out in the fuselage. No one saw the fighter, which may have been below the gunners' range of vision. The fire spread and soon the fuselage between the mid-upper and rear turrets was well alight. Smoke poured into the pilot's compartment, so that the captain was unable to see his instruments, and the bomber, still flying with three engines only, went into an uncontrollable spin. The captain ordered the crew to bale out.

26 April 1944 – Sgt Norman Jackson VC (No 106 Squadron)

Norman Cyril Jackson joined the RAF as an engine fitter but later became a flight engineer with 106 Squadron. In November 1943, the Squadron moved to Metheringham; on 26 April, his Lancaster was part of the force attacking Schweinfurt. His citation reads:

Bombs were dropped successfully and the aircraft was climbing out of the target area. Suddenly it was attacked by a fighter at about 20,000 feet. The captain took evading action at once, but the enemy secured many hits. A fire started near a petrol tank on the upper surface of the starboard wing, between the fuselage and the inner engine. Sergeant Jackson was thrown to the floor during the engagement. Wounds which he received from shell splinters in the right leg and shoulder were probably sustained at that time. Recovering himself, he remarked that he could deal with the fire on the wing and obtained his captain's permission to try to put out the flames. Pushing a hand fire extinguisher into the top of his life-saving jacket, and clipping on his parachute pack, Jackson jettisoned the escape hatch above the pilot's head and started to climb out of the cockpit and back along the top of the fuselage to the starboard wing. Before he could leave the fuselage his parachute pack opened and the whole canopy and rigging lines spilled into the cockpit. Undeterred, Jackson continued. The pilot, bomb aimer and navigator gathered the parachute together and held on to the rigging lines, paying them out as the airman crawled aft. Eventually he slipped and, falling from the fuselage to the starboard wing, grasped an air intake on the leading edge of the wing. He succeeded in clinging on but lost the extinguisher which was blown away.

By this time the fire had spread rapidly. Jackson's face, hands and clothing were severely burnt. Unable to retain his hold he was swept through the flames and over the trailing edge of the wing, dragging his parachute behind. When last seen it was only partially inflated and was burning in a number of places. Realizing that the fire could not be controlled, the captain gave the order to abandon the aircraft. Four of the remaining members of the crew landed safely; the captain and the rear gunner have not been accounted for. Sergeant Jackson was unable to control his descent and landed heavily. He sustained a broken ankle, his right eye was closed through burns and his hands were useless. These injuries, together with the wounds received earlier, reduced him to a pitiable state. At daybreak he crawled to the nearest village where he was taken prisoner. After ten months in hospital he made a good recovery, though his hands require further treatment and are only of limited use.

This airman's attempts to extinguish the fire and save the aircraft and crew from falling into enemy hands was an act of outstanding gallantry. To venture outside, when travelling at 200 miles an hour at a great height and in intense cold, was an almost incredible feat. Had he succeeded in subduing the flames, there was little or no prospect of his regaining the cockpit. The spilling of his parachute and the risk of grave damage to its canopy reduced his chances of survival to a minimum. By his ready willingness to face these dangers he set an example of self-sacrifice which will ever be remembered.

Jackson became a Prisoner of War, and was repatriated at the end of hostilities.

Two members of the crew who were in the nose of the aircraft – the navigator and flight engineer – baled out, acting on the captain's instructions. Then the air bomber reported that the fire had destroyed both gunners' parachutes and that his own had opened prematurely. The opening of the front escape hatch had by this time cleared the smoke from the pilot's compartment, and it was now possible to see the flying instruments; but the captain could not push the stick forward and the aircraft continued to lose height as it went round in a flat spin. Eventually, when indicated height was 3,000ft and speed only 100 kts, the stick responded. With the port engines throttled back and full power on the remaining starboard engine, the Lancaster came out of the spin. Lake Constance and the fires at the target were within sight, and the captain turned back, resolved to ditch the burning Lancaster on the lake, despite the fact that the front hatch had been jettisoned. A crash landing in such a mountainous region could not be risked, and he ordered the crew to their ditching stations.

Although there was no moonlight to help him and one engine was unserviceable, the captain made a perfect ditching with very little impact. Water rushed in over him, and the rear gunner had to be assisted out of the aircraft as both he and the mid-upper gunner had sustained injuries from the fire. However, all the crew (except the two who had baled out) were in the dinghy within 1 minute of ditching. After about 1 hour the crew reached the Swiss shore of the lake and landed safely on neutral territory. (Bomber Command Quarterly Review No 9)

The attackers lost 18 Lancasters, most of these to fighters in the target area; the raid, however, was deemed to have been highly successful, in that a number of war industries, especially tank production, were badly affected.

Also bombed in this period of 'D-Day' operations were Cologne, Düsseldorf, Karlsruhe, Munich, Essen and Schweinfurt.

Mid-1944

Reducing the Defensive Armament

The trade-off between weight and increased performance had led to a consideration to removing certain elements of the defensive armament from the Lancaster – primarily the front gun, as no significant night threat was perceived from this quarter. In April, Bennett, as AOC No 8 Group, had given verbal authorization for the removal of the Lancaster front turrets within his Group; the same policy was soon under consideration by Command HQ, which proposed the:

> Replacement of the front turrets by light metal fairings would cause a reduction of 600lb in the all-up weight. For every aircraft lost an expensive and intricate piece of equipment would be saved; and Lancasters with the metal fairings would be very slightly faster. ...A call for opinions from all Groups brought replies generally in favour of this modification and it was suggested that all new aircraft should be designed to take either fit. (Bomber Command ORB)

The entry went on to say that No 1 Group were less than enthusiastic and that, after 'further consideration, it had been decided to restrict this policy to aircraft of No 8 Group'.

The question of defensive armament was once more under discussion at Bomber Command HQ in April and May 1944, the Operational Record Book noting various developments:

> The C-in-C informed D Arm R that the Rose turret had completed its preliminary firing trials in this Command with complete success. He stated that the greatly improved accuracy of fire obtained with the Rose turret, the view from it, and the hitting power obtained from the 5in guns more nearly met his requirements than any other turret this Command had ever had or was likely to have for a very long time. In view of these facts, he pressed for an immediate production programme on a wide basis and urged immediate investigation into the question of equipping the Rose turret with AGLT...with reference to the Bristol B.17 20mm dorsal turret intended for Lancaster aircraft the C-in-C stated that the clear view from this turret was so limited as to render it almost useless for night work and emphasized the requirements for this Command in respect of future designs for turrets. (Bomber Command ORB, April/May 1944)

Lancaster JB375 was used by the BDU in July 1944 to conduct a test on the AGLT scanner in response to:

> Reports of seizing of the scanner mechanism of aircraft at Binbrook. It appears likely that the seizing of scanner mechanisms is due initially to rusting of the ball bearings and not directly to the use of Duralumin gear-wheels and that the use of inhibitor oil would overcome the trouble.

The problem is not mentioned again and so would appear to have been either solved, or ignored.

Training

It was suggested that, by mid- to late 1944, a further two Lancaster Finishing Schools would be required. However, as an interim measure, the UE of the existing units was increased in May from 18 to 24 aircraft, and 1654 HCU at Dishforth was given a six-aircraft Lancaster flight to train replacements for Lancaster units in No 6 Group. Within weeks, the plans had changed again, as lower loss rates and increased use of second-tour crews reduced the training requirement; it was proposed, therefore, to run four LFSs, along with 17 HCUs and 17 OTUs.

Even when a crew arrived on a squadron, their training was not over. Depending on the operational commitment of the unit, and the policy of the Flight Commanders and Squadron Commander, a new crew would fly a number of training sorties in the UK. Then, the pilot would go on an operational mission as 'second dickey', to observe procedures, before taking his own crew on ops. As Don Clay recalls:

> Having arrived on 100 Squadron on August 18 we were airborne three days later on our first Squadron exercise – a cross-country flight involving all the crew. My particular part of this was to carry out a high-level bombing exercise at 20,000ft at one of the targets designated to us around the country. I think this one was St Tudwals Island off the Welsh coast, where I did particularly well – or so I was told when we returned to Waltham. The results were summarized and phoned through by the Range staff who measured the distance from the target that our practice bomb (which gave off a small puff of white smoke) exploded. After a few days, during one of the ground theory lectures, we as a crew were told that on the next night operational sortie, Trev and I would be going along with an experienced crew to get a feel for what a real operation was like. On August 25 we attended the briefing and saw that the target was Russelheim – it looked to be a long trip with some nasty flak and enemy fighter areas to fly over; however, the route had been worked out for us to get there and back in the shortest possible time.
>
> We were in the air for 8 hours and successfully bombed the target – which at the time was home

to the Opel factory building military vehicles. We were very lucky on that op in that we met no fighter opposition at all and the searchlights and flak all missed us. (Don Clay, pers comm)

Russelheim was one of three major targets attacked that night; the others were Darmstadt and Brest. The Lancasters were concentrated against Russelheim (412 aircraft) and Darmstadt (190 aircraft). On the former target, the marking was accurate and the factory suffered damage, although this did not hold up production for more than a few days. The attackers lost 15 aircraft. The Darmstadt attack was a failure, as no Master Bomber was available; the primary crew turned back and both the deputies were shot down. Seven Lancasters were lost.

As part of the enhancement of Bomber Command's capabilities, designs were put forward for two long-range variants of the Lancaster, the Mk IV to be equipped with Merlin 68s and the Mk V with Merlin 85s; both would have extra fuel tanks and a change of armament to incorporate the Bristol B.17 turret with twin 20mm cannon. A trial installation was put into Lancaster III JB456 in May 1944, but, by the end of the year, the concept had been abandoned and the orders that had been placed with Vickers-Armstrong were cancelled.

Overlord and Tactical Employment

Operational control of Bomber Command had passed to SHAEF (Supreme HQ Allied Expeditionary Force) on 14 April and, for the next three months, the majority of effort was expended in direct or indirect support of the ground offensive. For the heavy bombers, the most important targets were rail communications, the idea being to isolate the invasion area and prevent the Germans from moving reinforcements to Normandy. Such target systems had been under attack for some while, but with SHAEF now dictating targets they were to receive an even greater weight of raids. (At the same time, Bomber Command continued its campaign against German cities.)

Direct military targets were also attacked. On 3/4 May, the Panzer barracks at Mailly-le Camp were hit by 348 Lancasters; the raid was a complete disaster, proving that by no means all targets in France were 'easy runs'. The bomber force lost 42 of their number. A second Lancaster force, of 84 aircraft, was airborne on the same night to attack the night-fighter base at Montdidier.

On the night of 26/27 May, the Command sent two separate missions to the railway targets of Nantes (100 Lancasters and four Mosquitoes of No 5 Group), and Aachen (162 Lancasters and eight Mosquitoes). Both attacks were accurate and effective, but losses from the Aachen raid were high – 12 aircraft (7 per cent) were lost, and others were seriously damaged. One of the Lancasters taking part was 'Fair Fighter' from 106 Squadron. Flight Engineer A. W. Downs recalled the mission:

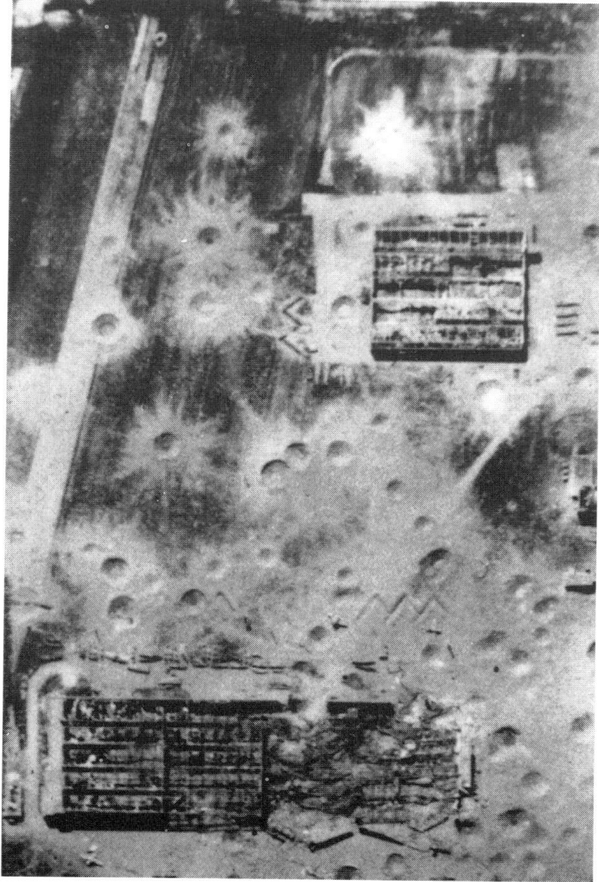

Before and after shots of an aircraft factory at Toulouse, attacked May 1/2, 1944. Ken Delve Collection

We had already done ten missions in 'Fair Fighter' and were half way to the Belgian coast on the way home from the Aachen mission when we were attacked by a Bf 110. The intercom was damaged and smoke filled the cockpit. The skipper motioned that he had lost control of the rudders; the port engine temperature was rising and we were losing power on the others. In the thick smoke the rear of the aircraft seemed to be alight and I went back to take a look. With the W/Op and mid-upper gunner we put the fire out and then found that the rudder control had been shot through and the rear gunner injured – as well as three of the parachutes having been riddled with incendiary bullets. I made a rough repair to the rudder control and went back up front. The skipper decided to make for Woodbridge. The rudder control gave way again and we had to blow down the undercarriage using the air bottle as the hydraulics had gone – we also had no flaps. It was a fast touchdown and almost at once the aircraft veered to starboard; the brakes had been damaged so we had to go where the Lancaster wanted to go! On reaching the edge of the runway we hit an incline and the aircraft was momentarily airborne again. A terrific roar and then the aircraft stopped; we had come to rest in a wood and all clambered out. After breakfast and a rest we took another look at our Lancaster and realized how lucky we had been to survive. That afternoon an aircraft came down from Kirmington to collect us and in due course we had a brand new aircraft – which we named 'Fair Fighter's Revenge'.

The priority being given to the equipping of the Lancaster force was once more evident in May with a Bomber Command decision to fit H2S to Lancaster Xs. The ORB recorded that this was:

> Possible because the delay in the Halifax programme would make sets available. It was further stated that it was proposed to fit some 100 aircraft and to change the 8,000lb bomb doors for small bomb doors. (Bomber Command ORB May 1944)

D-Day

The heavy bomber force was committed to support operations in the hours leading up to the D-Day landings and a number of units had a highly specialized role to play in the deceptions campaign. Under Operations *Taxable* and *Glimmer*, bombers, including 617 Squadron Lancasters, flew carefully planned race-track patterns dropping window to simulate the approach of a large naval force:

> The problem of creating just the right effect was principally one of navigation because the 'convoy' had to be made to appear to approach at a speed of 7 kts and this necessitated a window-dropping aircraft making a series of very accurate overlapping orbits for a period of up to 5 hours. The technique was developed by 617 Squadron, who carried out tests against our Type II radar, and the two operations were actually undertaken by 617 and 218 Squadrons respectively. (Harris, 'Despatch on War Operations'.)

The 218 Squadron Stirlings flew Op *Glimmer* to simulate a convoy near Boulogne.

The first wave of the Taxable operation was led by Sqn Ldr J. Munro; each aircraft had 10–14 crew on board, in order to keep up the correct level of window deployment (2,000 bundles of which were carried by each Lancaster). The Taxable mission was flown by 16 Lancasters to simulate a convoy off Cap d'Antifer. No 101 Squadron was also tasked to provide support for the landings, operating an ABC screen with 24 of their aircraft (losing LL833 which had an engine failure and had to ditch in the Channel).

The bombers were operating every night in the period after D-Day, most of the effort being expended against lines of communication; rail and road junctions and nodes were attacked by formations of Lancasters and Halifaxes – Acheres, Alencon, Amiens, Argentan, Arras, Caen, Cambrai, Chateaudun, Conde-sur-Noireau, Coutances, Dreux, Etampes, Fougeres, Juvissy, St-Lo, Lisieux, Massey-Palaiseu, Mayenne, Orleans, Pontabault, Rennes, Tours, Versailles and Vire were all hit within the week following the invasion.

The Tallboy

The specialist bomber unit, 617 Squadron, had been chosen to employ another new weapon – the 12,000lb HC Tallboy bomb, developed by Barnes Wallis. The Squadron was allocated replacement aircraft capable of carrying the bomb, and in June/early July undertook an intensive training programme (with standard bombs), in order to hone their operational skills ready for a new campaign using the new bomb:

> The 12,000lb MC bomb was not designed for attack on very hard targets but for the production of large craters and maximum earth shock by deep penetration into the ground with a large charge. Nevertheless, the cast-steel body is capable of withstanding impact against very heavy targets and the bombs will cause a penetration of reinforced concrete roofs as much as 18ft 6in thick… It is noteworthy that all the serious damage caused to the large V-weapon sites was caused by very near misses in which the structure was undermined by the crater. (ORS Report No 218 in SD719, Armament Vol I)

The first operational use of this new weapon was on 8/9 June. The target was the rail tunnel at Saumur – a key communication route that the Germans were using to move reinforcements to Normandy. Four Lancasters of 83 Squadron dropped illuminating flares, in the light of which the target was marked by Mosquitoes. In the space of a few minutes, 25 Lancasters of 617 Squadron had dropped their Tallboys with telling accuracy (one bomb actually piercing the tunnel), and succeeded in blocking the railway. Over the next few weeks, the Tallboys were used against a range of hardened targets, such as V-weapon storage bunkers and U-boat pens. Between 8/9 June and March 1945, 721 Tallboys were dropped on operations, 605 by day.

Cutting the Lines of Communication

Attack on Dreux

On the night of 10/11 June, Lancaster III NE177 of 90 Squadron was one of those not to make it back from the attack on Dreux marshalling yards. Most of the crew were on their first operational sortie, with only the pilot (Plt Off. T. A. Burnett) and mid-upper gunner (Sgt Munday) having flown a previous mission. The K report provided by three of the survivors told the story:

> The aircraft left Tuddenham at about 2245 hours and reached the target area without incident. The night was dark, but clear.
>
> Just as the Lancaster was making the bombing run, flying at 7,000ft it was attacked from ahead by an enemy aircraft, variously described as a Ju 88 and a Fw 190. The W/Op saw the fighter dive under the port wing, and the rear gunner saw it

come up on the starboard side. The rear gunner opened fire. The Lancaster had been hit in the port wing between the engines, and No 2 tank was badly holed, emptying almost immediately.

The flight engineer changed to another tank, as No 2 was in use during the attack. Meanwhile the pilot corkscrewed, and the aircraft overshot the target. The pilot turned to make another run and the bombs were dropped at 0103 hours. The aircraft was then hit (informants thought by flak) either on the port inner engine or between the engine and the fuselage. The engine caught fire and at the pilot's order the flight engineer feathered it and cut off the idle cock. The pilot then cut off the master cock. The propeller stopped and the flight engineer pushed the fire extinguisher button. However, the fire did not go out, and the engineer reported the whole wing on fire. The pilot then ordered the crew to bale out as the aircraft was falling very rapidly and was very bumpy.

The W/Op detonated the IFF set and took the flimsies giving stations, frequencies etc., putting them with his escape gear. He then put on his parachute and went to the rear exit. The exit was open when he reached it. He plugged in to report that he was baling out but got no reply. He then took off his helmet, climbed the step, put his head between his knees and rolled out. He remembered only that he pulled his rip-cord, but knew nothing of the descent or landing. The bomb aimer was still in the nose of the aircraft when the order was given to bale out. The escape hatch was covered with bundles of window, and in among these his intercom became unplugged so that he did not hear the order to bale out.

Meanwhile, the navigator and flight engineer put on their parachutes. The flight engineer went forward and saw the bomb aimer hesitating by the escape hatch. He made signs to the bomb aimer to bale out, the latter opened and jettisoned the hatch, which jammed for a short time. He then took his parachute, clipped it on and went out feet first, followed by the engineer. The aircraft at this time was falling very fast, and although the aimer stated he was about 5 minutes in the air, the engineer landed after 10 to 15 seconds. The aircraft was already burning when it hit the ground.

At least two of the crew, pilot and navigator, were still in the aircraft when it crashed.

Nantes and Cambrai

Lancasters were now flying some 75 per cent of the sorties and losses varied from under 1 per cent to over 5 per cent. Lancaster 'K' of 635 Squadron was on the 11/12 June mission to Nantes when it was hit by flak:

There was 10/10 cloud over the target with tops at 5,000ft when Lancaster 'K' reached the target area, and the Master Bomber was heard to order the main force to go down below the cloud base at 2,000ft. By the time that 'K' broke cloud, the target was directly below, so the captain continued, intending to turn to starboard and come in again to bomb. While they were turning, at 1,800ft, a light flak position suddenly opened up with intense and accurate fire. The tail of the aircraft was immediately hit at several points.

The rear gunner reported that his turret was on fire, ammunition was exploding, and the elevator trimming tabs became jammed in a downward position. With the Lancaster in a shallow dive, the captain ordered the crew to bale out, but while he was doing so the intercom system failed. He then jettisoned the bombs safe.

This Lancaster of 460 Squadron was one of those supporting the Allied invasion of 6 June 1944; its crew survived the forced landing. FlyPast Collection

12 June 1944 – P/Off Andrew Mynarski VC (No 419 Squadron)

Plt Off. Andrew Mynarski was awarded the Victoria Cross for his actions on 12/13 June. Ken Delve Collection

Andrew Charles Mynarski joined the RCAF as a wireless operator/air gunner and was posted to 9 Squadron in October 1943, moving to the Canadian 419 Squadron at Middleton St. George the following April. As part of the post D-Day bombing campaign, his Squadron took part in an attack on Cambrai on the night of 12/13 June. His citation reads:

The aircraft was attacked from below and astern by an enemy fighter and ultimately came down in flames. As an immediate result of the attack, both port engines failed. Fire broke out between the mid-upper turret and the rear turret, as well as in the port wing. The flames soon became fierce and the captain ordered the crew to abandon the aircraft.

Mynarski left his turret and went towards the escape hatch. He then saw the rear gunner was still in his turret and apparently unable to leave it. The turret was, in fact, immovable since the hydraulic gear had been put out of action when the port engines failed, and the manual gear had been broken by the gunner in an attempt to escape. Without hesitation Mynarski made his way through the flames in an endeavour to reach the turret and release the rear gunner. Whilst doing so, his parachute and his clothing, up to the waist, were set on fire. All his efforts to move the turret and free the gunner were in vain. Eventually the rear gunner clearly indicated to him that there was nothing more he could do and that he should try and save his own life. Mynarski reluctantly went back through the flames to the escape hatch. There, as a last gesture to the trapped gunner, he turned towards him, stood to attention in his flaming clothing and saluted, before he jumped out of the aircraft. Mynarski's descent was seen by French people on the ground. Both his parachute and clothing were on fire. He was found eventually by the French, but was so severely burnt that he died from his injuries.

The rear gunner had a miraculous escape when the aircraft crashed. He subsequently testified that, had Mynarski not attempted to save his comrade's life, he could have left the aircraft in safety and would, doubtless, have escaped death. Mynarski must have been fully aware that in trying to free the rear gunner he was almost certain to lose his own life. Despite this, with outstanding courage and complete disregard for his own safety, he went to the rescue. Willingly accepting the danger, Mynarski lost his life by a most conspicuous act of heroism which called for valour of the highest order.

One of the two surviving airworthy Lancasters – FM213 – is today flown as the 'Mynarski Memorial Lancaster' in memory of this gallant Canadian airman.

After much exertion he managed to get the control back, but then the aircraft started to climb at a steep angle to 2,800ft. Controls for both rudders and trimming tabs were completely useless, and the captain repeated by gestures the order to bale out. The flight engineer, air bomber, navigator and mid-upper gunner accordingly jumped from the front escape hatch. Meanwhile, the rear gunner, who had come forward into the fuselage, had been injured in trying to extinguish the flames, his parachute had been destroyed in the fire and the complete rear turret had fallen off. In the circumstances the captain decided to attempt to fly the damaged aircraft back to England, with whatever assistance the wireless operator and rear gunner could give him.

By using varying degrees of flap the captain managed to fly the Lancaster straight and level, although airspeed was much reduced. The other two members of the crew succeeded in extinguishing the flames and, although suffering from burns, the rear gunner took his station in the mid-upper turret. The wireless operator sent out distress signals, plotted the fixes he received on the navigator's Mercator chart, and was thus able to give the pilot necessary alterations of course. Making aileron turns, and with the help of the wireless operator in pushing the control column, the captain eventually made a safe landing at Warmwell about two hours after leaving the target. (Bomber Command Quarterly Review No 9)

A number of rail facilities were attacked the following day by 617 bombers (285 Lancasters). One of the targets was Cambrai and a 419 Squadron pilot, Andrew Mynarski, was awarded the Victoria Cross for this mission.

Continued Attacks

On 14 June Bomber Command returned to daylight operations, with 200 Lancasters attacking German naval targets that were threatening the invasion supply lines. Establishing a secure bridgehead and expanding it as rapidly as possible was essential to the Allies if the invasion was to succeed. The Germans were equally determined to drive the invading forces back into the sea. The Allies' main advantage was their overwhelming air superiority; the massive numbers of tactical aircraft represented the critical element within this air-land strategy, but the 'heavies' (RAF and USAAF) still had an important part to play. Cutting the enemy lines of communication, in particular the rail network, was considered vital to the overall plan and the work that the 'heavies' had begun in this respect months before D-Day was continued in the post-invasion period.

Over 1,000 RAF bombers (589 Lancasters) attacked rail and road centres on the night of 6 June to cut key approach routes to the Normandy battle area. It was the same routine the following two nights. The raids of 7/8 June included an attack by 112 Lancasters on an area in the Foret de Cerisy that was not only a key road junction, but was also believed to be an assembly area for German armoured units planning a counterstroke.

Improving Accuracy and Navigation

The value of H2S had been recognized from early on and, as part of the continued development of this system, H2S Mk III was due to enter service in late June, with:

> 32 MU working to a programme to fit 40 Lancasters per month with H2S III/IIIA. (Bomber Command ORB June 1944).

As part of the desire to provide accurate navigation and bombing systems, a trial installation for operational evaluation of Oboe II in a Lancaster was carried out; the following conclusion was drawn:

> There was no real requirement to equip a squadron, but perhaps it would be of value to 9 Squadron and 617 Squadron. It was not wanted by No 5 Group. (Bomber Command ORB July 1944)

No 8 Group also experimented with formation Oboe bombing where an Oboe-equipped aircraft (Lancaster or Mosquito) led a flight of aircraft, all of whom dropped their bombs when the leader did so. The intention was to achieve a greater concentration of bombs on a small target. This tactic was subsequently used on day attacks against Crossbow targets and involved up to 18 aircraft in formation. Indeed, on 23 July, a combined force of 30 bombers from No 8 and No 3 Groups used this tactic against the flying-bomb site at Mont-Candon, bombing through thick cloud, the results being assessed as 'good'.

A similar tactic, but using a G-H aircraft as the leader, was evaluated by No 3 Group, and used operationally for the first time on 27 July against the V-weapon site at Les Landes.

The attempts to improve both the firepower and accuracy of the Lancaster's turrets continued; by late June, Bomber Command was assessing the first reports from 460 Squadron (C Flight) regarding the trials they had been conducting with CGS III in their FN121 turrets since mid-April:

> Reports indicate that without exception all the gunners concerned indicate that this sight is prefered for night operations. The main advantages of this over other sights are considered to be:
>
> 1. Auto deflection.
> 2. Easier manipulation of the FN121 turret, thus improving steadiness of aim.
> 3. More successful dimming of sight for night use.
> 4. In conjunction with 3, easier to hold target in graticule at night.
> 5. Easier to hold target in graticule throughout corkscrew manoeuvre.'

Direct Support of Ground Forces

By mid-June, the target sets had expanded to cover communications, V-weapons, oil targets and troop concentrations. The Allied advance, particularly on the eastern (British/Canadian) sector, was stalling by early July and, despite the pounding that the road and rail system was suffering, a trickle of German rein-forcements was managing to reach the battle area. A series of strongpoints around Caen had held up the Allied advance to the east and, in an effort to break the deadlock, strategic heavy bombers were used in the tactical role in direct support of ground forces.

The first major use of this tactic was on 7 July – Operation *Charnwood* – when 467 heavies (283 Lancasters) dropped over 2,000 tons of bombs on two aiming points on the approaches to Caen. An original plan to bomb a number of fortified villages was modified when these were considered too close to the Allied front lines; the risk of such a huge weight of bombs falling on friendly troops was considered unacceptable. However, the two new target areas, both of which were accurately marked, contained little of significance to the German defence line in the area; to a large degree, the effort was wasted. Nevertheless, the principle of employing such a heavy bomber force had been established and the accuracy, if not the effectiveness, of this attack had been impressive.

With the battle around Caen continuing in stalemate, an attack on an even larger scale was planned. Operation *Goodwood* would involve nearly 1,000 heavy bombers (667 Lancasters) in support of the British 2nd Army's attack on Caen. The bombers were tasked to destroy five fortified villages to the west of Caen. The RAF bombers dropped over 5,000 tons (to which American bombers added another 2,000 tons) in accurate attacks on all the targets. A daylight attack from 5-9,000ft by such a large force of bombers could have been a disaster if German flak had proved effective; as part of the overall plan, however, known flak positions were engaged by artillery. Results of the attack were good and a number of German Divisions were disrupted.

On three more occasions, the RAF's heavy bomber force was used as a battlefield weapon. In a particularly successful attack on 30 July, 692 aircraft (462 Lancasters) were used to support an American push in the Villers Bocage-Caumont area; a week later, 7/8 August, over 1,000 bombers (614 Lancasters) were airborne to attack a series of positions in front of the Allied ground advance (although only just over half were actually called on by the Master Bomber to release their loads). The last of the major attacks took place on 14 August, with 805 aircraft (411 Lancasters) supporting 3rd Canadian Division's advance on Falaise; seven targets were hit. Generally, the bombing was well controlled and accurate; tragedy did strike, however, when some bombs fell on an area occupied by a Canadian unit.

The Anti V-Weapon Campaign

As with all Allied air resources, Bomber Command's heavies were involved in the anti V-weapon campaign. Such targets had been under attack since the discovery of the 'ski ramp' sites in France (and with attacks on Peenemunde somewhat earlier). However, with the launching of the first V-1s against London, in June, the Allied anti V-weapon campaign intensified, with Bomber Command attacking storage sites and launch areas. The first major attack of a new offensive took place on 16/17 June, when 405 bombers (236 Lancasters) hit four sites in the Pas de Calais, the Lancasters and Halifaxes dropping on targets marked by Oboe Mosquitoes.

Such missions were frequent in June and early July, although they decreased in frequency when Bomber Command returned to its strategic campaign against the German homeland in August.

Lancasters were involved in the following 15 attacks in the second half of June. (The first set of numbers represents the total number of bombers, while the Lancaster component is shown in brackets.)

Date	Total no. of Bombers (no. of Lancasters)	Location
16/17	405 (236)	Pas de Calais
17/18	114 (19)	Oisemont
19	21 (19)	Watten
20	20 (17)	Wizernes
21	322 (142)	Pas de Calais
22	234 (119)	Mimoyecques, Siracourt, Wizernes
23/24	412 (226)	Pas de Calais
24	339 (122)	Wizernes + 3 sites
24/25	739 (535)	7 sites
25	343 (123)	4 sites
27	111 (2)	Mimoyecques
27/28	721 (477)	6 sites
28	110 (2)	Wizernes
29	305 (286)	2 sites
30	107 (102)	Oisemont

Many of the attacks were made in daylight in an effort to improve accuracy against these small-area launch and storage site targets. Massive concrete constructions at Watten, Wizernes, Siracourt and Mimoyecques were not only attacked by Main Force but also by 617 Squadron with its 12,000lb Tallboys. It was a huge bomber effort against a set of weapons that could cause little damage to the progress of the Allied invasion (although a number of V-weapons were fired against ports). The political dimension – London was the weapon's major target – was, however, another matter. From a purely military point of view, it could be argued that concentration of effort to assist the ground advance and, thus, overrun these sites would have been more effective.

Activity in July was even more intensive:

Date	Total no. of bombers (no. of Lancasters)	Location
1	328 (6)	2 sites
2	384 (374)	3 sites
4	347 (23)	4 sites
4/5	246 (231)	St Leu d'Esserent
5/6	542 (321)	4 sites
6	551 (210)	5 sites
7/8	221 (208)	St Leu d'Esserent
9	347 (120)	6 sites
10	223 (213)	Nucourt
11	32 (26)	Gapennes
12	145 (64)	Rollez, Thiverny
12/13	230 (170	4 sites
14	19 (19)	St Philibert Ferme
14/15	115 (4)	Anderbelck, Les Landes
15	53 (47)	Nucourt
15/16	234 (58)	Nucourt, Bois-des-Jardins
16	33 (30)	St Philibert Ferme
17	132 (20)	3 sites
18/19	62 (2)	Acquet
19	144 (132)	2 sites
20	369 (174)	Wizernes, 6 sites
20/21	87 (23)	Wizernes, Ardouval
21	52 (2)	Anderbeck
22	60 (48)	4 sites
23	60 (48)	Foret-de-Croc, Mont Candon
23/24	116 (2)	Les hauts Boissons
24	36 (28)	Acquet, Prouville
24/25	112 (2)	
25	93 (81)	Watten, 2 sites
25/26	51 (36)	Bois-des-Jardins, 2 sites
27	72 (36)	5 sites
31	103 (97)	Rilly-la-Montage
31/1	202 (104)	Foret de Nieppe, 3 sites

(Although these operations were clearly intensive, in terms of the overall available bomber force of 1,000-plus aircraft, they represent only a small percentage of Bomber Command's resources.)

There are a number of interesting features in the July raids. After the daylight raid of 6 July, Wg Cdr Leonard Cheshire was taken off operations. Having completed four bomber tours, and pioneered the very risky low-level marking technique, he was ordered to rest from operational flying. The three Flight Commanders of 617 Squadron – McCarthy, Munro and Shannon – all of whom were Dams veterans, were also taken off flying.

The attack on Gapennes (11 July) was the first time an Oboe-equipped Lancaster led the marking force; Wg Cdr G. F. Grant of 109 Squadron flew an Oboe Lanc of 582 Squadron to act as Master Bomber. When Grant released his bombs, the rest of the formation did likewise, in an attempt to achieve concentration of bombing against small-area targets.

Tallboy bombs were used by 617 Squadron on 31 July to destroy both ends of a tunnel at Rilly-la-Montage, which was being used as a flying-bomb store. The other Lancasters on this mission dropped HE bombs to destroy the approaches to the tunnel.

With a massively powerful day and night bomber force at their disposal, the Allied air commanders looked at ways to use this as a decisive weapon – and promptly disagreed as to its most effective employment. The bomber chiefs were still of the opinion that they had a war-winning weapon, if only they could apply it to the right targets. In essence, they divided into supporters of the Transportation Plan and proponents of the Oil Plan; the former believed that the German economy and military could be 'strangled' through the destruction of its communication network, and especially rail communications; the latter believed that oil was Germany's weak link.

Communications had of course been targeted during the period either side of D-Day, and pressure on likely troop-movement routes was maintained, primarily through attacks on key cities containing rail nodes. A campaign designed to cripple the rail network was two-pronged – both tactical and strategic. The strategic aspect was to bring about the disruption of war industry, and of the movement of both raw materials and finished products. Harris was happy to accept such a policy, as it would allow him to return his bombers to German cities. Bomber Command had also proved that it now had the accuracy to attack small targets, such as oil plants.

The argument was to be on-going for some time, and Bomber Command attacked both target sets in the remaining months of the war.

Bomber Command Humour

Despite periods of heavy losses, the crews of Bomber Command seldom lost their sense of fun. This was often typified by the songs devised by the units – the following offering from 100 Squadron is not unusual:

'The 100 Squadron Boys' (to the tune of 'McNamara's Band')

1. We are 100 Squadron – we're the boys who know the score,
If anyone denies it we will spread him on the floor,
At bombing and beer and billiards and all the Cleethorpe Hops,
We have got the gen – we're the leading men – we certainly are the tops.

Chorus
While the bombs go bang and the flack bursts clang and the searchlights blaze away,
We weave all over the starlit sky
And wish we'd gone by day.
Pattison, Pattison save us now
We can't abide the noise.
A credit to Butch Harris, the 100 Squadron boys.

2. Oh we love to nip in smartly to a little buzz bomb site,
And smartly nip off home again and get to bed at night.
We're saving our night vision up for earthly joys.
And now we're safely in the Mess, meet the 100 Squadron boys.

3. My name is William Irving, and I'm from the Middle East
And what you think about me here, I don't care in the least
I'm in command of 'A' Flight though you may not think it so,
There is not a pub in Lincolnshire or a WAAF that I don't know.

4. My name is Hammy Hamilton, I'm an unpretentioous Scot,
And although in a way I have little to say I sometimes think a lot
If you ask my crew if I have any faults, they'll tell you in accents sweet
You can see the ants as I stooge over France at altitude ZERO FEET.

5. My name is Taff and I joined the RAF – well pretty near the start,
My trade is navigation, but I'm a bit of a wolf at heart.
I've a popsy here and a pospy there and I don't care if they're wed
So long as their husbands don't come home and find me still in bed.

6. I'm Flight Lieutenant Thompson, once a terror of Tobruk,
My desert dicing days would fill a pretty weighty book.
But since I got to Grimsby, they've demoted me by heck,
And now I'm one of the lesser Sheiks of Barnolby-le-Beck.

7. My name's O'Donoval-llant and I'm No 1 AG
And 190s and 109s are all the same to me
I'll man the mid-upper with any old skipper, so long as he's learned to fly
You can only live once – it's a matter of months – and it doesn't take long to die.

8. My name is Waite, and I'm sorry I'm late, my train has just got in
I've travelled up from Scunthorpe where I'm living in part-time sin
There's a girl named Lou – she'd appeal to you – if you haven't been introduced
She's big and blond and terribly fond of me and my plus 12 Boost.

9. I'm Otto (Bang on Target) Towers, and many an aiming point
Was chalked up to my credit over many a Nazi joint.
But now I'm in semi-retirement and whenever the red light blinks
I set off on my bike on a local strike – and will tell the 'Lifeboat' sinks.

Two oil targets were attacked on the night of 21/22 June; 133 Lancasters went to Wesseling and 123 to Scholven/Buer. The combined force lost 46 aircraft; the Wesseling sortie cost 37 Lancasters (almost 28 per cent), representing the worst lost rate ever recorded. Three squadrons – 44, 49 and 619 – each lost six aircraft. Damage was caused to both targets, leading to a temporary reduction in production.

It was almost a month before Main Force hit another oil plant. On 18/19 July, the Wesseling and Scholven/Buer plants were the targets once again, with 350 bombers involved. One record shows that 1,000 bombs fell within the target area at Wesseling, causing extensive damage and a significant drop in production. Oil plants at Bottrop and Homberg were hit two nights later; the Homberg raid cost 75 Squadron seven of its 25 aircraft.

Other oil installations attacked in July were Donges (twice) and Wanne-Eickel.

In addition to the rail, V-weapons, oil and army-support target types, Main Force returned to German cities at the end of the month, attacking Kiel (23/24), Stuttgart (24/25, 25/26 and 28/29) and Hamburg (28/29). Loss rates had been running at a reasonable level, but the last of the Stuttgart raids showed that the German defences could still give a nasty bite; thirty-nine of the 494 Lancasters (7.9 per cent) were lost.

CHAPTER SEVEN

August to December 1944

Production of Aircraft and Bombs

Lancaster production increased when Victory Aircraft of Malton, Canada, began turning out a variant of the Mk III with Packard Merlin 28s; it was given the designation Lancaster X. Aircraft were built and then ferried to the UK for fitting out with operational equipment such as gun turrets. The first Mk X flew on 6 August 1943 and the first aircraft was ferried to the UK on 17 September.

No 6 (RCAF) Group had had a brief association with the Lancaster in 1943 but had then re-equipped to become an all-Halifax command; deliveries of the Lancaster X meant that this Group could give up its Halifaxes, which many crews were reluctant to do. It was early 1945 before a significant number of Canadian squadrons had re-equipped with the Lancaster X.

On 12 August, Harris sent a letter to the Minster of Supply urging that it be sent to all those involved in Tallboy production:

> Bomber Command appeals to all those engaged on the manufacture and fitting of the 12,000lb Tallboy bomb to do their utmost to expedite delivery at this critical juncture... They have already wrecked the submarine pens at Le Havre and badly damaged those at Brest and La Pallice. The Tallboys are the only ferrets big enough to get these rats in their holes and every one of them is shoved into the burrows within hours of leaving your hands. Our stock today is exhausted and the rats may bolt elsewhere to continue their depredations. We know you will not fail us. (Bomber Command ORB September 1944)

The Tallboy had proved to be an effective weapon in the hands of 617 Squadron and Harris was keen to increase the employment of this weapon. Part of his strategy was the creation of a second specialist squadron – 9 Squadron at Bardney was selected.

August and September

V-Weapons, Airfields, Cities and Communications

The first half of August 1944 brought a continuation of the campaign against V-weapons, the majority of effort being expended against this target category. Within the first week, over 3,500 sorties (1,800 by Lancasters) had been mounted against such targets. One of these, attacked on 4 August, was the Trossy St Maxim launch site. Sqn Ldr Ian Bazalgette of 635 Squadron (*see boxed text*) was awarded the Victoria Cross for his actions in this raid.

Attacks on V-weapon sites remained, therefore, an important priority, but Bomber Command also carried out a number of attacks on oil and rail targets. Bomber forces also hit the U-boat pens at Brest, the Opel factory at Russelheim, and continued to take part in a number of ground support missions.

In preparation for the renewal of the night-bomber offensive on 15 August, Bomber Command made a maximum-

Lancs over the V-bomb storage site at Trossy St Maxim on 4 August 1944. Graham Pitchfork

Lancaster IIIs of 619 Squadron; the unit had formed in April 1943 at Woodhall Spa and, during its wartime career with No 5 Group, flew over 3,000 sorties for the loss of 77 aircraft. Andy Thomas Collection

effort attack on a number of key night-fighter airfields in Holland – Deelen, Eindhoven, Gilze-Rijen, Soesterberg, St Trond and Tirlemont were all hit, while the USAAF attacked a further nine fields in NW Germany. This raid comprised 1,004 bombers (599 Lancasters) and, in the absence of significant enemy defences, only three Lancasters were lost. Weather conditions were favourable:

> It was estimated that heavy damage was done to runways, and the raid so disorganized the night-fighters in the area that they were unable to make any determined resistance to Bomber Command's night raids in the next two weeks. (AHB narrative, 'Bomber Offensive', Vol VI/VII)

Paris was liberated on 24 August and the Allied advance made steady progress towards Germany, overrunning V-weapon installations and thus greatly reducing the threat from these weapons. The capture of such sites as Watten and Siracourt also enabled Bomber Command experts to assess the effectiveness of their attacks, and especially of the Tallboy bombs. Oil and transport targets remained a high priority, but Bomber Command was, in the latter

4 August 1944 – Sqn Ldr Ian Bazalgette VC DFC (No 635 Squadron)

Ian Willoughby Bazalgette was commissioned as a Second Lieutenant in the Royal Artillery, but in 1941 transferred to the RAF Volunteer Reserve as a pilot. His first operational tour was with 115 Squadron flying Wellingtons, and he was still with the Squadron when they converted to the Lancaster in early 1943, completing his tour in August. After an instructional tour with 20 OTU at Lossiemouth, Bazalgette returned to operational flying with the Pathfinders, joining 635 Squadron at Downham Market in April 1944. On 4 August of that year, the PFF marked the V-I storage site at Trossy St Maxim. Bazalgette was the captain of Lancaster ND811 (although he does not appear to have been acting as Master Bomber, as it states in his citation). His citation reads:

When nearing the target his Lancaster came under heavy anti-aircraft fire; both starboard engines were put out of action and serious fires broke out in the fuselage, and the starboard main plane, and the bomb aimer was badly wounded. Despite the appalling conditions in his burning aircraft, he pressed on gallantly to the target, marking and bombing it accurately. After the bombs had been dropped the Lancaster dived, practically out of control. By expert airmanship and great exertion Bazalgette regained control. However, the port inner engine then failed and the whole of the starboard main plane became a mass of flames. Bazalgette fought bravely to bring his aircraft and crew to safety; the mid-upper gunner was overcome by fumes. Bazalgette then ordered those of his crew who were able to leave by parachute to do so. He remained at the controls and attempted the almost hopeless task of landing the crippled and blazing aircraft in a last effort to save the wounded bomb aimer and helpless gunner. With superb skill, and taking great care to avoid a small French village near by, he brought the aircraft down safely. Unfortunately, it then exploded and Bazalgette and his two comrades perished.

The deed remained unrecorded until after the war, when survivors of Bazalgette's crew returned to the UK. Their accounts of the sortie led to the award of his Victoria Cross (LG, 17 August 1945).

part of August, back over German cities in force – Stettin, Kiel, Bremen, Russelheim and Konigsberg were all attacked. Konigsberg was attacked twice by No 5 Group (26/27 and 29/30). This town, almost 1,000 miles (1,600km) away on the east side of Germany, was being used as a supply centre for the Eastern Front, and the attack was made to support the Russians.
On the Stettin raid of 29/30 August 1944, Plt Off. Hawes was flying ME742 of 626 Squadron on his 25th op; the aircraft was shot down, but Hawkes evaded capture. The subsequent ORS 'K' Report included his account of the mission:

> 0021 fix, on track and on time, 14 miles from Swedish coast at 13,000ft steering 098 degrees, climbing to 18,000ft. Attacked without warning by two Ju 88s. Fishpond was fitted but not being monitored. Both fighters opened fire from dead astern with cannon tracer, no crew men were seriously injured but the hydraulics to both turrets were severed. Only the mid-upper could be rotated manually. A large hole was torn in the starboard wing and fire erupted in both starboard engines, a fire also broke out underneath. The elevator and rudder were holed but still had enough control to corkscrew. The flight engineer [Sgt Ockwell] three window; feathered the starboard outer but the inner would not feather. Ten seconds later the fires broke out again and spread to No 1 petrol tank. The mid-upper gunner [F/Sgt Allison] saw a Ju 88 on a parallel course and fired – it burst into flames and dived down through the cloud. We levelled at 9,000ft and headed for Sweden. The fire was now well spread and there was a danger to the spar and we therefore abandoned aircraft. All baled out OK and the aircraft crashed about 1 mile from Bastad. (Bomber Command ORS 'K' Report)

The Dortmund-Ems Canal was one of the main industrial arteries of north Germany, connecting the Ruhr to the northern ports. As such, it had been a frequent target for Bomber Command. It was considered that the 12,000lb bomb would prove an ideal weapon to cause critical damage to the canal. On the night of 5 September, eight aircraft of 617 Squadron took off for their second attempt to hit this target – the previous night's mission had been aborted because of bad weather (although nevertheless Sqn Ldr D Maltby, one of the Dams veterans, was lost when his aircraft hit the sea.) The crews for this second mission were:

8 September 1944 – Wg Cdr Leonard Cheshire VC DSO DFC (No 617 Squadron)

Leonard Cheshire (left) was one of the foremost bomber leaders. In September 1944 he was awarded the Victoria Cross in recognition of his combat record.
Ken Delve Collection

Geoffrey Leonard Cheshire was commissioned as a pilot in the RAFVR in 1937 and by June 1940 was flying Whitleys with 102 Squadron, completing his first tour the following January. He promptly volunteered for a second tour and was sent to join the Halifax-equipped 35 Squadron. Having completed his second tour of bomber operations, Cheshire was posted to No 1652 HCU as an instructor. In September 1942, he returned to ops once more as OC 76 Squadron. April 1943 saw the 25-year-old Cheshire promoted to Group Captain to take command of RAF Marston Moor. However, he so yearned to return to operational flying that he chose to revert to the rank of Wing Commander to become OC 617 Squadron at Woodhall Spa. Having flown his 100th operational sortie on 6 July 1944, Cheshire was withdrawn from operations; soon after this came the announcement of the award of his Victoria Cross (LC, 8 September 1944). His citation reads:

This officer began his operational career in June 1940. Against strongly defended targets, he soon displayed the courage and determination of an exceptional leader. He was always ready to accept extra risks to ensure success. At the end of his first tour of operational duty he immediately volunteered for a second. Again, he pressed home his attacks with the utmost gallantry. When he was posted for instructional duties in January 1942 he undertook four more operational missions. He started a third tour in August 1942 when he was given command of a squadron. He led the Squadron with outstanding skill on a number of missions before being appointed as a station commander. In October 1943 he undertook a fourth operational tour, relinquishing the rank of Group Captain at his own request so that he could again take part in operations. He immediately set to work as the pioneer of a new method of marking enemy targets involving very low flying.

Cheshire's cold and calculated acceptance of risks is exemplified by his conduct in an attack on Munich in April 1944. This was an experimental attack to test out the new method of target marking at low level against a heavily defended target situated deep in enemy territory. He was obliged to follow, in bad weather, a direct route which took him over the defences of Augsburg and thereafter he was continuously under fire. As he reached the target, flares were being released by our high-flying aircraft and he was illuminated from above and below. All guns within range opened fire on him. Diving to 700 feet he dropped his markers with great precision and began to climb away. So blinding were the searchlights that he almost lost control. He then flew over the city at 1,000 feet to assess the accuracy of his work and direct other aircraft. His own was badly hit by shell fragments but he continued to fly over the target area until he was satisfied that he had done all in his power to ensure success. Eventually when he set course for base the task of disengaging himself from the defences proved even more hazardous than his approach. For a full 12 minutes after leaving the target area he was under withering fire, but he came safely through.

Wing Commander Cheshire has now completed a total of 100 missions. In four years of fighting against the bitterest opposition he has maintained a record of outstanding personal achievement, placing himself invariably in the forefront of the battle. What he did in the Munich operation was typical of the careful planning, brilliant execution and contempt for danger which has established for Wing Commander Cheshire a reputation second to none in Bomber Command.

EE144	Sqn Ldr G. W. Holden
EE130	Flt Lt R. A. Allsebrook
EE150	Flt Lt H. B. Martin
EE146	Flt Lt D. Shannon
JB144	Flt Lt L. G. Knight
JA898	Flt Lt H. Wilson
EE131	Plt Off. G. Rice
JA874	Plt Off. W. Divall

The aircraft flew at a low level, below 100ft, over Holland in an effort to avoid radar detection, but things soon started going wrong. Sqn Ldr Holden was shot down by flak near Nordhorn, while Allesbrook, Wilson and Divall all crashed near the target; Flt Lt Knight clipped some trees and crashed. Of all the crews in these aircraft, only Knight's (but not the pilot himself) survived. Of the remaining three aircraft, Plt Off. Rice's aircraft was hit badly enough for him to jettison the bomb and return to base. Shannon and Martin managed to find the target, despite poor visibility, and dropped their Tallboys – both bombs missed.

Night and Day

On 2 July, HQ Bomber Command had informed the Group Commanders that, in future, deeper-penetration day missions would be tasked and that new tactics would have to be employed in order to take advantage of the promised fighter escort. The first such daylight raid on a German target took place on 27 August, when 216 Halifaxes of No 4 Group, with Mosquito marking provided by No 8 Group, attacked the Meerbeck synthetic oil plant at Homberg. This mission was escorted by nine Spitfire squadrons, but very little enemy air activity was evident. The target was marked by the Oboe aircraft and, despite heavy flak, there were no losses.

A daylight attack by 675 bombers (348 Lancasters) was made on 3 September, in order to keep up the pressure on the now over-stretched German night-fighter force. The next daylight raid took place over Emden on 6 September, when 181 aircraft (76 Lancasters) made an accurate attack on the city for the loss of one Lancaster.

Further daylight raids were made over the next few weeks on targets in the Ruhr; although German fighter activity was slight, concern was expressed over the level of fighter support. At the Versailles

The massive concrete structures of the U-boat pens were invulnerable to all but a direct hit from a Tallboy. Ken Delve Collection

12,000lb Tallboys explode on the U-boat pens in Brest, August 1944. Ken Delve Collection

Conference, Harris requested that a dedicated Mustang Wing be allocated to defend his bombers, on the grounds that he considered the Germans would use their night-fighters in a day-fighter role (he was right), and that the bombers' 0.303in guns were simply inadequate for defence. He concluded that:

> With long-range escort, day bombing could be considerably cheaper than night bombing. (AHB narrative, 'Bombing Offensive', Vol VI/VII)

Loss rates to night-fighters continued to be critical for much of 1944 and a great deal of attention was paid at Command level to devising both tactics and equipment that would ease the problem. The RCM war had become firmly established as a critical part of operations by early 1944, and numerous developments continued to be made during the year. Various analysis and trials organizations were involved in this work, none more so than the Bomber Development Unit.

In August, the BDU at Newmarket was trialling Lancaster ND584 with an improved RCM aid called Fishpond:

> ND584 was fitted with filter unit Type 189 to clean up the transmitter pulse and enable operators to obtain improved maximum range. Four flights were made using 60 Beaufighter/Mosquito attacks. The Lancaster also had ALGT and this was used for range measurement. The results were promising but more work needs to be carried out in respect of bonding to H2S. (BDU Report 61, 20 August 1944)

September Sorties

Considering the number of aircraft that Bomber Command had available, the total number of bomber sorties flown in early September was not high. There were very few days when more than 400 bombers were airborne. The range of targets had altered somewhat and a fairly large effort was expended between 5 and 11 September on the German defences around Le Havre, the raid of 10 September involving almost 1,000 bombers (521 Lancasters); the garrison surrendered the next day. A number of oil plants were targeted this month, too, and the Command also attacked cities such as Frankfurt, Darmstadt and Kiel.

Although command of the bomber force reverted to the Air Staff on 14 September, one of the first series of major operations was in support of the airborne landings in Holland as part of Operation *Market-Garden*. This daring plan was launched at the instigation of Montgomery in an attempt to achieve raid exploitation of his advance and secure a bridgehead over the Rhine. On the night of 16/17 September, a force of 200 Lancasters attacked the German airfields at Hopsten, Leeuwarden, Steenwijk and Rheine, as part of the air supremacy plan, prior to the launching of the air assault armada the following morning. A smaller force, 54 Lancasters, attacked a number of flak positions, without success.

The air assault by glider and paratroop forces met with mixed success on day one; Lancasters were airborne on 17 September to attack flak sites in the Flushing area, and that night over 200 bombers made diversionary raids to draw German fighters away from the assault areas.

The advance by XXX Corps was not as rapid as had been hoped. Although important gains were made, the final bridge, at Arnhem, held by British and Polish paratroops, fell to a determined German counter-offensive before the ground column could reach it.

One of the major problems with the Allied ground build-up was the logistics of landing men and material in France – the

Salvaging items from the *Tirpitz*: **the final attack by 9 and 617 Squadrons destroyed the ship.** Ken Delve Collection

Lancaster with impressive nose art, LL843 of 463 Squadron, at Waddington in late 1944; the aircraft eventually flew 118 missions. Andy Thomas Collection

capture of a major port was essential. The RAF's heavy bombers were called on to help with the assault on Calais. The first of a series of attacks took place on 20 September, with 646 bombers (437 Lancasters); further missions were flown on 24, 25, 26, 27 and 28 September, a number being disrupted by poor weather. The Germans eventually surrendered to Canadian forces, and the port was soon undergoing repairs.

On 23/24 September, No 5 Group sent five marker Mosquitoes and 136 Lancasters to breach the Dortmund-Ems canal,one of the main communication waterways. They succeeded, but unfortunately 14 Lancasters were lost.

Crews use a blackboard to recount the hits made on the Tirpitz; note the poster on the wall: 'The smaller the target, the more accurate you must be.' Ken Delve Collection

Operation *Paravane* and the *Tirpitz*

For much of the war, British Prime Minister Winston Churchill was prey to something verging on paranoia regarding German Capital ships. As a result, enormous bomber effort had been expended against such targets, with little result. In September 1944, the Admiralty believed that the battleship *Tirpitz* was about to leave the Kaa fjord in Norway. The destruction of this battleship became a high priority and the Lancasters of 9 Squadron and 617 Squadron were tasked to attack the ship using 12,000lb Tallboy bombs. However, with these bombs aboard, the Lancasters were unable to reach the Kaa fjord and return to their bases in England. The Russians were persuaded to accept the Lancasters at Yagodonik airfield near Archangel.

Operation *Paravane* called for the Lancasters to take off from Scotland, attack the *Tirpitz* and then land in Russia; Wg Cdr Willie Tait would lead 617 Squadron and Wg Cdr James Bazin would lead 9 Squadron. This plan was cancelled and, on 11 September, the Lancasters flew direct to Yagodonik, the intention being to fly the attack from there. Weather conditions over Russia were poor and six of the Lancasters had to make forced landings, the others being scattered over various airfields in Russia. Fg Off Ross was one of those who had to force-land:

> We had been circling for 2 hours 45 minutes, so I looked for a likely spot to land the aircraft, the surrounding ground appeared to be waterlogged. Finally, I selected a long stretch of wooden road void of telegraph poles for a distance of about 1,100 yards. The cloud base was 200ft in patches and two approaches were made. The first was too far to the right, the second was OK, but a lorry load of troops had stopped on it. I tried the reciprocal without success. The engineer reported about 30 gallons of petrol left, so I ordered the crew to crash stations, selected a marshy land, 20 degrees flap, and approached at 115mph. Aircraft touched down, the crew were all OK.

The first task now was to gather as many of the serviceable aircraft as possible at Yagodonik; the final attack force of 28 Lancasters took off on 15 September led by Tait. Twenty-one aircraft carried Tallboys, and the others had 500lb Johnny Walker mines. The attackers found the *Tirpitz* and made their runs, some having to go around twice, due to bomb release trouble or poor line-ups. Seventeen of the Tallboys were dropped and all the 500lb mines – although an effective smoke screen had been thrown around the ship. No significant opposition had been encountered and all the Lancasters made it back to Yagodonik.

There were conflicting reports regarding the damage caused to the targets; although one bomb may have caused some damage, the *Tirpitz* was still afloat and was thus considered still to be a threat. The Lancasters returned to the UK, and the Germans moved the *Tirpitz* to the Tromso fjord to act as a gun battery – this was not known by the Admiralty.

The move south brought the ship in range of Lancasters flown from Scotland and, on 29 October, Tait led 40 aircraft (20 from each squadron) from Lossiemouth to attack it. Of the 32 Tallboys dropped, none caused any significant damage; one Lancaster (NF920, Fg Off D. W. Carey) was hit by flak, but managed to land in Sweden.

The crew report of 9 Squadron's Fg Off Taylor (PD213) was typical:

> Primary attacked at 0855 from 12,000ft, bombs were observed entering the water in several directions about a mile from the ship. Bombed on 3rd run owing to cloud. Thick yellow/brown smoke appeared to be coming from the ship.

The bombers returned to their home bases on 30 October. They were back in Scotland on 4 November, but on this occasion no raid was mounted, and they flew south once more two days later. Both squadrons were back at Kinloss/Lossiemouth on 11 November; this time, the operation went ahead.

The third attack was mounted on 12 November, Tait leading 31 bombers (18 from 617 Squadron and 13 from 9 Squadron). Good weather, no smoke screen and an absence of fighters allowed the Lancasters to make accurate attacks and several hits were scored; the *Tirpitz* exploded and turned over. The destruction of the battleship was filmed by a Group film unit aboard PD329 of 463 Squadron. One Lancaster, Fg Off Coster of 9 Squadron, was damaged but landed in Sweden.

The 9 squadron ORB recorded the following:

> 13 aircraft T/O 0300-0330 for *Tirpitz*, a further 7 were u/s because of frost. Aircraft modified to carry overload petrol, no mid-upper gun carried, two aircraft took off late and missed the RV and had to abort, the other 11 attacked between 0945 and 0948 from 10-14,000ft. Crews report clear weather over target and bombs well concentrated around target. Hit observed amidships followed by explosion and fire, and many near misses seen. One crew reported ship appeared to be listing to starboard with fire amidships.

It was indeed the final demise of the *Tirpitz*, and the ship rolled over. Some years later, the Norwegian Government presented the RAF with a bulkhead from the ship, which was duly 'shared' by 9 and 617 squadrons.

Attacks on oil installations were a major part of Bomber Command's effort throughout the latter part of 1944; here, a 514 Squadron Lanc bombs Bec D'Ambes on 4 August. Ken Delve Collection

A daylight attack on 11 September on the synthetic oil plant at Kamen: 'L' of 514 Squadron drops a 4,000lb and sixteen 500lb bombs. Ken Delve Collection

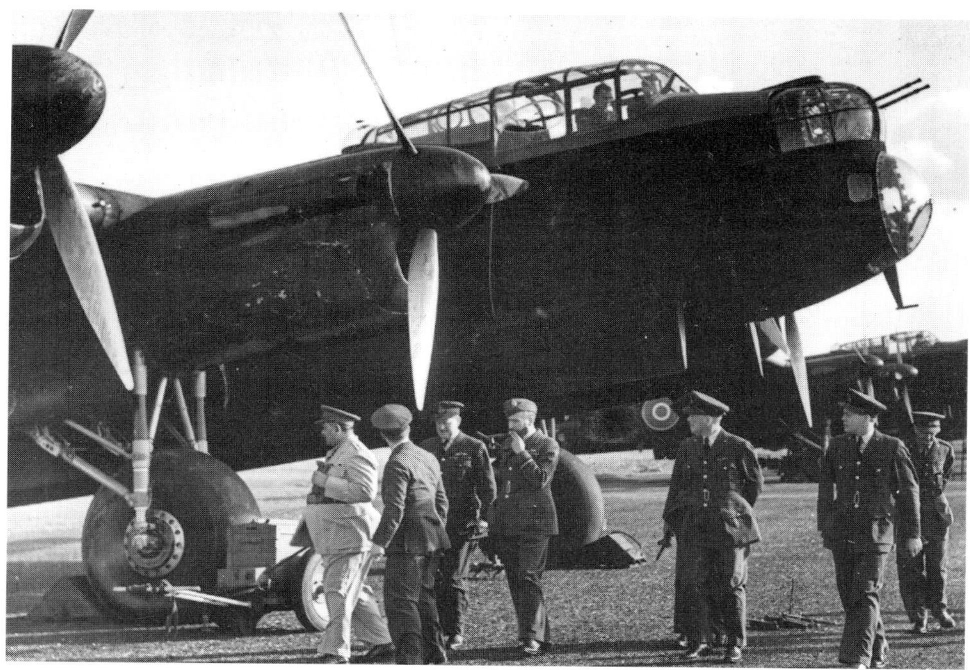

VIP visit to 35 Squadron at Graveley; the Squadron became a Lancaster unit with No 8 Group in March 1944. Ken Delve Collection

The 'battle of the bulkhead', in which each squadron endeavours to obtain it and put in on display, has been a part of RAF legend ever since.

October

The striking power of Bomber Command is aptly illustrated by the statistics for October 1944 – 17,000 operational sorties were flown, 13,000 to targets in Germany, and over 50,000 tons of bombs fell on German territory. In one 24-hour period, the Command dropped more tonnage of bombs on Duisburg than the Germans dropped on London in the entire war.

Early October established the pattern of day and night attacks on a variety of targets, which was now standard; some were connected with the Strategic Bombing Offensive, and others with the ground advance. Typical of the latter was the attack by 252 Lancasters on 3 October against the sea walls protecting Walcheren Island, the intention being to flood the low-lying island and destroy its various military installations, especially the gun batteries. The bombers succeeded in breaching the wall, and made a return visit on 7 October. Most of the bomber effort in the first half of the month was against German cities, although the occasional special op was also mounted, such as that by 617 Squadron on 7 October against the Kembs Dam – the Tallboys were dropped with the accuracy that had now become standard for 617 Squadron.

Operation *Hurricane* began on 14 October; the USAAF was to attack targets in the Ruhr by day, and Bomber Command was to attack them by night, with the intention of demonstrating the Allies' overwhelming air power. For many crews, this entailed flying on consecutive missions in the same 24-hour period, as 'maximum effort' was to be standard.

On the first raid, 1,000-plus RAF bombers hit Duisburg, crews landed back in England and, in many cases, snatched just a few hours' rest before taking off on the night attack. This was Bomber Command's biggest daylight operation to date: 1,013 bombers (519 Lancasters), escorted by fighters, plus an American contribution of 2,000 aircraft (1,251 bombers), which attacked Cologne. Over 4,000 tons of bombs were dropped by the RAF aircraft, causing major destruction.

A further 1,005 RAF bombers (498 Lancasters) were airborne that night, dropping another 4,500 tons. Another Lancaster force, 233 aircraft, attacked Brunswick the same night causing widespread destruction. The following day was quiet as the bomber force recovered from this intensive effort, although 9 Squadron sent 18 aircraft to attack the Sorpe Dam with Tallboys, a number of which hit the target but with no significant effect.

Mid-October saw large-scale formation attacks by 100-200 Lancasters of No 3 Group against targets in NW Germany. The ORS summarized this period as:

> A very successful form of attack with good concentration of bombs, approximately 180 tons per square mile and an average systematic error of 375 yards.

The first independent attack by AVM Harrison's Group using this tactic was against Bonn on 18 October by 128 Lancasters. With one-third of the Group now equipped with G-H, the tactic was for a non G-H aircraft to formate on a G-H equipped aircraft (which carried distinctive tail fin marks), thus ensuring bombing accuracy throughout the force. At a commanders' conference held on 2 October, Harrison had expressed his preference for escorted day attacks by small formations. On 6 October, HQ Bomber Command instructed the AOC to use a maximum G-H force 'day and night', aiming to achieve a concentration of 100 aircraft in a 6-minute window by day and of 100 aircraft in 4 minutes by night. A list of targets was issued but the actual choice of target was left to the AOC – Bomber Command was to be informed of the details before the take-off.

Such was the belief in G-H's accuracy that these missions were flown by day, when weather conditions such as cloud prevented other types from operating. This first attack was certainly accurate and much of the centre of Bonn was destroyed. While No 5 Group invariably operated as a separate force, the Lancasters of No 3 Group still worked as part of Main Force for night attacks, and were only employed as a separate entity when conditions were appropriate.

Other German cities were hit in the latter part of October. Essen suffered a raid by 1,055 bombers (561 Lancasters) on 23/24 October, and by 771 bombers (508 Lancasters) by day on 25 October. Much of this industrial city was hit and the once-mighty Krupps steelworks was, at last, seriously disrupted. A similar double blow was delivered on Cologne at the end of the month. Bomber losses had fallen dramatically on many of these raids – for example, not one of the 905 aircraft attacking Cologne on 30/31 October was lost.

New Devices and Aids

By late October, all of 617 Squadron's aircraft had been equipped with SABS (Stabilised Automatic Bombsight).

The crews undertook intensive training using Wainfleet bombing range, achieving averages of less than 100 yards from a bombing height of 20,000ft. In October, the Lancaster IIIs of 150 Squadron were using the Rose tail turret. The turret carried two 0.5in guns rather than the standard four 0.303in guns, and was part of Bomber Command's attempts to improve the defensive firepower of its bombers (even though fewer fighters were attempting to intercept the bombers). In his 'Despatch', Harris summarized these 1944 developments:

> Air Ministry informed me that the provision of four-gun mid-upper turrets for Stirling, Halifax and Lancaster was being pushed ahead, but they would not be available for use by Bomber Command before August 1943. It was also stated that the introduction of two 20mm guns into the dorsal turret of Lancaster aircraft would not be feasible because of Centre of Gravity considerations… owing to the lack of progress in the design of tail turrets with .5in guns, I directly encouraged Messrs Rose Bros of Gainsborough, who, with the assistance of Bomber Command personnel, designed and produced a tail turret carrying two .5in guns. This turret possessed novel features… [and] provided a large field of view, since the rear portion of the cupola was left open as a direct vision opening.

U-Boat pens at La Pallice showing the effect of the attack on August 9, 1944 by 617 Squadron. Ken Delve Collection

By the end of the war, 180 of these turrets had been installed in Lancasters of No 100 Gp.

This was not the first improved gun system to enter service in 1944. In mid-July, 460 Squadron had begun to fly with an AGLT (Automatic Gun Laying Turret) fitted; the system was code-named 'Village Inn'.

As early as late October 1942, the TRE (Telecommunications Research Establishment) had demonstrated a rearward-facing AI device that could be used as a blind-fire aid for the rear guns. An order was placed for 100 modified sets to be fitted to FN120 turrets (as FN121). Meanwhile, the BDU at Newmarket was undertaking intensive trials on the prototype AGLT in one of their Lancasters, and, although a few teething problems had to be overcome, they were, in general terms, satisfied with the equipment. They made various suggestions for modifications on technical and tactical grounds, most of which were adopted, and the first twelve operational aircraft were fitted out at SIU Defford, with 32 MU carrying out subsequent modific-ations. The first modified aircraft went to 460 Squadron in March, but the system was still giving problems; on the tactical side, the identification of friend and foe was perhaps the most significant drawback.

The BDU formed a special flight with six Lancasters in an effort to iron out the major problems, and intensive work solved a number of the difficulties. Thus, by late June, the first flight of 460 Squadron was undertaking a period of work-up, and the

Lancaster III JA918 served with 550 Squadron from March 1944 until its loss on the night of May 9/10. FlyPast Collection

Lancasters attack the L'Isle Adam V-bomb site on 2 August, one of a number of such sites hit this day by almost 800 bombers (385 Lancasters) without loss. Ken Delve Collection

On 25/26 August, 412 Lancasters attacked the Opel factory at Russelheim in an accurate and effective 10-minute attack; the reduction in production was short-lived, however. Ken Delve Collection

Squadron flew its first mission on 20/22 July. By the end of August, all the Squadron's flights had completed their training.

The general conclusion from this was the following:

> Whilst the equipment worked generally very well, it was obvious from the first that negative identification required great care and restraint by gunners. To make matters worse, trouble was experienced with IR filters fitted to the transmission lamps, and I decided to operate AGLT aircraft only under certain conditions and when other aircraft were not likely to be encoun-tered. (Harris, 'Despatch on War Operations')

The problems with the turret's serviceability continued. The second unit, 49 Squadron, undertook its first operation on 11/12 September, and reported similar difficulties. Harris later wrote:

> Both the squadrons experienced a considerable amount of unserviceability with AGLT and test gear was therefore fitted so that the gunner could try out the equipment during flight. When the equipment was working well, numerous contacts, chiefly friendly, were made. It was apparent, however, that gunners mistrusted Type Z ident and were loath to fire blind at what they thought might be friendly aircraft. As a tail warning device, the equipment was exceptionally good, giving both correct line and range of approaching aircraft.

Harris also wrote:

> Gun heaters became available in quantity in 1944, but they did not solve the problem in so far as Lancaster aircraft were concerned, since this aircraft was equipped with the FN tail turret, which, in order to afford a reasonable field of view, was used with the rear of the cupola removed. Moreover, the number of electrical gun heaters that could be used in Lancaster aircraft was limited by the power supply.

August 1944 saw the first significant use of ducting to feed warm air from the engines to the turrets; by the end of the war, approximately 50 per cent of the Lancaster force had been equipped with this system.

On 11/12 November, Loran, another blind-bombing aid, begin its operational career. No 5 Group sent 237 Lancasters to attack the Rhenania-Ossag oil refinery at Harburg; the industrial area of the city, including the oil installations, suffered moderate damage. On 11 November, Bomber Command had requested Loran for all its aircraft, starting with retrospective fitting to PFF aircraft as well as those of No 5 Group and No 100 Group, plus fitting on the production line for all new Lancs and Lincolns.

All the Lancasters of No 5 Group had

been equipped with Loran by the end of the year.

Towards the End of 1944

Pressure was maintained on the vulnerable German synthetic oil production industry in November, with a number of sites being hit by Bomber Command. On 21 November, the synthetic oil plant at Homberg was attacked by 160 Lancasters of No 3 Group (for the loss of three aircraft). For Lancaster 'H' of 514 Squadron, it proved a tricky mission:

> On the run-up to the target the aircraft was 50 yards to the port quarter of the leader, and slightly below. There was considerable flak, presumed predicted, during the run-up. Normally an aircraft in this position releases its bombs as soon as it sees the leader do so. Consequently, 'H' opened its bomb doors as soon as the leader did and the air bomber was waiting with his hand on the bomb release. Just as the formation neared the release point, the pilot and air bomber saw that the leader was jettisoning his bombs all together. They could see no reason why the leader was not bombing normally, and the air bomber prepared to release his bombs. Just as he did so there was a blinding flash below the leader, as though one of his bombs had exploded. The perspex in the air bomber's compartment, the pilot's cockpit, and the mid-upper turret was shattered, and the fuselage was scarred on the starboard side with small holes. The faces of both the pilot and air bomber were pitted with minute cuts, both were temporarily blinded by the flash, and by blood streaming over their eyes.
>
> The pilot lost control of the aircraft and, while he groped for the controls, with the wind lashing his face, the aircraft lost some 3,000ft. His intercom had gone unserviceable and, as he could not reach the emergency signal light, he waved the crew forward with his hand, indicating that they should bale out. While they were putting on their 'chutes, however, the pilot regained control and signalled the crew to wait. He could see better now, and managed to rejoin the bomber stream, though the aircraft was at 15,000ft, and well below the others. The engineer had previously tried without success to plug the pilot's intercom into a different socket, but the pilot was now able to do so himself, and called up the rest of the crew.
>
> All the crew replied, except the rear gunner, so the pilot told the wireless operator to go back and investigate. The wireless operator opened

CONFIDENTIAL.

RECOMMENDATION FOR HONOURS AND AWARDS.

Christian Names : ROBERT STANLEY. Surname : ROBERTS.
Rank : SERGEANT. Official No. : 1104382. ✓ R
Command or Group : PATH FINDER FORCE (NO.8 GROUP). Unit : NO. 7 SQUADRON, P.F.F.

Total hours flown on operations. 307.10
Total number of sorties. 31.
Total hours flown on operations since receipt of previous award. N/A.
Number of sorties since receipt of previous award. N/A.
Recognition for which recommended. IMMEDIATE D.F.M. ✓
Appointment held. WIRELESS OPERATOR.

This N.C.O. was Wireless Operator in the crew of a Lancaster aircraft detailed to attack Hamburg on the night of 28/29th July, 1944. After leaving the target, the aircraft was hit by Anti-Aircraft fire and burst into flames. The Captain gave orders to abandon, but this N.C.O. was unable to move from his position owing to the fires, and consequently became severely burnt in the face, hands and legs. The Captain subsequently was able to get the aircraft under control, and although all members of the crew, including this N.C.O., were injured, managed to bring this aircraft back to this country.

Throughout the return flight, this N.C.O. showed courage and forti tude of the highest order. Disregarding his own physical suffering through burns, he managed to put out the fires in the vicinity of his position and send a S.O.S. messag before his equipment became totally unserviceable. Realising that the Bomb Aimer ha received severe burns and was very ill, this N.C.O. administered First Aid and morphi and spent the whole of the return journey attending to his safety. Not until the aircraft had returned to this country and crash landed, did this N.C.O. make any mention of his own injuries, and his action throughout the flight was instrumental in relieving the badly injured Bomb Aimer of the serious effects of his burns.

This N.C.O. has proved himself to be an outstanding member of a gallant crew, and his conduct throughout the action, without consideration for his ow personal safety, is worthy of the highest praise.

R.W. COX,
Wing Commander, Commanding,
No. 7 Squadron, P. F. F.

Date:- 2nd August, 1944.
Covering Remarks of Station Commander,

I agree, this N.C.O's conduct in the face of extreme danger is worthy of the highest praise, most strongly recommended.

Group Captain, Commanding,
R.A.F. Station, Oakington.

Date: 3rd August, 1944.
Remarks of Air Officer Commanding, Path Finder Force.

Copy of the 'recommendation for honours and awards' for an immediate DFM for Sgt R. Roberts of 7 Squadron. Ken Delve Collection

Fg Off Denyluk and 50 Squadron crew pose by the tail of their aircraft at Skellingthorpe; the unit had flown its first Lancaster op on 30/31 May 1942, and had lost 112 Lancasters by the end of the war. Ken Delve Collection

Although this is an immediate post-war shot taken at Lindholme, it shows the range of bombs carried by the Lancaster. Ken Delve Collection

the bulkhead doors and saw through the inspection panels that the bomb doors were open and he could see the ground below; air was rushing through the fuselage with the force of a gale. The wireless operator reported this to the pilot, who ordered the mid-upper gunner to go instead. The mid-upper gunner, who had already left his turret when it was smashed, managed to reach the rear of the fuselage, where he found the rear hatch was open, and on opening the rear bulkhead doors discovered that the rear gunner had gone. His parachute was missing; he must have baled out within a few miles of the target.

The Lancaster was now flying normally and on track. Suddenly the starboard inner engine burst into flames, apparently due to an oil leak. The engine was feathered, the Graviner used, and the fire put out. A few minutes later the starboard outer engine revs began to fluctuate, and dense white fumes poured out of it, suggesting a coolant leak. This engine was also successfully feathered. The wireless operator sent a distress message back to base, although he did not think that the message would be received as the aerials were badly damaged. 'H' had now formated on another Lancaster and the wireless operator also signalled to this aircraft with the Aldis lamp.

The Lancaster had flown for some 20 minutes since the flash occurred when the port-outer revs began to fluctuate, and the engine finally burst into flames. Fire drill was again carried out correctly and with success. The intercom then failed completely. Thereafter, all the pilot's instructions had to either be given by gesticulation or written down on paper.

The aircraft, now flying on one engine and unable to maintain height, entered a belt of cloud at 12,000ft. Below this cloud the weather was bad with poor visibility. The pilot brought the aircraft down to 2,000ft and at this height passed over an airfield near Antwerp. It was impossible to turn the aircraft and land there, so he flew on and, seeing three suitable adjacent fields ahead, he decided to land. The pilot had managed to get the flaps down about 10 degrees, and he made a perfect belly landing. The aircraft came to rest after travelling about 50 yards over soft mud. No one in the crew was even bruised. The position of landing was Doorn, near Antwerp, behind our own lines. (Bomber Command Quarterly Review No 11)

The training system continued to evolve in the latter part of 1944, one of the most significant changes being the decision to re-equip the Stirling HCUs with 32 Lancasters each, and incorporate within them the role of the Lancaster Finishing Schools. First to be affected by this policy

10 September 1944 – the 'heavies' attack strongpoints near Caen to try to help the ground force advance.
Ken Delve Collection

were the No 3 Group units, 1651 and 1653 HCU. However, the remaining three Stirling HCUs – 1954, 1660, 1661 – also re-equipped in the period from November 1944 to January 1945. Indeed, in the latter part of 1944, the five remaining Halifax HCUs – 1656, 1662, 1666, 1667 and 1669 – also re-equipped, as Bomber Command became virtually an all-Lancaster force.

Specialist training units were also created towards the end of 1944. These included the Bomber Command Instructors School (BCIS) at Finningley in December (with ten Lancs amongst its UE), to train instructors for the OTUs and HCUs, and 1323 Flight, which formed at Bourn in November to train gunners for the three PFF squadrons equipped with AGLT Lancasters. On 29 December, the Gee-H Training Flight was formed at Hemswell, using eight Lancasters to train 20 crews per week.

The effectiveness of the Bomber Command campaign in late 1944 is aptly demonstrated by a memo, dated 7 November, sent by Reichsminister Albert Speer (responsible for armaments and war production) to Field Marshal Keitel:

> The continuous attacks directed by the enemy against the Ruhr are having the most serious effect on our entire armament and war production. In addition to the bombing of production plants in the Ruhr, the systematic attacks carried out on rail installations are largely responsible for the present critical situation, while the former can result in an appreciable drop in our total war output, the disruption of our communications network may well lead to a production crisis which will gravely jeopardize our capacity to continue the war.

617 Squadron used its expertise – and heavy bombs – to attack a number of important and difficult targets, such as the V-weapon site at Siracourt. Ken Delve Collection

The memo included various statistics – such as a 50 per cent drop in gas supply and the fact that ten railway stations, including Essen, Hamm, Cologne and Munster, were unusable, while 46 others were partly unusable.

The war against German industrial cities continued, with attacks on targets that had already received heavy raids in the past, such as Düsseldorf, and on new centres such as Koblenz (6/7 November), Freiburg (27/28 November) and Hagen (2/3 December), which either contained lines of communication or industries. With over 1,000 bombers available to him, a lower level of threat from the struggling German night-fighter force and improved bombing accuracy, Harris was now able to send smaller forces against a wider range of targets. Pinpoint targets, particularly oil installations, continued to attract a great deal of attention, and there was the occasional special task – for example, on 16 November, almost 1,200 RAF heavies supported the American ground advance towards the Rhine. Formations of bombers attacked Düren, Hülich and Heinsberg, causing massive destruction. A similar number of US heavies hit another range of targets in the same area.

Although the Allies had made steady advances in the latter part of 1944, the German Army was by no means a beaten force – a fact that was rammed home on 16 December, when it launched a massive armoured thrust through the Ardennes, aimed at reaching the Channel coast and destroying the cohesion of the Allied armies. Bad weather ensured that Allied air power could play little part in the battle, and the German thrust made significant gains, despite a few determined pockets of resistance. Three days later, the weather had improved sufficiently for air power to be used, and, while tactical types played the major role, the strategic bombers did have a part to play. On 19 December, No 3 Group sent 32 Lancasters to attack the railyards in Trier, bombing through cloud with reasonable results:

> Henceforward the heavy bombers were to be instrumental in halting the impetus of the German advance. (AHB narrative)

The cross marks the Aiming Point as other Lancs drift over the target area (Rheydt) beneath Fg Off Peek's 195 Squadron aircraft. Ken Delve Collection

Trier was hit again on 23 December and three days later, on 26 December, a force of 294 aircraft (146 Lancasters) attacked troop positions near St-Vith in direct support of the battle. The same day, a smaller force of Lancasters had attacked the Gremberg railyards at Cologne; one of the Oboe aircraft was flown by Sqn Ldr Robert Palmer. This 582 Squadron Lancaster completed its Oboe run, despite flak damage, and hit its target, but crashed shortly afterwards. Sqn Ldr Palmer was subsequently awarded the Victoria Cross.

1944 Summary

The War Room Manual of Bomber Command Operations for 1944 states that Lancasters flew 84,131 sorties for the loss of 1,641 aircraft by night and 180 by day. Some 1,200 Lancasters were on squadron strength, in 53 squadrons, by December 1944, a virtual doubling of aircraft strength since the previous December.

23 December 1944 – Sqn Ldr Robert Palmer VC DFC* (No 109 Squadron)

Robert Anthony Maurice Palmer joined the RAF as a sergeant pilot in 1939 and flew tours with 75 Squadron and 149 Squadron. After completing his first operational tour, he went to 20 OTU at Lossiemouth as an instructor. Commissioned in January 1942, he returned to operational flying with 109 Squadron at Warboys in January 1944, flying Mosquitoes. By December 1944, he had flown over 100 operational sorties but, rather than take a much-deserved rest, he stayed with the Squadron. On 23 December, Palmer was Master Bomber for a raid against marshalling yards at Cologne, flying a 582 Squadron Lancaster. His citation reads:

This officer has completed 110 bombing missions. Most of them involved deep penetration of heavily defended territory; many were low-level 'marking' operations against vital targets; all were executed with tenacity, high courage and great accuracy. The finest example of his courage and determination was on December 23, 1944, when he led a formation of Lancasters to attack the marshalling yards at Cologne in daylight. He had the task of marking the target, and his formation had been ordered to bomb as soon as the bombs had gone from his, the leading aircraft. The leader's duties during the final bombing run were exacting and demanded coolness and resolution. To achieve accuracy he would have to fly at an exact height and airspeed on a steady course, regardless of opposition.

Some minutes before the target was reached, his aircraft came under heavy anti-aircraft fire, shells burst all around, two engines were set on fire and there were flames and smoke in the nose and the bomb bay. Enemy fighters now attacked in force. Palmer disdained the possibility of taking avoiding action. He knew that if he diverged the least bit from his course, he would be unable to utilize the special equipment to the best advantage. He was determined to complete the run and provide an accurate and easily seen aiming point for the other bombers. He ignored the double risk of fire and explosion in his aircraft and kept on. With his engines developing unequal power, an immense effort was needed to keep the damaged aircraft on a straight course. Nevertheless, he made a perfect approach and his bombs hit the target. His aircraft was last seen spiralling to earth in flames. Such was the strength of the opposition that more than half of the formation failed to return.

CHAPTER EIGHT

1945

Equipment

Bombs

Bomber Command had carried out attacks on enemy targets with such intensity in the latter part of 1944 that in early 1945 it found itself short of 1,000lb bombs. In May 1944, when there had been a similar shortage, the Command had acquired 6,500 American 1,000lb SAP bombs (AN-M57), fourteen of which could be carried by a Lancaster. The temporary solution in 1945 was an increased use of 250lb bombs, but this was not without its problems:

> Two recent explosions [in which 22 people had been killed] were probably due to the instability of fusing in the 250lb bombs. Instructions were issued that all 250lb bombs now to be fused 'Tail Instantaneous' only and that detonators were to be removed from the nose. (Bomber Command ORB January 1945)

Armament

A conference was held at HQ Bomber Command on 5 January to decide the allocation of new type turrets, the general conclusions were as follows:

> 1. Ten squadrons of No 1 Group earmarked for the Rose-Rice turret.
> 2. One squadron in No 1 Group and one squadron in No 5 Group equipped with AGLT.
> 3. The PFF to re-equip throughout with AGLT before any further Middle East squadrons.
> 4. Lancasters with FN82 turret, but not fully equipped with AGLT, to be allotted to No 3 Group and later No 1 Group.

The Operational Research Section submitted a number of reports in the New Year on various aspects of gun armament. Report S.205 dealt with 'Initial operational experience with AGLT':

> One thousand plus night sorties by trained crews have been flown since its introduction to service in July 1944. The failure to return has been 1.4 per cent, against the standard of 1.7 per cent, but in the first few months the rate was markedly lower. There were only four instances of tail warner/blind fire and six visual pick-ups. There has been a 40 per cent unserviceability rate but some of these were due to faulty manipulation.
>
> The principal reason for failure of gunners to open fire blind is considered to be their lack of confidence in the Type Z ident, which has resulted from the occasional failure of an aircraft, later seen to be friendly, to give a Type Z response. This will have to be remedied by ensuring that all aircraft with Type Z transmitters, preferably by auto switching and by maintaining a high standard of efficiency of the receiver. It is suggested that there is a need to select and train suitable gunners, perhaps by establishing a training flight in No 7 Group.

Report S.210 covered the 'Operational record of the Rose turret to December 1944':

> The proportion of returning aircraft attacked by fighters is, for aircraft with Rose turrets, only about half what it is for otherwise comparable aircraft with standard turrets. This may be accounted for by the increased field of view from the turret which would assist evasion of attacks. Only 13 instances are recorded of the turrets being fired – and 60 per cent had one or more stoppages (the average is 23 per cent for standard turrets). It seems possible that the high tendency of the .5in gun to jam has been responsible for the lack of effect on loss rates. Although the total number of attacks may have been reduced by about 25 per cent by the improved field of view, the number of bombers shot down by fighters appears to be unaltered. It is thus possible that fighters who were able to make an attack had success above the average in shooting down aircraft with Rose turrets. Such a result might well follow from the apparently lower reliability of the Rose turret armament. Additional attempts to improve the armament are therefore highly desirable.

In January 1945, the BDU was tasked to compare AGLT performance with that of the American AN/APG 8 system; the latter was fitted to an American Emerson turret in a Lancaster X. The report (No 75) concluded the following:

> Radar gun laying has been found to be by far the best form, so far, of electronic warfare device. In this role AGLT is very good, but APG 8 should be better still by virtue of:
> i. its larger cone;
> ii. its range mechanism;
> iii. its likely better reliability due to design and the sealing of components in airtight containers.
>
> APG 8 is not a really practical method of blind firing since experience shows that deflection shooting, whether due to relative movements, bullet trail or gravity drop, is the rule rather then the exception. It seems likely that combining the best points of both APG 8 and AGLT would provide an equipment superior to either.

Engines

The Lancaster's Merlin engines gave very few problems; indeed, there are numerous reports of how resilient and reliable they were. One of the main problems for the pilot and flight engineer was that of synchronizing the four engines in order to prevent airframe vibration. Avro developed a simple system – the Avro Synchroscope – for this, and in early 1945 it was being evaluated by the BDU using Lancaster III DV273. In Report No 76 (dated 20 February 1945), the BDU stated the following:

> The Avro Synchroscope is an instrument used for synchronizing the engines of four-engined aircraft. It consists of three small lamps, spaced equally about the face of the instrument and connected to the Engine Speed Indicator (ESI) generators so that the phase rotation of the

Fg Off Cowling in the cockpit of his 619 Squadron Lancaster 'G-George', with its 'Going my way' nose art. Frank Slater

generator causes the lamps to light in rotation. A switch mounted in the centre of the instrument face is so connected that one ESI generator is used as the Master, and the other ESI generators referred to it in turn, by three positions on the switch. The direction of rotation of the lights indicates whether the engine under consideration is fast or slow with reference to the Master. When the engine under consideration has been accurately synchronized with the Master, the rotation ceases and one of the lights remains steady. The procedure is repeated until all engines have been synchronized to the Master.

It is considered that the Synchronoscope is a most useful instrument. It will without doubt reduce crew fatigue, not only because of a marked reduction in vibration and noise, but because ideal conditions can be easily and positively maintained.

1 January 1945 – Flt Sgt George Thompson VC (No 9 Squadron)

George Thompson joined the RAF as a wireless tradesman but transferred to flying duties as a wireless operator in 1943. He eventually joined 9 Squadron at Bardney in September 1944; on 1 January 1945, his aircraft was involved in a daylight attack on the Dortmund-Ems Canal. His citation reads:

The bombs had just been released when a heavy shell hit the aircraft in front of the mid-upper turret. Fire broke out and dense smoke filled the fuselage. The nose of the aircraft was then hit and an inrush of air, clearing the smoke, revealed a scene of utter devastation. Most of the perspex screen of the nose compartment had been shot away, gaping holes had been torn in the canopy above the pilot's head, the inter-communications wiring had been severed, and there was a large hole in the floor of the aircraft. Bedding and other equipment were badly damaged or alight; one engine was on fire.

Thompson saw that the gunner was unconscious in the blazing mid-upper turret. Without hesitation he went down the fuselage into the fire and exploding ammunition. He pulled the gunner from his turret and, edging his way round the hole in the floor, carried him away from the flames. With his bare hands, he extinguished the gunner's burning clothing. Thompson himself sustained serious burns on his face, hands and legs. Thompson then noticed that the rear turret was also on fire. Despite his own severe injuries he moved painfully to the rear of the fuselage where he found the rear gunner with his clothing alight, overcome by flames and fumes. A second time Thompson braved the flames. With great difficulty he extricated the helpless gunner and carried him clear. Again, he used his bare hands, already burnt, to beat out flames on a comrade's clothing.

Flight Sergeant Thompson, by now almost exhausted, felt that his duty was not yet done. He must report the fate of the crew to the captain. He made the perilous journey back through the burning fuselage, clinging to the sides with his burnt hands to get across the hole in the floor. The flow of cold air caused him intense pain and frost-bite developed. So pitiful was his condition that his captain failed to recognize him. Still, his only concern was for the two gunners he had left in the rear of the aircraft. He was given such attention as was possible until a crash-landing was made some 40 minutes later.

When the aircraft was hit, Flight Sergeant Thompson might have devoted his efforts to quelling the fire and so have contributed to his own safety. He preferred to go through the fire to succour his comrades. He knew that he would then be in no position to hear or heed any order which might be given to abandon the aircraft. He hazarded his own life in order to save the lives of others. Young in years (24 years old) and experience, his actions were those of a veteran.

Three weeks later, Flight Sergeant Thompson died of his injuries. One of the gunners unfortunately also died, but the other owes his life to the superb gallantry of Flight Sergeant Thompson, whose courage and self-sacrifice will ever be an inspiration to the Service.'

A New Year

By January 1945, Bomber Command included 53 Lancaster squadrons in its front line – a total established strength of around 1,200 aircraft. The remaining 30 or so squadrons were primarily equipped with Halifax or Mosquito, although some of the Halifax units would soon re-equip with Lancasters.

On New Year's Day 1945, 102 Lancasters of No 5 Group attacked the Dortmund-Ems Canal; this often-repaired German waterway was breached once again. One of the Lancasters lost on this sortie was from 9 Squadron; the Wireless Operator, F/Sgt George Thompson, was awarded the Victoria Cross for his actions.

Pressure on the rapidly crumbling German oil industry was kept up in the new year, and Bomber Command sent almost daily raids against such targets, often by formations from No 3 Group using Gee-H. It was a similar story with the other routine target systems – various German cities and towns were attacked, the aiming points often being the railway yards. A few special operations were also flown, including one by 32 Lancasters of 9 and 617 Squadrons to the U-boat pens at Bergen. A number of Tallboys scored direct hits, smashing through the concrete structures, but four Lancasters were lost, three of them from 617 Squadron.

It was to be a similar routine in February. On 7/8 February 1945, the broadcaster Richard Dimbleby flew with John Gee in Lancaster 'U' of 153 Squadron on the mission to Kleve. This attack by 295 Lancasters, in conjunction with a raid the same night on Goch (by 292 Halifaxes and 156 Lancasters), was an attempt to assist the ground advance by XXX Corps. Both towns had been incorporated by the Germans in their defence line.

No 100 Squadron sent 15 aircraft on the Kleve attack:

> Although a small objective demanding absolute accuracy, the attack was a complete success. The Master Bomber, having brought the Main Force down to bomb from 5,000ft below cloud,
>
> summed up their efforts with a congratulatory 'good bombing, boys'. (100 Squadron ORB February 1945)

The following night, Bomber Command sent out three major raids – 475 Lancasters to Pölitz, 228 aircraft (primarily Halifaxes) to Wanne-Eickel, and 151 Lancasters to Krefeld. The 100 Squadron diarist had this to say:

> The mission to Bohlen/Leipzig was cancelled and replaced with one to the Politz oil plant, north of Stettin. Thus the squadron participated in a historic precedent – bombing in support of the Allied armies in the West one night and in support of the Russian forces in the East the next. The round trip of 1,550 miles took them within 18 miles of the Russian spearhead at Stettin, the attack achieved a first-class concentration.

Operation Thunderclap

On 13/14 February, a force of 800 Lancasters and Mosquitoes undertook Operation *Thunderclap* – the attack on Dresden. This operation was intended as a 'knockout blow', to provide a final dislocation to the German system that would end the war – the bomber theorists were maintaining their 'war-winning' doctrine to the bitter end. With this objective in mind, the choice of targets might seem somewhat illogical (but for the influence of the Russians).

The Russians had made spectacular advances in the latter part of 1944 and, as part of their offensive strategy for 1945, requested bomber attacks on key node points, such as Dresden, Chemnitz and Leipzig. The fact that these towns were packed with refugees as well as active military forces was either overlooked or ignored.

The operation was planned as a combined RAF/USAAF offensive, with the Americans being scheduled to attack

23 February 1945 – Capt Edwin Swales VC DFC (No 582 Squadron)

Edwin Swales trained as a pilot in the SAAF and was seconded to the RAF in August 1943, joining 582 Squadron at Little Staughton in mid-1944. On 23 February 1945, Swales was chosen as Master Bomber for a raid against the Pforzheim rail junction. His citation reads:

As 'Master Bomber', he had the task of locating the target area with precision and of giving aiming instructions to the main force of bombers following in his wake. Soon after he had reached the target area he was engaged by an enemy fighter and one of his engines was put out of action. His rear guns failed. His crippled aircraft was an easy prey to further attacks. Unperturbed, he carried on with his allotted task; clearly and precisely he issued aiming instructions to the main force. Meanwhile, the enemy fighter closed the range and fired again. A second engine of Swale's aircraft was put out of action. Almost defenceless, he stayed over the target area issuing his aiming instructions until he was satisfied that the attack had achieved its purpose.

It is now known that the attack was one of the most concentrated and successful of the war. Captain Swales did not, however, regard his mission as completed. His aircraft was damaged. Its speed had been so much reduced that it could only with difficulty be kept in the air. The blind flying instruments were no longer working. Determined at all costs to prevent his aircraft and crew from falling into enemy hands, he set course for home. After an hour he flew into thin-layered cloud. He kept his course by skilful flying between the layers, but later heavy cloud and turbulent air conditions were met. The aircraft, by now over friendly territory, became more and more difficult to control; it was losing height steadily. Realizing that the situation was desperate, Swales ordered his crew to bale out. Time was very short and it required all his exertions to keep the aircraft steady while each of his crew moved in turn to the escape hatch and parachuted to safety. Hardly had the last crew member jumped when the aircraft plunged to earth. Captain Swales was found dead at the controls. Intrepid in the attack, courageous in the face of danger, he did his duty to the last, giving his life that his comrades might live.

Capt Edwin Swales (rear, standing) was awarded the Victoria Cross for his actions on 23/24 February 1945. Ken Delve Collection

'The bombing run'. Mac Mackay took this snapshot of 'Lofty' Walls in 'W-Whisky'. Ken Delve Collection

Waddington early 1945 – squadron personnel watch as PB754 of 467 Squadron taxies by.
Andy Thomas Collection

Dresden by day on 13 February. Bad weather, however, prevented this and so the first assault was made by Bomber Command on the night of 13/14 February. In two separate attacks, 807 bombers (796 Lancasters) attacked the city, causing widespread devastation and perhaps 50,000 casualties. The city was then bombed again on the following day by the Americans.

Continuing Operation *Thunderclap*, Chemnitz was hit by 717 aircraft (499 Lancasters) on 14/15 February, but, owing to the poor weather, the bombing was scattered and damage only moderate.

Both raids suffered only light losses as the strain on the German defences had reached breaking point. The night-fighter force was, however, still taking a regular toll of the bombers – although it was now impossible for this to have any significant impact on the offensive campaign.

Pforzheim

The last Bomber Command VC of the war was won by Capt Edwin Swales on 23/24 February, when he acted a Master Bomber for the attack on Pforzheim. This target was attacked by 367 Lancasters in a destructive 22 minutes that flattened over 80 per cent of the town; ten Lancasters were lost on this attack.

Lancaster PB945/O of 625 Squadron (Plt Off. Paige) was hit by incendiaries from another bomber; details of the incident are included in the No 1 Group 'K' Reports:

> Take-off 1629 from Kelstern en route to Pforzheim. Bombed primary on mixed salvo of Red and Green TIs at 2002 hours, 7,400ft. No flak or searchlights and no fighters seen.
>
> Approximately 1 minute after bombing the pilot saw a shower of incendiaries coming down immediately ahead. He could not see the aircraft from which they came and was unable to avoid flying straight into them. Fifteen to twenty 4lb incendiaries entered the fuselage from just astern of the main spar. Three incendiaries which were burning fell directly behind the W/Op and which he immediately threw out of a hole in the fuselage made by another incendiary. One incendiary came in the front of the W/Op on the starboard side and this he stamped out with his foot. One incendiary struck the rear turret, coming down behind the rear gunner. It hit the starboard side of the turret and exploded inside, going out through the bottom of the turret. The turret was jammed and one door would not open, but it left no fire. Some incendiaries damaged the intercom to the gunners, much damage was caused near the rest bed, all the wiring was ripped from the main spar astern. There was an incendiary in each wing in the proximity of each No 3 tank almost behind the outboard engines. There was another incendiary in the wing inboard of the starboard inner, which probably did some damage to the coolant system, causing the starboard inner engine to vibrate. The starboard inner then caught fire about 1 minute after the aircraft was hit. The engine was feathered and the fire went out.
>
> The pilot altered course south on to the next leg and almost immediately turned west in order to get back to our own lines. They flew for 5 minutes when the incendiary in the No 3 starboard tank blew up and the starboard outer caught fire. The starboard outer was feathered and the flight engineer managed to put out the fire with the Graviner almost immediately.
>
> Two minutes later the Captain asked the navigator to give him a course to steer to regain

the main bomber stream. They crossed the Rhine at the bend east of Bischweiler at 4,000ft and then took up a course for Juvincourt – where they intended to make an emergency landing. At approximately 2022 the incendiary in the port outer blazed up furiously and the captain gave orders for the crew to bale out, the W/Op relayed the message verbally to the gunners. Both gunners and the W/Op went out at the rear door, the W/Op used the spare parachute as his own had caught up in the broken wiring while he was throwing the incendiaries out and was partially open. The remainder of the crew went out the front escape hatch. The aircraft crashed on the outskirts of Luttenheim.

All the crew were OK except for minor injuries and three days later they were taken by Dakota to Croydon. The crew were: pilot – Fg Off D. Paige; navigator – W/O J. P. Sullivan; W/Op – F/Sgt J. Bettany; FE – Sgt R. B. Bennett; bomb aimer – F/Sgt J. A. Puttick; mid-upper – F/Sgt K. E. Campbell; rear – F/Sgt K. J. McRorie.

The Grand Slam and the Tallboy

The January Bomber Command ORB updated progress with the Grand Slam bomb, another special weapon from the design genius of Barnes Wallis:

> Production figures for the bomb and modified aircraft have been given as follows: 8–10 aircraft by the end of January, 10–12 bombs by the end of January. No live drops with this store have been attempted, but it is expected that a crater of some 160x35ft – and much earth disturbance – will result. (Bomber Command ORB January 1945)

The Grand Slam was a truly massive weapon – 25ft 5in long, 3ft 10in in diameter and with a filling of 9,200lb of Torpex; the terminal velocity of the weapon was calculated as 4,580 fps!

The following month, the Air Ministry agreed to the formation of an extra flight within 617 Squadron as it was expected that the workload for Tallboy and Grand Slam operations would need one flight for the former and two for the latter.

In these final months of the war, the Lancaster once again proved its adaptability and the BI (Spec) was modified to take a 22,000 Grand Slam bomb. Trials took place in February, using PB592, and the first production aircraft was PB995; the first two aircraft joined 617

A 22,000lb Grand Slam being lifted onto a bomb trolley. Ken Delve Collection

Armament trials were on-going as Bomber Command tried to improve the self-defence of its bombers; the Martin turret (in mid-upper position here) was not a great success. Ken Delve Collection

Note the AGLT radar beneath the rear turret of this 635 Squadron aircraft. Graham Pitchfork Collection

Squadron on 13 March and that same afternoon one aircraft joined the attack on the Bielefeld viaduct. The following day, 32 Lancasters returned to the Bielefeld and Arnsberg viaducts. Sqn Ldr C. Caldwell dropped the first operational 22,000lb Grand Slam bomb on the Bielefeld target; Calder dropped his Grand Slam from 14,000ft and scored a near miss (30 yards), which collapsed two of the arches of the viaduct. Tallboys dropped by other Lancasters caused further damage.

The Arnsberg viaduct was undamaged, so the Lancasters were next tasked to destroy this using Grand Slams. The attack of 15 March was unsuccessful because of the weather, but six Grand Slam and 13 Tallboy aircraft returned to this target the following day; all dropped within 200 yards and the viaduct was destroyed. In the second half of the month, other bridge targets were also destroyed by these awesome weapons.

Bombing results achieved by the two specialist squadrons – 9 and 617 – were analysed by the Bomber Command ORS:

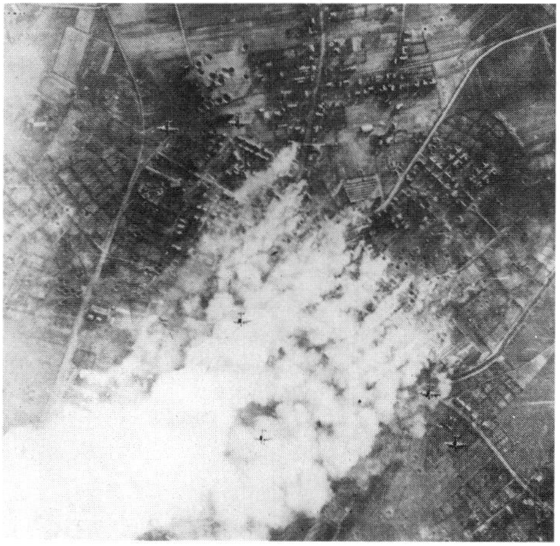

Another daylight raid, on 21 March 1945; by this stage of the war formations of Bomber Command aircraft ranged over Germany with virtual immunity from fighters – although flak still took its toll. Ken Delve Collection

> The bombing accuracy achieved in a series of Tallboy operations carried out by 9 and 617 Squadrons during the period December 1944 to March 1945 have been analysed from crater plots. No 9 Squadron are equipped with the Mk XIV bombsight and No 617 Squadron with the SABS Mk IIA, and consistently greater accuracy has been achieved by the latter squadron. All bombs falling more than 400 yards from the aiming point have been classified as gross errors. On this basis, one of 69 bombs plotted for 617 Squadron and five of 50 bombs plotted for 9 Squadron have been counted as gross errors. The random errors of 617 Squadron are smaller than those of 9 Squadron and an overall estimate of the effectiveness of the two forces in achieving a given density at the aiming point is approximately 2:1 in favour of 617 Squadron... the results of the two squadrons accordingly provide a comparison between the two sights.
>
> The proportion of gross errors with the Mk XIV is greater than that with the SAB Mk IIA, in the order of 2:1 in favour of SABS. It must be pointed out, however, that this is only true in those operations in which the tactical freedom of the Mk XIV or the necessity for a small and well-defined point of aim for synchronization with the SABS do not confer an advantage on the former sight. For instance, SABS IIA could not be used satisfactorily in large-scale ground-marking attacks by night. (ORS Report S.226, dated 25 July 1945)

Gelsenkirchen

On 23 February 1945, No 3 Group sent 133 Lancasters to attack the Alma Pluto benzol plant at Gelsenkirchen; a Lancaster of 186 Squadron was one of those to encounter trouble:

463 Squadron Lancasters during an attack on the Weser Bridges, Bremen, 22 March 1945.
Ken Delve Collection

NE165 while on loan to Rolls-Royce at Hucknall in late 1944; the aircraft returned to 83 Squadron and went missing on the night of 21/22 February. Ken Delve Collection

We dropped our load and made our usual quick exit from the heavily defended target area, the sky around us being filled with bursting shells. Some seconds later the Flight Engineer reported a loss of hydraulic power – this was serious as without hydraulics we would not be able to lower flaps or undercarriage. The Captain decided to lower both while hydraulics were still available, and then try and land at an Allied base as with flaps and undercarriage down we would never make it back to Stradishall. Lying in the nose I was the first to spot the emergency landing area – not ideal for a Lancaster as it was only a narrow and short stretch of metal planking but our Captain was one of the best and decided that he could get the aircraft down. We landed OK and taxied to the end of the strip; the Captain ordered us to man the guns – if the field was held by the Germans he wanted to fight it out rather than give up an intact Lancaster. Fortunately, the troops that came to meet us proved to be Royal Engineers.

A few days later, on 27 February, another No 3 Group attack on Gelsenkirchen by 149 aircraft brought a dramatic end to the operational career of a 186 Squadron Lancaster:

The target once more was Gelsenkirchen and we were going to finish off the job started earlier – to destroy the railway marshalling yards. It was around 3pm on that wintry day that we made our approach to the target. The target area was obvious from a long way off with the HE and incendiary bombs exploding on the ground and defending ack ack shells bursting in the air all round the bombers. It was our turn to go in. As Air Bomber it was my job to direct the pilot so that the target was lined up in the Sperry Bombsight. My bomb load consisted of a 4,000lb bomb and the remainder a mix of 1,000lb HE and incendiaries. The bombs were programmed to release in a set order – the streamlined bombs going first, followed by the clusters and, lastly, the 'Cookie', the theory being that all the bombs would arrive on the ground at the same area. To my horror the 'Cookie' dropped almost immediately the release button was pressed, it

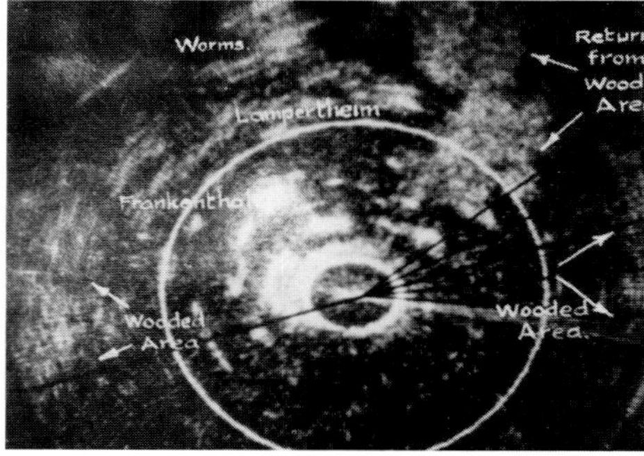

Photo of H2S screen showing the Mannheim-Ludwigshaven area, March 1945. Ken Delve Collection

soon caught up with the lighter bombs, scattering them all over the sky until one, and then, it seemed, all the rest, simply blew up.

The aircraft was caught in the blast and disintegrated. Aircrew members are trained to react to emergencies, I am thankful for the drills which, though boring at the time, proved their worth on this day. My first duty was to listen for instructions from the Captain but there was no response from the intercom to my request. My next duty was to jettison the escape hatch in the nose, absolutely vital if the cockpit crew are to escape. This was accomplished without difficulty but I was aware of the ground getting closer – we were diving almost vertically and on fire! At this point I fitted my parachute and dropped away from the aircraft. I came to on the ground, in great pain and very cold, and surrounded by German soldiers. My boots had gone – either in the descent or 'acquired' by one of the Germans whilst I was still out cold; they patched my arm wound and took me to HQ – where, to my great surprise, I met my Wireless Operator.

(According to Bomber Command records, the target on this raid was not actually the railyards but, once more, the Alma Pluto benzol plant.) A conference was held at HQ Bomber Command on 26 February to discuss Air Sea Rescue:

Various suggestions were put forward regarding a

NN801, the Mk VII prototype on test April 1945. Ken Delve Collection

A peaceful but vital role for the Lancasters – Operation *Manna* **dropping supplies to the people of Holland.** John Carson

> suitable dinghy drill for Lancaster aircraft which are being fitted with the Glen Martin and FN150 mid-upper turrets. These turrets made it practically impossible to pass from the rear of the aircraft to the fore in an emergency. As it was not likely that these aircraft would come into use for some considerable time, no decision on this drill was made. (Bomber Command ORB, February 1945)

Spring 1945

On 17 March Harris was informed by Portal that:

> Owing to manpower deficiencies, a reduction in RAF first-line squadrons must be made during the next few months and it was suggested that this Command's share should be disbandment of certain Mosquito and Halifax squadrons.

Harris replied a few days later that, if a reduction was totally unavoidable, he recommended:

> The whole of the reduction be made in terms of Halifax squadrons as they were unsatisfactory as a Heavy Bomber and uneconomical in maintenance personnel, airfields and overheads. (Bomber Command ORB, March 1945)

By late March, the bomber effort was often no more than 400 aircraft a day, usually split between two or three targets – the typical target categories now featured. The pace was more intensive on a few of the daylight operations; for example, on 27 March, 268 Lancasters hit Paderborn, 150 attacked a benzol plant at Hamm and 115 another oil target at Farge. It was a similar picture into April with oil targets being among the most frequently attacked. There was still the occasional large-scale Main Force attack on a city – for example, on 8/9 April on Hamburg, on 9/10 and 13/14 on Kiel, and on 14/15 on Potsdam.

An attack on Pilsen, on 16/17 April 1945, involved 222 Lancasters, one of which failed to make it back to England. Lancaster III MD733 of 463 Squadron was flown by Fg Off J. A.Hagley:

> Aircraft was on track on outward route and climbing at position 5020N 0932E, 0310 hours, 7,200ft when suddenly in the light of a half moon the aircraft was attacked by an aircraft of unknown origin. The attack came from slightly to port in front, approx 200 yards above, at 4-600 yards range. 463/L received strikes on starboard inner, starboard mainplane, engineers panel, starboard side of pilot's cockpit, oil supply in starboard outer, No 1 tank on starboard – which was losing fuel, main fuselage above W/Op, and navigator's compartment, plus the hydraulic and electrical systems. The aircraft was flooded with

Another Lancaster load of supplies is dropped to the waiting Dutch crowd. FlyPast Collection

hydraulic oil. The strike on the starboard inner set it on fire, but this was feathered and the Graviner was applied successfully.

Immediately prior to 463 being attacked, a Lancaster was seen flying on port bow above at 4-600 yards. A second or two after the sighting, the rear gunner and air bomber heard machine gunning, and almost simultaneously 463 was attacked. No tracer was seen. The aircraft, with its starboard inner on fire, dived to port to avoid revealing position of bomber stream. After corkscrew it was found that the starboard outer was losing oil rapidly, and it was then decided to set course for the English Cannel via Juvincourt. The English Channel being the nearest jettison area for bombs. However, these good intentions were foiled, because height could not be maintained, and thirteen 500 MC bombs were jettisoned safe at 0325 hours. After jettison action had been taken, aircraft was able to climb to 4,800ft, at which height, course was set for Juvincourt by aid of stars, as navigator's equipment was unserviceable.

The flight engineer nursed starboard outer, although for an hour this engine was not registering an oil pressure. Juvincourt eventually appeared 20 miles on the port side at 0500 hours, when starboard outer seized, imparting considerable vibration to the aircraft. Crew were then told by the captain to 'put on parachutes, stand by'. The rudder was then lashed with rope to assist the pilot by the air bomber and flight engineer. The 4000lb HC was then jettisoned. Aircraft was flown over Juvincourt at 2,500ft, with starboard outer on fire and unable to feather same owing to lack of voltage, due to failure in electrical circuit. The aircraft was in danger of immediate explosion owing to the petrol still flowing in the nacelle by the windmilling action of the starboard outer. The order 'emergency, jump, jump, jump' was given and all the crew escaped.

It was concluded – but not proved – that this aircraft had been the victim of 'friendly fire' from another Lancaster.

Bomber Command's biggest single raid for weeks took place on 22 April, when 767 aircraft (651 Lancasters) attacked Bremen, the aiming point being the SE part of the city in preparation for an assault in the area by XXX Corps. Two Lancasters failed to return.

The last major raids of the war took place on 25 April, with 482 bombers (375 Lancasters) attacking gun positions on Wangarooge Island and 359 Lancasters attacking the Berghof (Hitler's 'Eagle's Nest' chalet) and the associated SS barracks at Berchtesgaden in the Bavarian Alps. Two Lancasters were lost from each mission.

The final Lancaster bombing operation of the Second World War took place that night, when 107 aircraft attacked an oil refinery at Tonsberg, Norway. The only loss was a Lancaster of 463 Squadron, which crashed in Sweden. The crew were interned but released a few days later.

New Tasks for the Lancaster

Operation Manna

The next major task for the bombers was a far more peaceful one – the dropping of food supplies to the hard-pressed population of Holland. As early as February, a 115 squadron aircraft (HK696) had been at Netheravon for trials in supply dropping; five panniers were fitted into the bomb bay, each pannier capable of holding 70 25lb sacks. Trials suggested a delivery speed of 11-120 kts, with half flap, from 2-500ft.

Operation *Manna* commenced on 28 April, the first sorties being flown by Lancasters of 115 Squadron. John Gee was involved in the planning stages:

> We adapted the bomb bay of the Lancaster so that supplies could be hung on meat hooks on cables stretched between the bomb release points. An engineering company in Gainsborough helped by making thousands of meat hooks at short notice. To test the system out I did a practice drop from a Lancaster loaded with sandbags. A number of senior officers from No 1 Group HQ attended to watch the flight test, which proved successful, and preparations were put in hand for a series of food dropping operations over Holland. (John Gee, *Wingspan*)

John Carsons was a navigator on some of these drops:

> Our fourth *Manna* flight took place on a Saturday, take-off being shortly after 0600 hours in BQ-H; the previous day the bomb aimer and myself had written a number of personal leaflets to drop with the supplies. We crossed the coast at Overflakkee and flew east to the Hoekse Waard, an island south of Rotterdam, and around which we flew very low for quite some time. We were constantly greeted by countless people waving at us enthusiastically. Next to a smallish village we dropped our manna and the self-written leaflets and then after a spot of sightseeing flew back to North Killingholme. Back at base I drew a sketch of the Dutch village and surroundings as I had forgotten to pinpoint the location. I moved to Holland in 1957 and two years later a Dutch magazine published my sketch; I then heard from a number of people that the village was Maasdam – and I was even sent pictures of our Lancaster making the drop.

Bart van der Klaauw was one of those witnessing the food drops:

> The image of a large formation of Lancaster bombers coming in low and dropping food supplies will remain in my mind for ever. They were indeed most welcome as the nearly five million people in the Occupied West were nearing starvation. I could hardly believe it and together with some friends I climbed a nearby church tower to get a better view – a large stream of Lancasters were heading for the Duindigt racecourse, preceded by a Mosquito which dropped some flares to mark the target area. The Lancasters opened their bomb doors and masses of brown packets fell through the sky, like manna from heaven. The bombers returned again over the next few days, and Duindigt racecourse was just one of many drop zones.

In a two-week period, the Command flew 3,000 sorties and dropped 7,000 tons of food.

The ruins of Essen, one of the most bombed cities in Germany, since it was home to major industry such as the Krupps works. Ken Delve Collection

Operations Exodus *and* Dodge

The war with Germany ended on 8 May. Even before that date, a massive repatriation plan was under way. Under Operation *Exodus*, aircraft were used to fly ex-PoWs back to England and a number of Lancasters were converted to carry 25 passengers. The first Exodus sortie was flown out of Brussels on 4 May; during the month, 3,000 such sorties were flown and 74,000 PoWs were flown home. Operation *Dodge* was a similar operation, which brought the troops home from Italy and the Central Mediterranean.

In late June and early July a number of squadrons were involved in Exercise *Post Mortem*. The purpose of this was to:

> Test the efficiency of the German radio location under scientific supervision by the Allies' (100 Squadron ORB June 1945).

This involved bombers flying simulated operational profiles against various targets.

For UK-based bomber squadrons, one of the major tasks in the months immediately following the end of the war was the disposal – in the sea – of unwanted stocks of incendiary and HE bombs. This, combined with the latter part of Operation *Dodge*, accounted for the majority of flying hours in the remaining months of 1945.

Tiger Force

Although the war with Germany was over, the war with Japan still raged fiercely. The Allies were inexorably advancing towards Japan itself, but there was still a great deal to do. Part of the planned build-up of air power was the creation of Tiger Force, making use of squadrons no longer needed for the war in Europe. Among the units earmarked for Tiger Force were three bomber groups, each comprising ten Lancaster squadrons. The designated squadrons were equipped with Lancaster I (FE – for 'Far East') and Lancaster VII (FE), and undertook long-range training flights as part of their work-up. The aircraft themselves were given more a appropriate camouflage scheme of white upper surfaces and black undersurfaces.

The aircraft were given extensive modifications, including avionics fit with Gee III, Rebecca II, Loran I and H2S III, as well as armament mods that included an FN82 rear turret (twin 20mm guns), removal of the dorsal turret, an extra 400-gallon fuel tank in the rear of the bomb bay (giving a total fuel load of 2,554 gallons and a 3,000-mile range with a 7,000lb bomb load). Both specialist units – 9 and 617 Squadrons – expected to be part of Tiger Force with Mk VII (Spec) Lancasters for carriage of Tallboy and Grand Slam.

At one stage, there was a plan to use half the aircraft as refuelling tankers for Lancaster air-to-air refuelling) but this would, obviously, have had a major effect on the bombs-on-target tonnage of the overall force, and was therefore abandoned. Two aircraft, HK541 and SW244, were flown with saddle tanks but, again, the idea was not taken up.

The planned deployment date of Tiger Force slipped from summer to autumn, but the dropping of the atom bombs on Japan in early August brought the war

Lancasters wait at Pomigliano for the next batch of PoWs for the flight to England. Ken Delve Collection

in the Far East to an end. On 2 September, the Tiger Force deployment was cancelled.

Loss Rates

There has always been much debate as to the relative merits of the Lancaster and the Halifax; the latter could be seen to have suffered something of a bad press, much to the chagrin of many of its crews. The AHB Narrative dealing with the Bomber Command Operational Research Section's reports into aircraft loss rates draws this conclusion:

> It was a matter for speculation whether the lower loss rate of the Lancaster was due to the fact that the Halifax was more easily susceptible to interception and what the loss rate would have been had Bomber Command had a homogeneous force. There were a few operations on which only Lancasters flew and they were compared with those when they were operating in a mixed force. The results showed that when operating alone the loss rate increased by about 50 per cent and in fact appeared to be even higher than that of the mixed force. This was no doubt partly due to the lower level of saturation of the defences due to the small forces engaged, but it seems very likely that the lower loss rates of the Lancasters on general operations was due partly to the presence of lower performance and more visible aircraft in the force.

The final words regarding the Lancaster are best left to Sir Arthur Harris:

> Suffice it to say that the Lancaster, measured in no matter what terms, was, and still is, incomparably the most efficient. In range, bomb-carrying capacity, ease of handling, freedom from accident, and particularly in casualty rate, it far surpassed the other heavy types. Hence the constant pressure brought by HQ Bomber Command for concentration on Lancaster production at the expense of other types, and hence the policy to employ every available Lancaster in the front line, even at the expense of an uneconomical training set-up.

Repatriation of ex-PoWs from southern Europe under Operation Dodge. Ken Delve Collection

Bari, 29 October 1945 – another Dodge **aircraft awaits passengers.** N. Cosslett

CHAPTER NINE

The Lancaster's Post-War Career

Reorganization

With the Second World War over, it was time to attempt to return the nation to a peaceful footing as soon as possible, for economic and other reasons. The inevitable consequence was a rapid run-down of squadrons; within a matter of months, almost 30 Lancaster squadrons had gone. Commonwealth and Allied units were released from RAF service and, in many cases, especially the Canadian No 6 Group, the airmen returned home with their aircraft.

The RAF itself underwent a rapid reorganization as the politicians and military attempted to determine the shape of the post-war world, and the necessary nature of the military commitment. Britain had extensive commitments throughout the world and it would take some time to adjust to the new world situation after six years of war. The Lancaster was no longer needed in such numbers as a bomber. However, pending its replacement by the 'next generation' bomber – the Avro Lincoln – it remained the main type within Bomber Command. Squadrons established a training routine based on the tactics developed by Main Force in the latter part of the war.

By late 1946, Bomber Command had been through the initial, often painful and difficult, transition from war to peace, many of the bomber squadrons had started re-equipping with Lincolns and the 'non-RAF' units had vanished, with the Canadians taking their aircraft home. The first Lincolns had gone to 57 Squadron at East Kirkby in September 1945, for service evaluation. A further 13 Bomber Command squadrons had given up their Lancasters in 1946 and, by 1950, the remainder had also either disbanded or received replacement types.

The last Lancaster unit was 49 Squadron at Upwood; when it said farewell to its Lancasters in March 1950, an era for Bomber Command came to an end.

Photo Reconnaissance

Photo reconnaissance had proved vital in the Second World War and Bomber Command had a requirement for pre- and post-attack photography. No 106 Group took over the post-war reconnaissance task within Bomber Command and was allocated three Lancaster squadrons from No 3 Group. The Air Photographic Development Unit (APDU) of the Central Photographic Establishment (CPE) at Benson undertook development work on PR and photo survey. The Lancaster PR.1 had all its turrets removed and faired over and was given a range of cameras to suit its various survey tasks. First of the squadrons to re-equip was 541 at Benson, the home of

In the white scheme that was adopted for Tiger Force, but then retained for many Bomber Command aircraft, NX683 of 40 Squadron is seen over Eygpt in 1946; in the post-war period, Lancasters went to various squadrons in the Middle East. Andy Thomas Collection

149 squadron fly-by at Mildenhall as part of the visit by the RAAF Chief of Air Staff. Ken Delve Collection

RAF Photo Reconnaissance. The Squadron formed an extra flight equipped with PR.1s in mid-1946. It was, however, a short-lived association with the Lancaster; in September, the Squadron disbanded, and the Lancaster PR.1 Flight became 82 Squadron.

In May 1947, the Squadron was sent to Africa to undertake a major survey; the detachment went to Eastleigh to undertake a survey of Kenya, an undertaking that also involved a detachment of PR Lancasters from 683 Squadron at Fayid. These African survey tasks, flown primarily from Takoradi and Eastleigh, kept 83 Squadron busy to the end of 1953, with Nigeria, the Gold Coast, Sierra Leone, Gambia, Kenya and East Africa all being covered. On its return to the UK, the Squadron took up residence at Wyton and bade farewell to its Lancasters in December 1953.

No 683 Squadron had re-formed at Fayid, in the Canal Zone of Egypt, on 1 August 1950 as a survey unit operating Lancaster PR.1s. Various survey tasks, including support of the 83 Squadron work in Africa, kept the unit fully occupied. In December 1951, the Squadron moved to Aden, and in the following year moved again (in May) to Habbaniya, Iraq, where it finally disbanded in November 1953.

Although the Lancasters were not involved in any offensive operations post-VE Day, aircraft of 683 Squadron were called upon to provide reconnaissance and supply in support of British involvement in the Buraimi Oasis crisis in August 1952.

Re-Deployment

A number of Lancaster units were re-deployed to the Middle East in the bomber role and by late 1945 there were four Lancaster units in the Middle East: 40 and 104 Squadrons at Abu Sueir, 178 Squadron at Fayid, and 214 Squadron at Shallufa were all tasked with ensuring the security of the Suez Canal. The first Lancasters had become operational in the Middle East in November 1945. This was a mix of Mk Is (214 Squadron), Mk IIIs (178 Squadron) and Mk VIIs (104 Squadron), with 40 Squadron receiving their aircraft two months later (B.7s). It was to be a very short-lived re-deployment for most of the crews – 178 Squadron was disbanded in April 1946, followed a year later by 40 and 104 Squadrons. Although 214 Squadron kept its Lancs until February 1950, it disbanded by April 1946 and re-formed at Upwood in November with Lancaster Is as part of Bomber Command.

Maritime Patrol

In the maritime role, the Lancaster was seen as an interim pending the introduction of the MR version of the

Lancaster VII NX612 serving with 1689 Flight. FlyPast Collection

Lincoln; surplus bombers were plentiful and, using experience of the MR/ASR Warwicks, the Lancasters were duly modified. Air Sea Rescue aircraft were given Merlin 224s and fitted with the airborne lifeboat Mk II (soon replaced by the IIA), and designated as Lancaster ASR.III. Other modifications included removal of the dorsal turret – with the fuselage being faired over – removal of the guns from the rear turret, and the provision of additional windows (and a larger astrodome), as crew look-out was a key part of the ASR task. The lifeboat was hung on a hook attached to a gantry fitted into the modified bomb bay; the bomb bay doors had to be cut away in certain places to allow for the fit of the suspended lifeboat. Avro used ND589 as a pattern aircraft for the conversion, although subsequent conversions were carried out by Cunliffe-Owen at Eastleigh, Southampton.

The first unit to re-equip was 279 Squadron at Beccles (September 1945), which received Lancasters in place of its Sea Otters and Warwicks, although in March the following year the unit disbanded. Based at St Eval, 179 Squadron received the first of its ASR.IIIs in February 1946 – but only operated the type until September. Two further squadrons also held a number of ASR.IIIs on strength; for 203 and 210 Squadrons, their main equipment was the GR.3. The variant also served in the Middle East from July 1946 in 38 Squadron, along with GR.3s.

In the three-year period from July 1945 onwards, 131 aircraft were converted, all but one of these being Lancaster IIIs. In addition to the full-strength squadrons, Lancasters also equipped 1348 ASR Flight from January 1946 at Pegu, Burma.

The Lancaster also served in the true Maritime Patrol (MP) role with a specialized ASV radar fitted to the GR.III variant in 1946, partly in response to the disposal of the Lend-Lease Liberators that most MP squadrons were then operating. The first Lancaster GR.III unit was 210 Squadron at St Eval, the unit reforming in June 1946 from 179Y Squadron, having disbanded the previous year. Three squadrons within Coastal Command's No 19 Group were soon re-equipped – 203, 210 and 224 – all at St Eval. From August 1937 they were involved in rotating detachments to Ein Shemer in Palestine to support Operation *Bobcat*, the search for ships carrying Jewish immigrants to Israel; the majority of this work was undertaken by the Middle East squadrons.

The Leigh Light had been the main means of night illumination by maritime aircraft during the war, and the need to turn night into day continued into the post-war period. Trials took place with the 'Glow worm' system, the Lancasters being equipped with rockets carrying flare heads – but with no great promise. Another tactic was to use the Lancasters to drop flares to light up the target, so that it could be attacked by other aircraft. In spring 1952, this 'light strike' tactic was trialled by 203 Squadron, providing illumination for 25 Squadron's Vampires.

Lancaster GR.3s had replaced Liberator GR.8s with 203 Squadron in August 1946 and, in common with the other Coastal Command Lancaster units, these were retained until 1953 and the arrival of the Neptune MR.1 and the Shackleton. The last Lancaster MR.3 left service in October 1956, having served with the School of Maritime Reconnaissance.

Trials

Throughout the wartime career of the Lancaster, Sir Arthur Harris, as Commander-in-Chief of Bomber Command, fought every attempt to siphon off what he considered to be his most effective bomber. In order to do this, he accepted an inefficient training system that kept to a minimum the number of Lancasters. He was also against using the aircraft for trials use, other than the bare minimum required for operational evaluation. However, despite Harris' efforts, and for obvious good reasons, numerous Lancasters were used by both industry and Service establishments for a wide range of trials and evaluations. Such work took place from the earliest days of the Lancaster – beginning with the initial Boscombe Down evaluations on BT308, for example – and became more extensive as the type appeared in increasing numbers and variants. As this work peaked, well over 100 Lancasters were involved with such trials.

The Lancaster had a comprehensive career in trials and evaluation work both with industry and the RAF. Its major involvement with industry was in engine development.

Lancaster dropping an airborne lifeboat; aircraft conversions were carried out by Cunliffe-Owen at Eastleigh. FlyPast Collection

Lancaster ASR.III RF310 fitted with an airborne lifeboat. FlyPast Collection

Aircraft of 115 Squadron in late 1945; the rear aircraft, TW893, served with a number of RAF units and was subsequently transferred to the Egyptian Air Force in August 1950. Ken Delve Collection

Shallufa 1958, a 'Sunray' detachment by 149 Squadron. Ken Delve Collection

Aries

Lancaster PD328 was delivered to the Empire Air Navigation School (EANS) at Shawbury in October 1944. As 'Aries', it undertook a number of record-making flights.

One of the first long-range trial flights (later to become the Aries series) made by PD328 was undertaken by the Empire Central Navigation School (ECNS) in October 1944. The aircraft departed from the UK on 21 October en route to New Zealand, via Reykjavik, Montreal, Washington, Honolulu and Samoa. It arrived on 1 November, and returned a few weeks later via Masirah, Cairo and Malta.

In November 1944, initial plans were made for a North Polar flight to take place the following May. This was the best period for flying over the geographical and magnetic poles, in order to take advantage, for navigation, of sun/moon fixes with a good angle of cut:

> The plan was to carry out a series of polar flights with the multiple aims of studying navigation under the peculiar conditions imposed by polar flying; examining the behaviour of navigation instruments, especially compasses, radar installations and automatic dead reckoning gear; collecting magnetic and meteorological data; observing the effects of polar flying conditions on aircraft efficiency; examining the application of the Greenwich grid system of co-ordinates; and obtaining examples of H2S and Loran photography. However, navigation research was the prime object and the intention was to investigate everything which had a bearing on Arctic air navigation in a modern aircraft. (*Air Clues*, July 1986)

A full suite of navigation equipment was fitted to the Lancaster, including H2S, Gee and Loran, plus various items of test equipment – as well as Arctic survival kits and dehydrated rations. Departing Shawbury on 10 May 1945, the aircraft flew, via Prestwick, to Reykjavik in Iceland, where a few days were spent making final preparations. On 12 May, the aircraft flew a rehearsal sortie to the Greenland coast and this showed various problems with the astro fixing technique and certain items of equipment. There was bad weather on 15 May, and the aircraft transferred to Meeks Field; it was from there at 0300 the following day that Aries left on the first of its trans-Polar flights. Unfortunately, the flight had to be abandoned after five hours, when weather conditions once more proved unfavourable.

With a forecast for improving weather, the crew refuelled the aircraft and took off again. There was still a fair amount of cloud to be avoided or flown through, and fixing the aircraft's position proved difficult. However, sufficient fixes were obtained, and the Lancaster flew over the geographic North Pole en route to Reykjavik. After refuelling and topping up the oxygen, the aircraft flew back to Meeks Field. Taking off again at 0400, the Lancaster was forced to divert to Goose Bay with a generator problem; this was soon fixed and on 19 May Aries made its flight over the magnetic North Pole, landing at Dorval.

The Lancaster flew to Montreal on 23 May, making a stop-over at the RCAF Central Navigation School, to prepare for its next series of polar flights from Whitehorse. Aries finally landed back at Shawbury on 26 May, having flown a total of 20,000 nms, over half of which had been above the Arctic Circle.

Aries was not the only Lancaster undertaking such evaluation work, and other specialist organizations had Lancasters on strength for a range of tasks. The Empire Air Armaments School's (EAAS) Lancaster PB873 'Thor' undertook tours of the Far East and South Africa.

Interim maritime aircraft were required in the post-war period and various Lancaster conversions fulfilled this requirement; here, a GR.3 (SW370) of 210 Squadron at St Eval. Andy Thomas Collection

Among the many trials units to employ Lancasters was the Central Bomber Establishment (CBE), here using LL870 to test remote-controlled 'barbettes' armed with 20mm cannon. Ken Delve Collection

Air Refuelling

In October 1945, the BDU, now based at Feltwell, issued Report No 84 covering its recent flight refuelling trials. Four Lancasters on loan from Flight Refuelling Ltd – two as tankers and two as receivers – were taken on charge, the objects of the trial being:

> 1. To determine the operational use of flight refuelling.
> 2. To ascertain the feasibility of carrying out the operation using crews of varying experience.
> 3. To report on the working conditions of the operations.
> 4. To ascertain the possibility of refuelling by night and under any weather conditions.
> 5. To determine the time taken to complete the refuelling operation.

The tanker aircraft carried a 'Hose Drum' in its bomb bay, with a 250ft length of 2 ⅛in bore hose; in front of this were the two 600-gallon 'give-away' fuel tanks:

> Initial contact between the two aircraft was made by the tanker operator firing a securing line (a fixed forward-firing gun was mounted at the rear of the operator's station). The tanker pilot positions his aircraft below, aft and to starboard of the receiver. When in the correct position (wing tip in line with the black and white markings on the hauling line) he gives the order 'Fire'. The operator in the receiver aircraft confirms contact and then uses his winch to wind in the cable and its attached refuelling hose, the hose is thus wound in to the coupling. The refuelling operation is carried out at 135 kts and the fuel line is pressurized to 880-920lbs/sq.in. When refuelling is complete the toggles gripping the hose nozzle are released and the hose and hauling line separate, at a weak link in the line, to be wound back inside the tanker.

Four pilots and eight 'equipment operators' had been detached from the BDU to Flight Refuelling at Staverton for ground and air instruction; the actual trial comprised 36 sorties and a total of 99 hours' flight time at heights between 5,000ft and 20,000ft. The significance of the trial is such that it is worth quoting BDU Report No 84 at some length:

> Owing to the tanker operator's station being limited to the rear portion of the bomb bay, the operation became increasingly difficult at heights much above 15,000ft. The low air temperatures and the amount of oxygen necessary tended to impair the efficiency of the operator.
>
> Receiver Aircraft.
>
> During the whole period of the trials, the receiver equipment operated satisfactorily, with the exception that on two occasions hydraulic failures were experienced. The operation merely

Lancaster GR.3 SW329 of 203 Squadron; the unit operated Lancasters from August 1946 to March 1953. Andy Thomas Collection

The hose-drum and hose fitted in the bomb bay of the tanker Lancaster. Ken Delve Collection

G-AGJI (ex-DV379) was the first of the civil registered aircraft; acquiring its registration in late 1943, it was used to develop a transport version of the Lancaster. FlyPast Collection

requires straight and level flying at a steady airspeed on the part of the pilot and the operator has few controls and requires very little training. Two flight engineers of 149 Squadron were detached to the BDU and trained as receiver aircraft operators. It was found that 2 hours' ground training and 4 hours' experience operating the equipment in the air was sufficient to enable the operators to be considered efficient.

Tanker Aircraft.

The tanker aircraft equipment operated satisfactorily, with the exception that on four occasions, on breakaway, the hose nozzle broke away from the hose owing to failure of the drogue to act correctly. The success of the operation depends infinitely more on the tanker than on the receiver and both pilot and operator need careful training. Two pilots of BDU with 2,300 and 1,700 flying hours' experience respectively, and no flight refuelling experience, each carried out one refuelling operation as tanker pilot.

Two pilots of 149 Squadron were detached to BDU with 1,150 and 650 hours respectively, four-engined aircraft flying being limited to 90 hours and 190 hours. Total formation experience was 6 hours and 15 hours on Anson and Wellington aircraft. In the case of these pilots it was necessary to give 5 hours' formation practice before the refuelling operation could be attempted. Five hours' ground training and a further 10 hours' flying training was necessary before these pilots could be considered capable tanker pilots. The two flight engineers of 149 Squadron already trained as receiver operators were given training as tanker operators. The operation of the tanker is more complicated than that of the receiver and as a result 6 hours' ground training and 14 hours' experience operating the equipment in the air were necessary before these operators were efficient.

Times taken to carry out the operation were noted. The average times were:

Ht.	Prepare-Contact	Contact-Break	Pass 1100 galls
10,000	5 mins	19 mins	11 mins
15,000	5 mins	19 mins	12 mins
20,000	6 mins	24 mins	12 mins

The method of intercommunication used between the two aircraft can be either by R/T or by Aldis lamp signalling. Assuming that R/T silence would be necessary Aldis lamp signalling was used during the trials.

Conclusions:

Flight Refuelling is undoubtedly a successful method of increasing the range and/or bomb load of an aircraft and the number of unsuccessful sorties during the trials was only two in a total of 36 flights, both of these being due to hydraulic failures of the receiver windlass. Using the equipment as installed in the Lancasters employed for these trials, both No 1 tanks can be refuelled, giving an extra range of approx 1,000 miles. Whilst, however, a single aircraft can be refuelled with little difficulty, the question of refuelling large numbers of aircraft in a short space of time, as would have been necessary during the recent war, becomes rather more complicated.

Refuelling by night is not practicable with the present lighting arrangements. In order to ensure the greatest possible safety it would be necessary to illuminate the receiver aircraft, both underneath for the contact position and above for the refuelling position. During daylight, refuelling can be carried out in unstable air conditions providing that such instability is not too great. The operation can be carried out in rain except when the rain is so heavy that the tanker pilot's vision is obscured.

Another Lancaster involved in AAR development work, G-33-2, formerly PB972, spent two years with Flight Refuelling Ltd. Ken Delve Collection

Throughout the war, various Lancasters were used for engine trials; perhaps the most unusual modification was made to TW911 in 1949 when it was given Python engines in its outboard positions. Ken Delve Collection

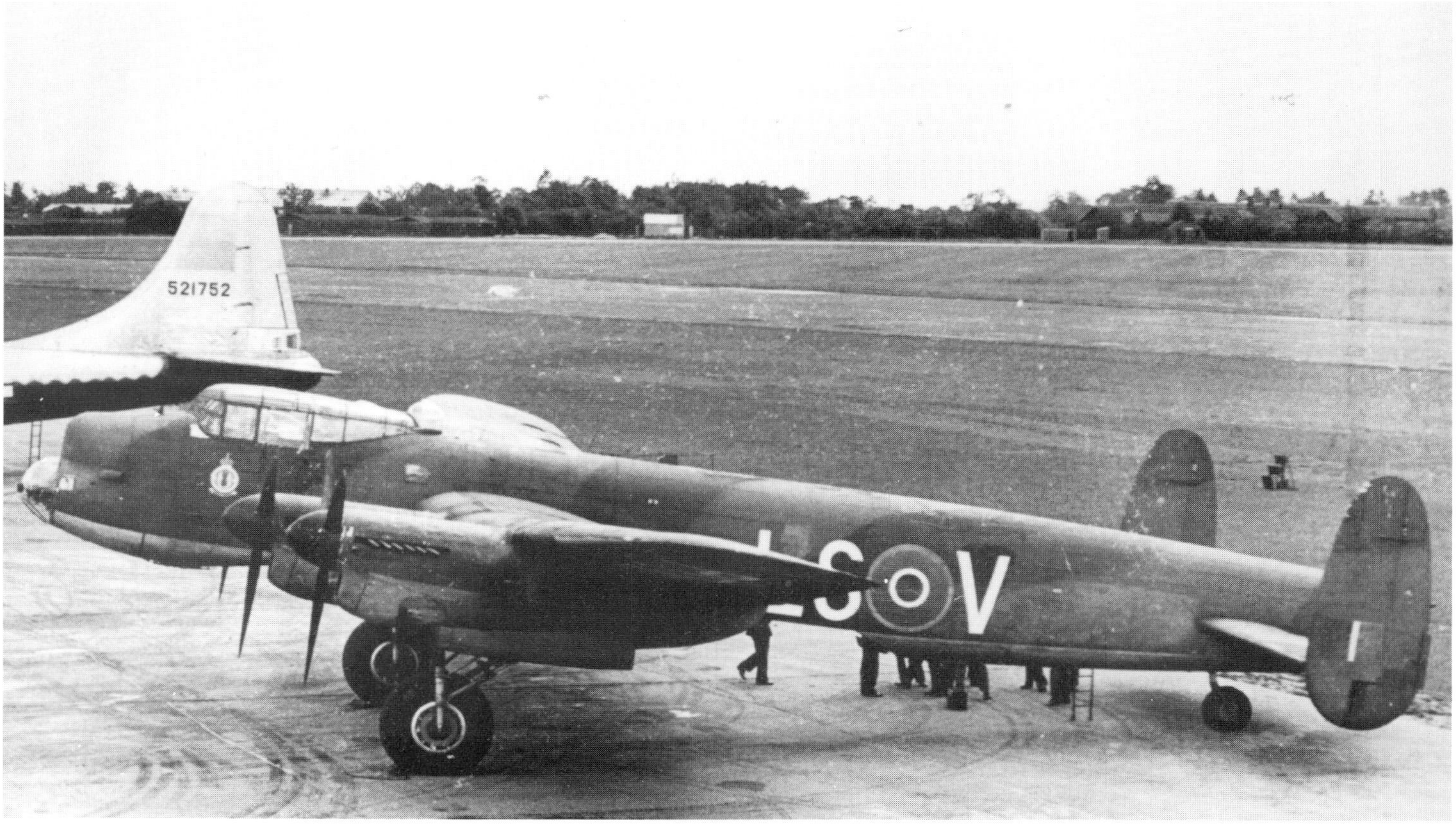

Lancaster BI (Spec) PD131 of 15 Squadron, used in the months after the war to drop Tallboy and Grand Slam bombs on test targets. Norman Roberson

The Empire Air Armament School (EAAS) fleet included one Lancaster in this March 1945 shot. Ken Delve Collection

LANCASTRIAN

The range and carrying capacity of the Lancaster made it an obvious choice for conversion to civil use. The first conversion was undertaken in 1941 using Lancaster III R5727, which became CF-CMS when it moved to Canada and operated with Trans-Canada Airlines, TCA, on its transatlantic route. First of the true Avro 691 Lancastrians was, however, G-AGLF, which was converted from VB873 and operated by the BOAC Development Flight at Hurn in early 1945. The post-war period brought an urgent need for such long range transports and BOAC received a further twenty conversions during 1945 as Lancastrian C.1s.

The RAF also operated the type, the main military usage being thirty-three Lancastrian C.2s (of which ten were later converted for civil use) and eight C.4s, which went on to either civil use or were taken up by the Argentine Air Force as VIP transports.

The only other production variant was the C.3, eighteen of which were built for a variety of civil operators such as British South American Airways Corporation, Skyways Ltd and Silver City Airways. Never a great success as a passenger aircraft, the C.1 could only carry nine passengers, they did fill an important niche in the mid-1940s before true long-range commercial aircraft were available; in the freight role they proved somewhat more useful and it was with such tasks that they remained in service until 1951 as 'bulk fuel carriers'.

Development of the Lancaster included the Avro Lancastrian transport. FlyPast Collection

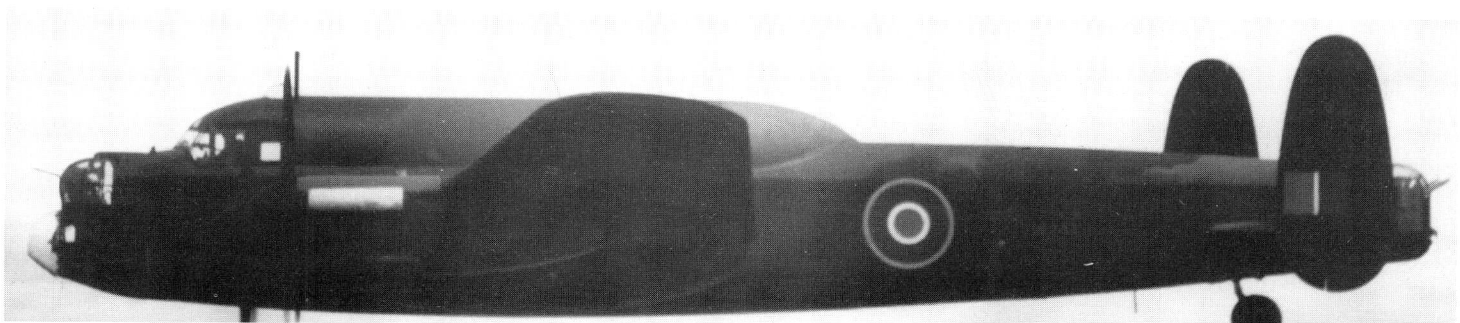

An ugly Lancaster; aircraft fitted with a 'saddle tank' of fuel to extend its range. FlyPast Collection

Lincoln II RE418 was one of a batch of aircraft built by Avro at Chadderton and delivered in mid-1945; it remained as a trials aircraft and was eventually struck-off-charge in February 1953. FlyPast Collection

AVRO LINCOLN

The development of the Avro Type 694 was a direct consequence of an Air Ministry request in 1942 for an 'extended range' Lanacaster that would, over longer operational ranges, maintain the same high bomb load as the current Lancasters. Chadwick and his team began the design by keeping as much of the basic Lancaster structure as possible, although in part this was also due to a requirement for the aircraft to enter service by 1945. Extra fuel capacity was provided in wing and fuselage areas that had been extended by 10 per cent and 13 per cent respectively, the only other significant changes at this stage being enhanced Merlins and a stronger undercarriage to cope with the increased all-up weight.

Under Specification B14/43 an order was placed for three prototypes, designated Lancaster IV. However, by the time the prototype (PW925) flew on 9 June 1944 the new aircraft had been named Lincoln. Early trials showed a mixed bag of results in respect of the requirements: the range of 4,450 miles with a 3,000lb bomb load was achieved but the speed and ceiling criteria were not. Adjustments were made and the LIncoln entered service in August 1945, with 57 Squadron at East Kirkby. Production orders had been issued for almost 3,000 aircraft, but these were rapidly cut back in the immediate post-war period and only 82 Mk Is and 447 Mk IIs were built, 60 of the latter subsequently being converted to Mk 4 standard for the ECM role.

The Lincoln B.I and B.II became the mainstay of post-war Bomber Command in the late 1940s and early 1950s, until replaced by the B-29 Washington and the new Canberra jet bomber. The Lincoln did, however, have two brief periods of operational use, in 1950 against communist terrorists in Malaya and in 1953 against the Mau Mau dissidents in Kenya. In its ECM role with Signals Command the Lincoln remained in RAF service until May 1963 (151 Squadron) but it had long since given up its bomber role.

The Lincoln was operated by twenty-eight squadrons and a wide range of trials units and establishments; the type was also used by Argentina and Australia. Sadly, there are no Lincolns flying today.

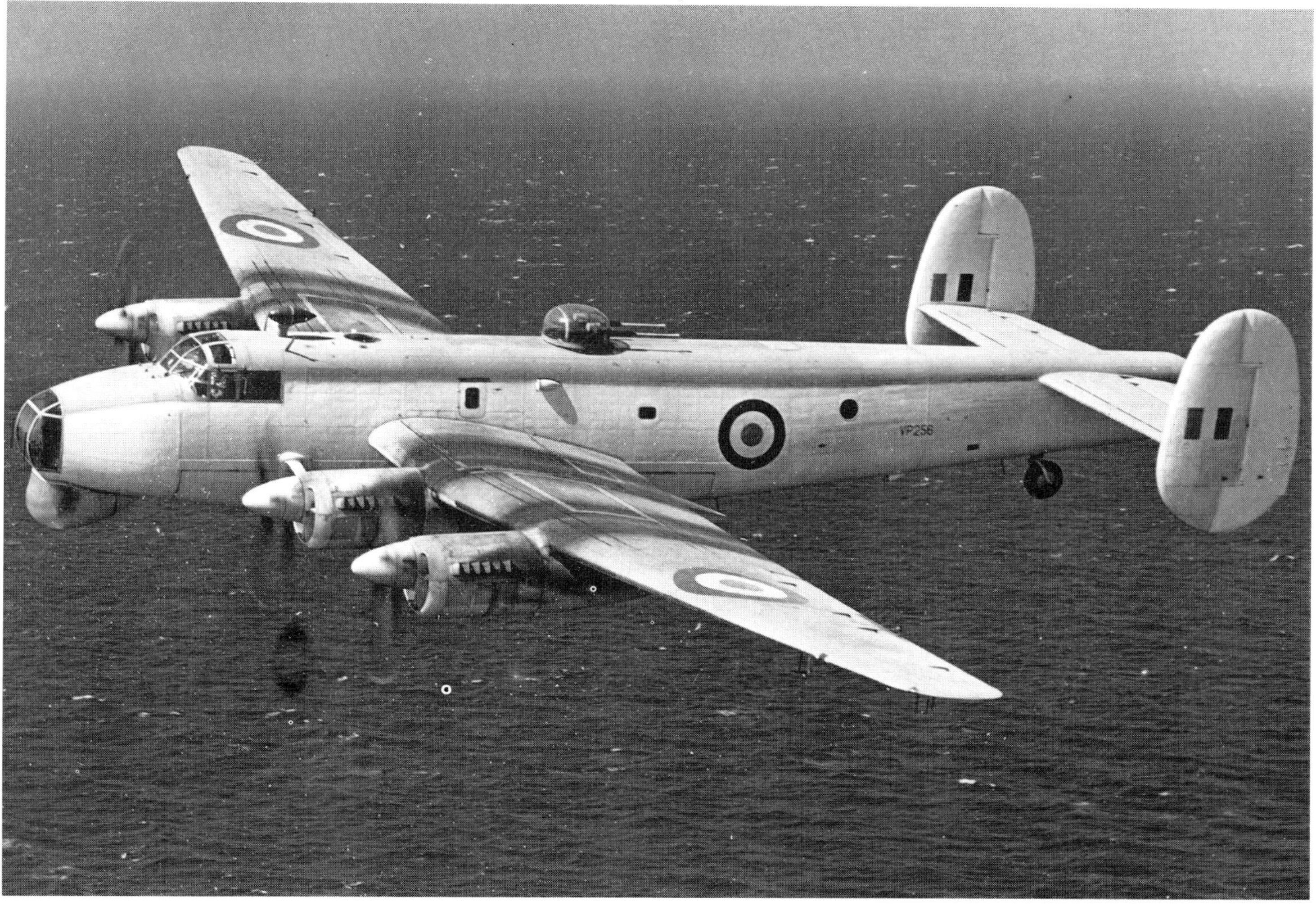

Shackleton VP256 in its operational environment at low level over the sea. This GR.1 served with 224 and 269 Squadrons before ending its days in a take-off accident at Ballykelly on 26 October 1954. FlyPast Collection

AVRO SHACKLETON

Although not a 'Lancaster follow-on', the Avro Type 696/716 Shackleton is still worthy of mention in this history of the Lancaster as it also came from the Chadwick design stable.

Designed to suit Specification R5/46 for a maritime reconnaissance aircraft, the Shackleton had Lincoln wings (more or less) but a new fuselage and Griffon engines powering contra-rotating propellers.

The prototype GR.1 (VW126) flew on 9 March 1949 and the type entered service with Coastal Command's 120 Squadron at Kinloss in April 1951.

Subsequent variants, the MR.2 and MR.3, duly entered service incorporating a number of improvements, and between the three variants some 180 production

Shackletons were built for the RAF, a further eight MR.3s serving with the South African Air Force.

Modifications to a number of the early production aircraft produced the T.4 trainer for use by 236 OCU.

The final RAF variant was the AEW.2, twelve aircraft being modified to carry the APS-20 radar so that the 'Shack' could take on the Airborne Early Warning role; in this capacity the type remained in service, with 8 Squadron, until replaced by the E-3D Sentry in 1991.

The Shackleton was operated by sixteen RAF squadrons and a single SAAF squadron. A number of aircraft have been acquired by private owners and at least two of these are still flown at air displays.

CHAPTER TEN

Overseas Users and Survivors

Lancasters Overseas

Canadian Lancasters

With the war in Europe over, the Allies turned their attention to the continuing conflict with Japan and the creation of Tiger Force. As part of the run-down of Bomber Command, eight of the RCAF squadrons from No 6 Group returned with their Lancasters to Canada in the summer. As part of the preparations for Tiger Force, the RCAF now created No 664 Wing at Greenwood, Nova Scotia. However, the end of the war with Japan came before this Wing was even fully constituted and, in common with the other Allied nations, Canada looked at its post-war military requirements. Most of the Lancasters were placed in storage, and before long a number of aircraft were either sent for scrapping – in most cases, these were aircraft with combat records and, therefore, higher flying hours – or for modification to other roles. No true bomber requirement was seen for the Lancasters within the RCAF.

Over the next 20 years almost 230 Lancasters served with the RCAF in a number of roles, primarily of a maritime nature, and in all cases this required modification of the basic Mk X airframe. The modification work was carried out by Avro Canada, successor to Victory Aircraft; from 1951 onwards, Fairey Aviation was also involved with this work. The major variants to be used by the RCAF post war were:

10AR – Arctic Reconnaissance, cameras, extended nose and rear observation windows. Three aircraft.

10BR – Bomber Reconnaissance, extra

Canada was the most significant non RAF post-1945 user of the Lancaster; here bomber Lancs sit at Malton awaiting modification. Hawker Siddeley Canada

fuel, radar torpedoes, depth charges.

10DC – Drone Carrying, two underwing pylons to carry Ran Firebee target drones. Two aircraft.

10MR/MP – Maritime Reconnaissance/ Patrol – extra fuel and nav kit, sonobouys, depth charges.

10N – Navigation trainer, unarmed flying classroom. Five aircraft, including 'Northern Cross' (FM206), 'Polaris' (FM208), 'Zenith' (FM211) and 'Orion' (KB986).

10O – Engine test-bed, FM209 was modified to take the Orenda jet engine.

10P – Photographic reconnaissance and survey, unarmed but with range of cameras plus extra fuel and improved nav fit. Nine aircraft.

10S – Standard post-war bomber with mid-upper turret removed.

10SR – Sea Rescue. Eight aircraft.

10U – Unmodified wartime bomber.

One of the most significant post-war tasks for the RCAF was that of photo mapping the remote areas of the country and it was into this that a number of Lancasters were introduced in the late 1940s (along with a range of other aircraft types). Initial Lancaster sorties were flown by 7 (Photographic) Wing out of Rockcliffe. The aircraft required extensive modification and numerous difficulties had to be overcome in this early period of use by 13 (later 413) Squadron; however, in due course, the 10Ps proved invaluable and they flew thousands miles of survey lines in service with 408 Squadron – even discovering a number of new islands. The survey work was carried out in the spring and summer, with detachments operating out of various remote locations and only returning to Rockcliffe when the weather deteriorated towards the end of the year. While survey was the main task, the Squadron also had a variety of other missions to perform during the height of the Cold War, including searching for and photographing Russian research stations that had been set up on floating ice islands. The Squadron kept its Lancasters until 1964. Arctic reconnaissance and ice patrols were also carried out by Lancasters with a variety of units.

FM128 of 404 Squadron; the aircraft was finally scrapped in May 1956. FlyPast Collection

Sporting a Ryan Firebee drone under its starboard wing, KB851 was one of two Lancaster's converted to 10DC standard for trials in connection with the CF-100 programme. Larry Milberry

The Cold War and the threat posed by Russia was also the motivation behind the formation of three Lancaster-equipped anti-submarine squadrons. First of these was 405 Squadron, which formed at Greenwood in March 1950, followed by 404 Squadron at Greenwood and 407 Squadron at Comox. It was to be a short period of activity for the Lancasters; by the mid-1950s, the squadrons were receiving Neptunes as replacements (although 407 Squadron did not bid farewell to its last Lancs until 1959).

Trials and evaluation work using Lancasters had continued into the post-war period, one of the first tasks being carried out by the Test and Development Establishment's (Rockcliffe) KB739, which, in September 1945, was involved with propeller de-icing trials. A wide range of trials [use kept various Lancasters busy]; however, the most famous of these was the fitting of two jet engines (Orenda) to FM209 in place of its outboard Merlins. The first flight by this modified aircraft was on 13 July 1950 and it was in use until 1954 when it was lost in a hangar fire at Malton. Firebee drones were carried by two aircraft (KB848 and KB851), in association with trials by the Central Experimental and Proving Establishment's programme of development with the CF-100, between June 1955 and February 1957.

Four RCAF Lancasters were transferred to the civil register: FM222 (CF-IMF), KB907 (CF-IMG) and KB909 (CF-IMH) all going to Spartan Air Survey, and KB976 (CF-TQC) becoming a water bomber (although later going to the Strathallan Collection as G-BCOH). A fifth Lancaster received a Canadian civil registration as CF-GBA, but this was an ex-RAF aircraft, TW870.

The Egyptian Air Force received nine Lancasters in 1950, but they saw very little service. FlyPast Collection

French Lancasters

Like most of the colonial powers, France attempted to re-impose its control over its former overseas territories and as part of this came a requirement for a maritime patrol aircraft for the Aéronavale. The only aircraft that was available was the Lancaster and an agreement was reached whereby the Western Union (later to become the Western European Union) funded the acquisition and modification of 54 such aircraft from Avro at Woodford. Fairly extensive mods were carried out, including fitting ASV, observation windows, new nav fit, and, on most aircraft, the provision to carry an airborne lifeboat. Initial deliveries took place in 1951, the aircraft finished in Aéronavale blue (later changed to white for those operating in tropical regions), and the Lancasters were numbered WU1 to WU54. The final deliveries were made by 1954 and the units to operate this batch of aircraft were 10F and 9S at Lann-Bihoué, Brittany, 10S at St Raphael, 2F at Port Lyautey, Morocco, with 52S, 55S and 56S also operating in Morocco, whilst Algeria was home to 11F (at Lartigue) and 5S.

Most of the Lancasters were replaced by Neptunes in the late 1950s, few Lancasters were left in service by the early 1960s, but one unit, 9S, continued to operate the type in the Pacific region, based at Tontouta, New Caledonia up to 1964.

Argentinian Lancasters

Argentina received 15 Lancasters in the latter part of 1948 (delivered by BSAA and Skyways Ltd pilots between May 1948 and January 1949) to serve with Grupo 2. Ten of these aircraft crashed whilst serving with the FAA; three others had been modified to act as transports (B-038, -040, -045).

Egyptian Lancasters

The only other country to use the Lancaster was Egypt. In May 1948, nine aircraft were ordered; it seems, however, that these ex-RAF aircraft, delivered in 1950, saw very little use. Their exact fate is uncertain; it is believed that, by 1953, only three were still airworthy.

Sweden

Sweden acquired a single aircraft, ex-RA805, which was delivered in June 1950 (serialled 80001) to act as an engine test-bed.

Russian Lancasters

It is known that the Russians flew at least two Lancasters, put together from aircraft that had force-landed in Russia. These included, it seems, substantial parts of ME559, a 617 Squadron aircraft that had force-landed on 18 September 1944, during the *Tirpitz* operations.

Lancaster Survivors

Of the 7,377 Lancasters that were built, Bomber Command lost 3,500 on operations (with seven crew per aircraft); others were lost in training, or damaged beyond repair. A few years after the end of the war, there were still hundreds of Lancasters in open storage at various airfields. Sadly, the number of complete airframes still in existence is less than 20. Of these, only two are at present airworthy, although a number of others could be made to fly. (Strong rumours are currently circulating regarding an airworthy Lancaster in Russia, but these are not confirmed.)

B.1 PA474 RAF Battle of Britain Memorial Flight

The RAF's PA474 is the best known of the surviving Lancasters. It is presently operated by the RAF BBMF, based at the ex-wartime Lancaster base at Coningsby in Lincolnshire. The aircraft has been flown as a 'warbird' since November 1967, and the RAF now presents it at a wide range of airshows and other events each summer season.

The aircraft was built by Vickers-Armstrong's Chester plant in 1945 and was intended for Tiger Force operations; when this plan was abandoned, the aircraft went into store with 38 MU at Llandow, having flown for just 3 hours in total! It spent little time in store, however, before undergoing a modification programme and joining 82 Squadron at Benson. The Squadron was tasked with photo survey in Africa, and PA474 joined the detachment operating out of Takoradi in West Africa.

On its return to the UK, the Lancaster was allocated to Flight Refuelling Ltd at Tarrant Rushton, where it was to be turned into a drone. Once again, the plan changed, and PA474 was re-allocated to the College of Aeronautics at Cranfield as a flight trials platform. During this period

The French Aéronavale acquired 54 ex-RAF Lancasters at the end of the war for maritime use. Ken Ellis Collection

it grew extra wings as different aerofoil sections were attached to the fuselage. In 1964, the Lancaster was returned to RAF control, handed to the Air Historical Branch as a preserved historic airframe, and put into store at Wroughton. It was given wartime markings ready for a place in the planned RAF Museum. A little while later, it moved into open store at Henlow (along with a Lincoln that, sadly, did not survive), and carried on waiting for the promised museum. At this point, the Commanding Officer of 44 Squadron suggested that the aircraft should be allocated to his Squadron, and looked after in a hangar. The one-off ferry flight to Waddington was made on 18 August 1965. Impressed with the condition of the aircraft, the engineers decided to put it into full airworthy condition, and the Squadron persuaded the 'powers that be' to allow the Lancaster to make 'occasional commemorative flights'.

Thus, in the appropriate hands of 44 Squadron, an RAF Lancaster was seen at UK airshows. The aircraft was transferred to the Battle of Britain Memorial Flight, at Coltishall, in November 1973, and has remained with this unit (with a move to Coningsby in March 1976) ever since. In the mid-1990s, it was feared that the aircraft would be grounded, as it needed a re-spar; however, this work was carried out at St Athan in the winter of 1995/96, and PA474 looks set to thrill airshow crowds for years to come.

B.1 R5868 RAF Museum, Hendon

One of few survivors with a wartime record, the RAF Museum's R5868 'S for Sugar' is the oldest surviving Lancaster, and one of only a handful of Lancs to have flown over 100 operational missions (137, in fact). The aircraft was built by Metropolitan Vickers (Metrovick) in Manchester and actually started life as a Manchester airframe,

The French bought five more ex-RAF Lancasters for search and rescue duties, including FCL-03 (ex-RT689); note the transparent radar blister. Ken Ellis Collection

although it was completed as a Lancaster. Delivered to 83 Squadron at Scampton in June 1942, the Lancaster was soon in action, carrying out its first operational sortie to Wilhelmshaven on 8/9 July.

When the Squadron moved to Wyton to join the new Pathfinder Force, it took R5858 with it. However, in August 1943, the aircraft was transferred to 467 Squadron, moving with them to Bottesford, where it became PO-S. Operational sorties continued and the bomber took part in the Battle of Berlin; on one sortie it was hit by flak and collided with another bomber, but the pilot nursed the Lancaster back to England and landed at Linton-on-Ouse. Extensive repairs were required and the aircraft went back to the manufacturers, returning to operations the following February.

R5858's final sortie was flown on 23 April. During its three-year career it had flown over 500 operational hours, but, sadly, this record was not enough to guarantee its preservation in the post-war run-down, and it was put into storage at Wroughton. In 1956, it was transferred to the RAF's Historical Aircraft Collection and in 1959 it was sent to Scampton as a gate guard. The return of PA474 to airworthy status prompted those planning the RAF Museum to look for another airframe. R5868 was chosen, moved to Hendon and underwent a restoration programme that enabled it to form part of the initial collection when the Museum opened in November 1972.

B.1 W4783 Australian War Memorial, Canberra

Another war veteran, W4783 notched up 90 operational sorties with 460 Squadron RAAF before going to Australia in 1944 on a 'war drive'. It adopted the RAAF serial A66-2 and undertook a War Bond tour, with those who donated certain sums of money being given flights in the aircraft. The Lanc remained in RAAF service to 1950 when it was presented to the AWM for preservation.

B.VII NX611 Lincolnshire Aviation Heritage Centre, East Kirkby

'Just Jane' presently carries the markings of two squadrons – 57 and 630 Squadrons – both of whom had been based at this ex-wartime airfield. The aircraft has been restored to a condition in which it can make taxi runs around the site – this is done a few times a year, at night, and East Kirkby is one of the most atmospheric places at which to 'experience' a Lancaster in these modern times.

The aircraft was built by Austin Motors, Longbridge, and was delivered in April 1945, the first of 150 production B.VIIs, to B.VII (FE) standard with a Martin mid-upper turret. It was un-allocated at the end of the war and went into store at Llandow, being one of a number of Lancasters subsequently sold to the Aéronavale. With the Aéronavale it became WU15 and was collected in May 1952. Used for maritime patrol and ASR, WU15 spent its next 10 years of operational service in places as far apart as Brittany and Agadir. In 1962, the aircraft was overhauled and sent to Noumea, New Caledonia, for similar tasks over the Pacific Ocean. This role was short-lived and in 1964 the aircraft was withdrawn from use.

FM218 became a Lancaster 10P and served with 408 and 413 Squadrons. National Aviation Museum

Having left RCAF service, a small number of Lancasters were acquired by civil operators; Spartan Air Services bought three aircraft for aerial survey work. Larry Milberry

Around the same time, the UK-based Historic Aircraft Preservation Society (HAPS) was on the lookout for a Lancaster to put back in the air. In due course, WU15 was donated to HAPS and in August it was flown to Bankstown, Australia. It was not until 25 April 1965 that NX611, as G-ASXX, left Australia en route to the UK, arriving at Biggin Hill on 13 May. It was not, however, to be a successful period of ownership and HAPS found few airshow bookings for the aircraft, especially after the appearance of the RAF's PA474. The aircraft was transferred to Reflectaire Ltd and moved to Lavenham, later going to Hullavington and, finally, Blackpool (June 1970). The Blackpool plans came to nothing and the aircraft was sold at auction to Lord Lilford, moving to Scampton to act as a gate guard. Ten years later it was purchased by Fred and Harold Panton, remaining at Scampton for another five years until plans for the East Kirkby museum were properly developed.

The official Lancaster phase-out celebration held at Downsview in April 1964. Larry Milberry

B. VII NX662 Air Force Association, Bull Creek, Perth

This aircraft followed a similar route to NX611 in its early years, being sold to the Aéronavale for maritime duties (registered as WU16). It was eventually moved to the Pacific area, operating from Tahiti and New Caledonia. Taken out of service in 1962, it was presented to the Air Force Association (Western Australian Division) and flown to Perth. The aircraft is now in the AFA's Heritage Museum at Bull Creek.

B. VII NX665 Museum of Transport, Technology and Social History, Auckland

An Austin Motors aircraft delivered in 1945, NX665 saw no RAF use. It was acquired by the Aéronavale, becoming WU13. Assigned to a training unit at Agadir in 1959, the Lanc saw subsequent service with 55S at Agadir and Khourigba. However, like other Aéronavale Lancs, it moved in the early 1960s to the Pacific area, operating with Esc 9S from Noumea, New Caledonia. Retired from service, it was flown to New Zealand as a gift. It ended up in the museum at Auckland and has been looked after ever since by a team of volunteers. The aircraft wears codes for 101 Sqn (SR-V) and 75 Sqn (AA-O).

B.X FM104 Canadian National Exhibition Grounds, Toronto

All Lancaster Xs were built by Victory Aircraft in Canada, this example serving in the UK with 428 Squadron before returning to Canada in 1945. It remained in service, modified to 10MR standard, based at Torbay, Newfoundland. Retired in 1962, the aircraft was, by 1965, on a plinth in Toronto. Sadly, years of external display have taken their toll and the aircraft is looking very much the worse for wear. However, it is reported that moves are afoot to take the aircraft down and put it into restoration.

B.X FM136 Calgary Aerospace Museum

Built by Victory Aircraft, FM136 was sent to the UK but went straight into storage (20 MU and 32 MU), and saw no service before being returned to Canada. In

Airworthy Survivors

B.1	PA474	RAF Battle of Britain Memorial Flight, Coningsby
B.X	FM213	Canadian Warplane Heritage, Hamilton

Static Survivors

B.1	R5868	RAF Museum, Hendon
B.1	W4783	Australian War Museum, Canberra
B.1	W4964	Newark Air Museum
B.1	DV372	Imperial War Museum, London
B.VII	NX611	Lincolnshire Aviation Heritage Centre, East Kirkby
B.VII	NX622	Air Forces Association, Perth
B.VII	NX664	Ailes Anciennes, Paris
B.VII	NX665	Museum of Transport and Technology, Auckland
B.X	FM104	National Exhibition Ground, Toronto
B.X	FM136	Calgary Aerospace Museum
B.X	FM159	Lancaster Society Museum, Nanton
B.X	FM212	City of Windsor, Ontario
B.X	KB839	Canadian Forces Base, Greenwood
B.X	KB848	St Jacques Airport, Edmunston
B.X	KB889	Imperial War Museum, Duxford
B.X	KB994	National Aviation Museum, Rockliffe
B.X	KB976	Weeks Air Museum, Polk City

Avro Canada's Malton facility, work under way on an unidentified ex-wartime Lancaster. Larry Milberry

Lancastrian VM734. FlyPast Collection

A number of foreign air forces adopted the Lancastrians; with T-101 in Argentinian service. Ken Delve Collection

Bomber Command's next 'heavy' was the Avro Lincoln; many Lancaster squadrons received this type in the late 1940s. Ken Delve Collection

common with most surviving B.Xs, it was converted to MR10 standard and served in the maritime role with 407 Squadron at Comox, British Columbia. The aircraft was retired in April 1961, moving the following year to Calgary, where it was put on a plinth. Like the Toronto example, it suffered from this external display until it was rescued from its perch in April 1992 and put on display in the museum. Restoration work has been progressing ever since; the interior of the aircraft is now superb and, once indoor accommodation has been secured, the exterior of the airframe will be restored.

B.X FM159 Nanton Lancaster Society Museum

Delivered to the UK from Victory Aircraft, this aircraft was another to spend its time in storage before returning to Canada. The intention was to prepare the aircraft for operations in the war against Japan, but this plan was abandoned, and in the latter part of 1945 FM159 went into store at Fort Macleod. After some years in storage it was converted to 10MR standard (1953) and sent to join 103 Rescue Unit at Greenwood, Nova Scotia. It was subsequently given a second series of mods before joining 407 Squadron at Comox. Withdrawn from use in 1960, the Lancaster was acquired by a group of enthusiasts and put on display at Nanton. Once again, external display played havoc with the aircraft and it rapidly deteriorated. It was taken on by the town of Nanton and in 1985 the Nanton Lancaster Society took over its care. Fund-raising activities paid for a building and in the early 1990s Lancaster FM159 was safe indoors.

B.X FM212 City of Windsor, Ontario

After a period of storage this B.X was modified to 10MR standard and served with 408 Squadron for a short period before

PA474 is probably the most famous of the surviving Lancasters; now operated by the RAF Battle of Britain Memorial Flight at Coningsby, it is seen here at Finningley in 1984. FlyPast Collection

The only other airworthy Lancaster is FM213 of the Canadian Warplane Heritage, Hamilton, Ontario; this Lancaster is presently marked as KB726, the 'Mynarski Memorial Lancaster'. FlyPast Collection

March 1984 – PA474 undergoes a major servicing at Abingdon. FlyPast Collection

going back into storage. Retired in October 1964, the Lancaster went to Jackson Park Gardens, Ontario and, in typical Canadian fashion, was placed on a plinth. Given regular attention, at least externally, FM212 does not look too bad – although, without a thorough inspection of its condition on a regular basis, there must be doubts as to its long-term future.

B.X KB839 Canadian Forces Base Greenwood

One of the few surviving B/Xs with a wartime record, KB839 served with 419 Squadron, flying its last sortie on 25 April 1945. It returned to Canada and was converted to 10AR standard for ASR use. It served on into the early 1960s, but by 1965 was on display at Greenwood.

B.X KB882 St Jacques Airport, Edmunston

This Lancaster arrived on a UK-based RCAF squadron, 428 Squadron, just before the end of the war. Returned to Canada in June, it was subsequently modified to 10AR

R8568 graces the Bomber Command display at the RAF Museum, Hendon. FlyPast Collection

The BBMF acquired PA474 in 1973, although it had been operated by 44 Squadron since 1967. FlyPast Collection

Although FM136 spent many years on a pole at Calgary Airport, it is now in the care of the Calgary Aerospace Museum, and restoration work is under way. Larry Milberry

standard and joined 408 Squadron at Rockcliffe. Retired in May 1964, it was flown to St Jacques Airport for display and, unlike most surviving Lancs, has kept its post-war Canadian colours.

B.X KB889 Imperial War Museum, Duxford

This sister aircraft to KB882 arrived on 428 Squadron in April 1945, and saw no operational service. Back in Canada, it had a short period of storage before being modified to maritime configuration, as a 10MP, to serve with 107 Rescue Unit at Torbay, Newfoundland. Sold for scrap in 1963, it was rescued and was acquired two years later by Age of Flight Ltd at Niagara Falls. A few years later it was sold again as a project for restoration to flight. In 1984, the Lancaster was acquired by Warbirds of Great Britain and shipped to the UK as G-LANC. Within two years, it had been acquired by the IWM and, after a restoration programme, now appears as a 428 Squadron aircraft.

B.X KB944 National Aviation Museum, Ontario

KB944 arrived in Britain in March 1945 to join 425 Squadron at Tholthorpe. Returned to Canada in the summer, it went into store at Fort Macleod, but was subsequently modified to 10S standard. It served with 404 Squadron and was finally retired in February 1957, going into store at Dunnville, Ontario. It was allocated to the National Aviation Museum in May 1964 and now appears as NA-P of 428 Squadron.

FM121 left RCAF service in 1964 and was put on display in Jackson Park Gardens, Windsor, Ontario. Larry Milberry

With a ghostly groundcrew figure under the fuselage, NX611 fires up for a night taxi run at the Lincolnshire Aviation Heritage Centre, East Kirky. FlyPast Collection

ND458 'Able Mabel' completed 121 operations, primarily with 100 Squadron. Ken Delve Collection

Another 467 Squadron veteran, LL843, which flew 118 missions. Andy Thomas Collection

The Centurions

Bomber Command statisticians estimated that a Lancaster could be expected to achieve 10-15 operations (averaged across the fleet of aircraft); a few were lost on their first operational sortie, while, at the other extreme, some managed to survive over 100 operational missions. The following list details of the 34 Lancasters that broke the 100-mission barrier.

Mk	Total ops	Sqns	Fate
Mk I			
R5868	137	83, 467 Sqns	RAF Museum
W4964	106	9 Sqn	SOC 12.44
DV302	121	101 Sqn	FTR 30.1.44
ED588	128	50, 97 Sqns	FTR 30.8.44
LL806	134	15 Sqn	SOC 15.12.45
LL843	118	61, 467 Sqns, 1659 HCU	SS 7.5.47
LL885	113	44, 622 Sqns	SOC 4.3.47
LM227	100	467 Sqn	SOC 19.10.45
ME746	116	166 Sqn	SS 2.46
ME758	108	12 Sqn	SOC 19.10.45
ME801	114+	576 Sqn	SOC 19.10.45
ME803	105	115 Sqn, 1659 HCU	SOC 20.11.45
ME812	105	153, 166 Sqns	SOC 25.10.46
Mk III			
DV245	119	101 Sqn	FTR 23.4.45
ED611	113	44, 463 Sqns	SOC 20.6.47
ED860	130	61, 156 Sqns	Xxd on T/O 28.10.44
ED888	140	103, 576 Sqns	SOC 8.1.47
ED905	100+	103, 166, 550 Sqns,	Xxd on T/O 20.8.45 1 LFS, 1656 HCU
EE136	109	9, 189 Sqns	4.46
EE139	121	100, 550 Sqns, 1656/1660 HCU	SOC 19.2.46
EE176	122	7, 61, 97 Sqns, 1653 HCU	5.45
JB138	123	5, 61, Sqns LFS	4.45
JB603	111	100 Sqn	FTR 6.1.45
JB663	111	106 Sqn	SOC 26.10.46
LM550	107	153, 166 Sqns	SOC 15.5.47
LM594	104	576 Sqn, 1651 HCU	SOC 13.2.47
ND458	127	100 Sqn, BCIS	SOC 29.8.47
ND578	121	44, 75 Sqns	SOC 27.10.45
ND644	115	100 Sqn	FTR 17.3.45
ND709	111	35, 582, 635 Sqns, 1667 HCU	SOC 28.8.47
ND875	100+	7, 156 Sqns	SOC 8.47
NE181	101	75, 514 Sqns	SOC 30.9.47
PA995	101	550 Sqn	FTR 8.3.45
PB150	100+	625 Sqn	SOC 22.5.47

The Lancaster in Detail

The following photographs were taken of the Battle of Britain Memorial Flight's PA474 at Coningsby, Lincolnshire, and of Fred and Harold Panton's NX611 at the Lincolnshire Aviation Heritage Museum at East Kirkby. The publishers wish to thank both organizations for their support and for unlimited access to the aeroplanes.

The cockpit of NX611. To the left of the control column is the P4 compass and below this, the flap indicator. The standard RAF blind flying panel is in front of the column with the throttles, mixture controls and propellor speed controls to the right. Above these are the engine instruments with the magneto switches above and, to the right of these, the feathering buttons, fire extinguisher and oxygen controls.

To the right of the pilot's seat is found the elevator, rudder and aileron trim wheels, and the undercarriage selector which is safely wired shut on NX611.

The left-hand side of the cockpit houses the radio pushbuttons and intercom, flap controls, radiator shutter controls and pilot's seat adustment.

The right-hand side of the cockpit has an observer's/second pilot's seat which can be folded away. In front of this can be seen the entrance to the bomb aimer's position and, behind, the flight engineer's panel which houses the fuel cocks, starter switches, and fuel and oil gauges. Nearest the camera is the drift sight.

Close-up of the flight engineer's panel.

Above: The only armour plate on the Lancaster was behind the pilot's head.

Left: Inside the bomb aimer's position showing the bomb selectors. Bombs would be dropped in a set pattern to maintain the trim of the aeroplane.

The massive bomb bay on the Lancaster was made possible by having the main spar running through the fuselage. The limited amount of space above it can be clearly seen; this could make escape from a damaged aeroplane very hazardous.

Looking forward from the rear spar past the ASV radar set that was fitted to maritime Lancasters, to the front spar, with the radio operator's position. NX611 retains some internal fittings from its French service, but the Panton brothers are gradually returning the interior to stock condition.

The tailplane halves are joined by four massive bolts and these, too, run through the fuselage. The elevator push rod can be seen on the right and beneath it are the runners for the 0.5in rounds for the rear turret. The Elsan lavatory would be situated in front of the tailplane.

The main entrance door of the Lancaster was in front of the tailplane. The door opened inwards, to make escape easier in flight. Just inside the door is the flare chute.

Emergency escape from the Lancaster could be made through the hatch in the nose. This view of PA474 also shows the optically flat panel on the nose perspex and the brackets that hold the bombsight.

The inside of the bomb bay showing the double curvature inside the doors, the pipework inside the bomb bay and the bomb shackles.

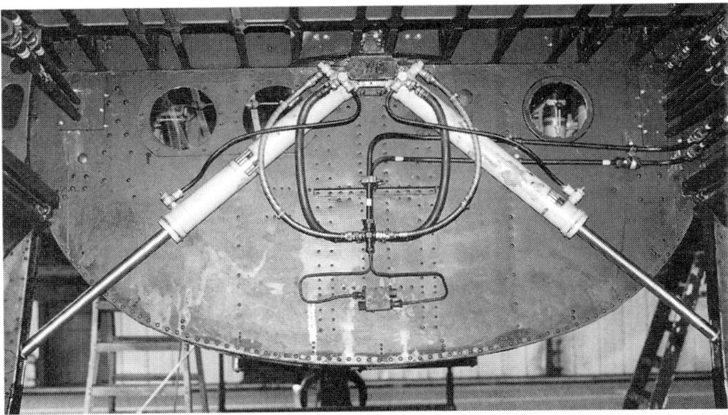

The rear end of the bomb bay showing the operating jacks for the doors and the small windows that allowed the crew to check that no bombs had 'hung up'. Similar jacks were at the forward end of the bomb bay.

The inside of the inner engine nacelle on PA474. At the top are two fire extinguisher bottles; beneath these are the connections for a trolley accumulator and lower right from these are the engine priming pumps. A ground crewman would have to climb on to the wheel and on to the retraction jacks, which had footrests fitted, in order to reach the primers.

Undercarriage detail and engine mountings on the starboard inner engine of PA474.

The tailwheel of PA474 whilst tresteled for maintenence.

Inner flap detail on PA474. Note the cutout on the inner end to clear the open bomb bay doors.

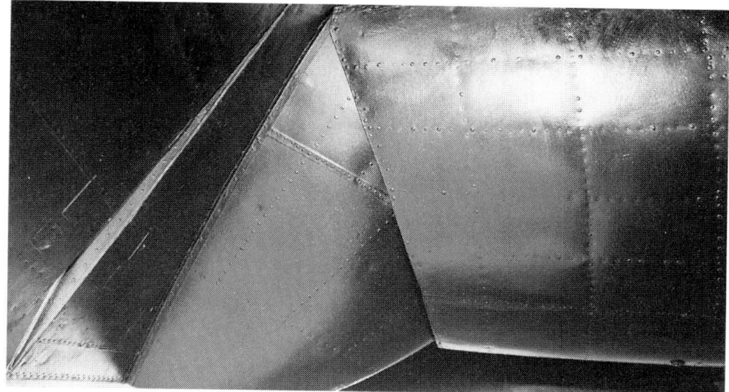

The outer part of the inner engine nacelle pivots when the flaps are lowered.

Access to the engine controls and pipework is achieved through an opening section of the leading edge. The wing jacking point can be seen beneath the pipework junction on the right, just inboard of the oil tank and the massive casting that holds the undercarriage.

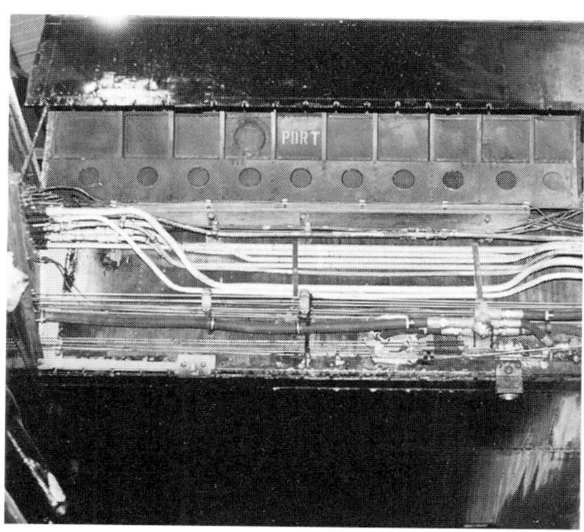

Good detail of the FN5 front turret on NX611.

The rear turret on PA474 is the FN20 with four 0.303in Browning machine-guns.

The rear turret on NX611 is the later FN82, with two 0.5in Brownings.

APPENDIX II

Lancaster Production and Deliveries

PROTOTYPES

BT308	Avro	first flight Jan 1941
DG595	Avro	first flight May 1941
DT810	Avro	first flight November 1941
DT812	Avro	cancelled

PRODUCTION

[a]Serial range	Mark	No	Manufacturer
L7527-L7584	I	43	Avro
R5472-R5763	I	200	Avro
R5842-R5917	I	57	Metrovick
W4102-W4384	I	201	Avro
W4385-W4700	I		Avro, cancelled
W4761-W5012	I/III	200	Metrovick
DS601-DS852	II	200	Armstrong Whitworth
DV155-DV407	I/III	200	Metrovick
ED303-ED999	I/III		Avro
EE105-EE202	III		Avro
FM100-FM229	X	130	Victory Aircraft
HK535-HK806	I	200	Vickers Armstrong
JA672-JA981	III		Avro
JB113-JB748	III		Avro
KB700-KB999	X	300	Victory Aircraft
LL617-LL739	II		Armstrong Whitworth
LL740-LL977	I		Armstrong Whitworth
LM100-LM296	I		Armstrong Whitworth
LM301-LM310	I	10	Avro
LM311-LM756	III		Avro
ME295-ME551	I/III	200	Avro
ME640-ME868	I	250	Metrovick
ND324-ND996	III		Avro
NE112-NE181	III		Avro
NF906-NF999	I		Armstrong Whitworth
NG113-NG503	I		Armstrong Whitworth
NN694-NN816	I	100	Austin Motors
NX548-NX794	I/VII	200	Austin Motors
PA158-PA509	I		Vickers Armstrong
PA964-PA999	III		Avro
PB112-PB998	I/III		Avro
PD112-PD139	B.I (Spec)		Avro
PD198-PD444	I	200	Metrovick
PP663-PP792	I		Vickers Armstrong
RA500-RA805	I		Metrovick
RE115-RE226	III		Avro
RF120-RF197	I		Armstrong Whitworth
RF198-RF326	III		Armstrong Whitworth
RS102-RS225	I		Vickers Armstrong, cancelled
RT140-RT456	VII		Vickers Armstrong, cancelled
RT670-RT699	VII		Austin Motors
SR707-SR907	IV/V		Vickers Armstrong, cancelled
ST477-ST790			Metrovick, cancelled
SW243-SW279	I		Metrovick/Avro
SW283-SW316	I/III		Armstrong Whitworth
SX558-SX921			Vickers Armstrong, cancelled
TG758-TG799			Austin Motors, cancelled
TW647-TW911	I(FE)		Armstrong Whitworth
TW915-TW929	I		Metrovick
TX263-TX283	III		Avro

DELIVERIES

The MAP (Ministry of Aircraft Production) Statistical Bulletins are an amazing source of contemporary data; the table below is created from the monthly summaries of new aircraft deliveries for the Lancaster, with annual summaries showing the cumulative deliveries by manufacturer.

The figures for 1942 include Manchesters but the MAP tables do not differentiate between the types or state when the Manchester acceptances cease. As is often the case with official statistics, the numbers do not always add up!

1942

Jan	31	Feb	21	Mar	27
Apr	40	May	46	Jun	53
Jul	67	Aug	61	Sep	84
Oct	97	Nov	71	Dec	106

Cumulative deliveries to 31.12.42

Lancaster I		
	Avro	539
	Metrovick	128
Lancaster II		
	Armstrong-Whitworth	10
Lancaster III		
	Avro	34

1943		
Jan	116	
Feb	128	
Mar	137	
Apr	126	
May	156	
Jun	144	
Jul	145	
Aug	140	1 (Canadian production)
Sep	187	2
Oct	198	2
Nov	189	5
Dec	181	6

Cumulative deliveries to 31.12.43

Lancaster I		
	Avro	595
	Metrovick	343
	Castle Bromwich	2
	Armstrong-Whitworth	7
Lancaster II		
	Armstrong-Whitworth	264
Lancaster III		
	Avro	1212
	Metrovick	135

1944					
Jan	224	7	Feb	199	9
Mar	257	11	Apr	228	12
May	259	17	Jun	260	9
Jul	217	12	Aug	298	24
Sep	266	21	Oct	268	19
Nov	257	17	Dec	200	23

Cumulative deliveries to 31.12.44

Lancaster I		
	Avro	787
	Metrovick	799
	Castle Bromwich	164
	Armstrong-Whitworth	676
	Austin	71
	Vickers	46
Lancaster II		
	Armstrong-Whitworth	300
Lancaster III		
	Avro	2512
	Metrovick	136

APPENDIX III

Lancaster Losses

The losses shown in this table relate to operational losses only.
*marks the squadron with the highest number of losses in that year.
Many thanks to Bill Chorley for allowing me to use data from his excellent series of books on Bomber Command losses – this six-volume set, published by Midland Counties, covers the period 1939 to 1945 on an annual basis.

Sqn	1942	1943	1944	1945	Total
7		36	53		89
9	14	55	41	9	119
12		66	55	16	137
15			43	8	51
35					
44	31*	49	59	11	150
49		46	51	11	108
50	12	48	55	18	133
57	10	53	56	7	126
61	29	43	49	16	137
75			43	11	54
83	17	36	48	6	107
90			27	5	32
97	22	46	44	5	117
100	3	56	45	9	113
101		64	68	13	145
103	5	69	64	20	158*
106	23	52	53	8	136
109					0
115		38	78	5	121
138				1	1
148					
149			2	4	6
150			2	6	8
153			6	18	24
156		67	52		119
166		18	95*	22*	135
170			1	13	14
186			4	9	13
189			4	15	19
195			11	2	13
207	20	41	69	12	142
214					
218			10	9	19

Sqn	1942	1943	1944	1945	Total
227			8	11	19
300			23	14	37
405		13	38		51
408		11	32		43
419			31	16	47
420					
424				7	7
425					
426		18	15		33
427					
428			15	8	23
429				1	1
431			2	12	14
432		4	6		10
433				4	4
434				7	7
460	1	70*	69	18	158*
463		2	59	16	77
467		44	53	11	108
514		6	64	7	77
550		4	48	16	68
576		7	45	17	69
582			29		29
617		17	9	4	30
619		28	50	12	90
622			38	7	45
625		8	51	1	60
626		4	44	12	60
630		5	57	8	70
635			31		31
Year Total	**187**	**1124**	**2005**	**498**	

Total Lancaster operational losses: 3814 aircraft

APPENDIX IV

AFDU Tactical Trials Report

AFDU REPORT NO 47

Tactical Trials – Lancaster Aircraft

In accordance with arrangements with HQ Bomber Command, trials of the Lancaster I commenced on 24.4.42 at Duxford with a crew from No 44 Squadron to discover the fighting capabilities of a single aircraft. A tactical circus of 3 Spitfires then visited all the Lancaster squadrons in No 5 Group and carried out a series of affiliations, both with single aircraft and with various formations.

The Lancaster I is a mid-wing monoplane powered with 4 Merlin XX engines developing 1280 hp each. The present gross all-up weight is 60,200lb, and the max bomb load carried at present on operations is 12,000lb, though there is provision for carrying 14,000lb when necessary. With 12,000lb of bombs the total air mileage that can be covered is 1,100-1,200 miles. The max air mileage available is about 2,000 miles, in which case the bomb load must be reduced to 4,000lb.

Crew

The crew consisted of several whose duties were as follows:

Captain and 2nd pilot	at controls
Air Observer	navigator and bomb aimer
1st W/Op air gunner	W/T
2nd W/Op air gunner	front turret
Air gunner	mid-upper turret
Air gunner	tail turret

It is understood however that the 2nd pilot will shortly be replaced by the Pilots Assistant who will aid the pilot and also act as flight engineer and front gunner. An air bomber whose duties are map reading and bombing will be carried in place of a second wireless operator.

Standard bomber wireless installation is carried. The TR.9 for intercommunication has proved fairly satisfactory, but a very high standard of maintenance is necessary if this is to be relied on for formation fighting control.

De-icers are provided for the propellers but there is no protection for the main or tail planes other than de-icing paste.

Balloon cutters are fitted along the leading edge of the mainplane.

The Lancaster is at present armed with .303 in Browning guns in three Frazer-Nash turrets. The FN.5A in the nose and the FN.50 in the dorsal turret position have two guns each, with an ammunition supply of 1,000 rounds per gun. The FN.20 in the tail has four guns with servo-feed mechanism and 2,500 rounds per gun. There is also provision for an under-turret – the FN.64, with 2 guns and a periscopic sight. This is not yet in service but was fitted to the aircraft while at Duxford so that trials could be carried out to discover the tactical value of the turret.

The FN.5A turret in the nose has a good field of view and is satisfactory in all respects except that there is no foot rest for the gunner. This is extremely inconvenient when the bomb aimer is in position as the gunner is likely to tread on the bomb aimer's head in moments of stress.

The FN.50 in the dorsal position is a comfortable and roomy turret although the seat design is unsatisfactory. This results in the gunner having great difficulty in entering and leaving the turret. The field of vision is very good and attacks can be seen from any angle except a very steep climbing attack from dead astern. The turret has rotation through 360 degrees and its movement when the guns are elevated about 20 degrees is fast and smooth. Cut-outs are provided for the tail fins and a taboo cam track runs round the turret to prevent damage to the wings, propellers and the tail unit. A restrictor valve is fitted to the hydraulic system to slow down the movement of the guns when they are depressed on to the taboo cam so that a violent movement does not damage the fuselage or fairings. This restriction, however, is not at all satisfactory since the movement of the guns is slowed down so much that it is impossible to follow a fighter who breaks away at fairly close range. As this is usually the air gunner's best opportunity to shoot the fighter down, the loss of rotational speed at this critical moment is serious. While some restriction in speed is clearly necessary it is considered that the present reduction in speed is too great for reasonable operational requirements. The fairing which has been introduced aft of the turret for streamlining purposes is also too high, as the cam track which runs over it cuts down the field of fire between the fuselage and the fins.

The FN20 turret in the tail is satisfactory and accurate, and fast traversing is possible. The vision is somewhat naturally restricted by the armour and gun mountings, but it is impossible to have armour and perfect vision and a reasonable compromise has been affected. Unless the base of the turret is kept perfectly dry, oil is liable to be forced to the rear perspex by the slipstream, but a clear vision panel 6in wide by 30in long has much improved this position. This makes the gunner very cold under icing conditions, but the excellent vision and reduction of searchlight glare more than compensate for the discomfort. One other minor criticism of this turret is that the doors are liable to burst open when taking violent evasion as the locking catch is not sufficiently positive.

The FN.64 in the rear under position is smooth in operation and the view through the periscopic sight is remarkably good, although limited to 60 degrees cone. However, the turret rotates through 180 degrees and search can be carried out without difficulty. A cut-out is provided for the tail wheel and the lower part of the fins which are just within the field of fire.

The GJ3 reflector sight is fitted in all turrets except the under turret which has a prismatic sight with 25 and 50mph rings. The four guns of the rear turret are harmonised on a point at 250 yards by night and on a 7ft 6in square by day. The upper and front guns are usually harmonised

5ft square at 400 yards.

Apart from normal turret armour for the air gunners, the main protection for the crew consists of an armoured door 7mm thick behind the wireless operator's position. The pilot also has two plates of armour, each of 4mm thickness, behind his seat and a head piece 8_mm. Bulletproof glass 2_in thick is provided behind the 2nd pilot's position. The petrol and oil tanks are self-sealing but the engines have no protection.

Tactical trials

The Lancaster is reasonably manoeuvrable for a large aircraft. The controls are positive and moderately heavy under normal cruising conditions, but tend to stiffen appreciably as speed is increased over 200mph. When any evasive manoeuvres are attempted, however, there is a considerable lag in the aileron control and this is very marked indeed when the aircraft is fully loaded. This means that considerable practice is required before violent evasion is possible at ground level. The cruising speed is approx 185mph IAS with full load and about 220mph IAS when light. The max speed near the ground at a weight of 60,000lb is approx 220mph.

The combined all-round view from the Lancaster is good. Owing to the raised position of the cabin the pilot's general view, although slightly restricted on the starboard side, is satisfactory towards the beam and quarter, and of considerable assistance in taking evasive action. The Fighting Controller can stand just behind the 2nd pilot but this gives a poor view downwards and even if he uses the astro-hatch beside the wireless operator, he is still given a large blind area by the mainplane. For this reason control is mainly carried out by the mid-upper gunner who is able to see all attacks except those from beneath and directly astern. For this he relies on the rear gunner so that with practice a good commentary can easily be maintained.

It is considered, however, that it is a mistake for air gunners to carry out fighting control as it is extremely difficult to combine control with good shooting. If therefore a low-level sortie is to be made, with the result that attacks must be made from above, the fighting control should be carried out from the astro-hatch.

Fighting manoeuvres for single aircraft

The trials were carried out with the object of discovering the best method of evasion by the Lancaster against all types of attack both by single fighters or by a number of fighters simultaneously.

It has already been found in previous trials with heavy bombers that the only really effective evasion against the astern, quarter or beam attacks is the corkscrew, or the tight turn towards the fighter. Other forms of evasion, such as skidding, undulation and throttling back are useful but not as effective.

Corkscrew: This evasion consists of a steep diving turn of about 30 degrees and 500ft, followed by a steep climbing turn of 30 degrees and 500ft in the opposite direction. The manoeuvre must be as violent as possible, particularly at the top and bottom of the corkscrew, to avoid giving an easy deflection shot. It should begin when the first fighter attacking is at 600yds and should be continued throughout the engagement unless all the fighters attacking can be clearly seen by the Controller to be out of position, when normal flight can be resumed. This evasion is tiring for the pilot and must be stopped immediately it is clear that immediate attacks are developing. The main advantages of corkscrewing are that the bomber can make good its course, while the fighter is given difficult deflection in two dimensions in that it has to aim in front and below during the diving turn, and in front and above during the climb. Assessment of fighters' cine camera gun films proved in the case of Lancaster, as with other 4-engined bombers, that even the most experienced fighter pilots who knew that the evasion was to be were able to obtain moderate results. Height can be maintained without any extra throttle opening when the Lancaster is without bomb load, but when fully loaded slight opening is necessary to regain height in the climbing turn. This evasion does not affect the air gunner's shooting as much as a tight turn and did not prevent them from obtaining good cine camera gun results when they became used to the movement.

Tight turn: The Lancaster is sufficiently manoeuvrable to be able to do a very tight turn and if this is timed correctly, a fighter who is making an attack at a fast overtaking speed is given a difficult deflection and only a short burst of fire. Against a steep diving attack, a slightly climbing turn is advisable but against a normal astern attack, a diving turn is best as it enables the Lancaster to gain speed. The tight turn is the best evasion against a single fighter provided that it is correctly timed – at about 600 yards – and that there is no question of shortage of petrol or other fighters coming up to engage the bomber. Under the latter circumstances, or if more than one fighter is attacking, the corkscrew evasion is more effective, because it enables the bomber to maintain a course and height instead of flying circles.

Head-on attacks: Were carried out against the Lancaster but were difficult to deliver owing to its high speed. It is often possible for the Lancaster to prevent the attack developing by edging towards the fighter when it is trying to get into position. If the attack is delivered, a diving turn at about 800 yards is effective and gives the fighter an extremely difficult deflection allowance. The mid-upper gunner, who will be facing forwards for this type of attack, is given a reasonable shot.

Fighting manoeuvres for formation

Low-level attacks: It is recommended that a formation of more than three Lancasters is unwieldy if adequate individual evasive action is to be taken. The three aircraft should be in Vic formation with Nos 2 and 3 only slightly behind the leader at about 1_ wing spans' interval. The leader can fly at about 50ft with Nos 2 and 3 slightly above, to give them a small margin if the leader has to climb up suddenly to avoid ground obstacles.

Fighter affiliation carried out with the Squadrons has proved that if a formation of Lancasters simply relies upon low flying, it will always provide an easy target for the fighters. If the formation is intercepted it should therefore climb up to about 600-700ft. This is absolutely essential to give the bombers room to manoeuvre. It cannot be over-emphasised that flying at ground level is not in itself an adequate form of evasion when attacked.

In the past it has usually been considered that tight turns in formation are the best form of defence against fighters but it is almost impossible with heavy bombers to make turns sufficiently steep to upset the fighters' aim. Turns also have another very serious defect as they have to be begun early in order to make them at all effective, and this results in the formation turning through nearly 180 degrees. It can be seen that a series of turns results in the bombers flying in circles so that they waste petrol and are unable to maintain their track towards the target.

It has also been found in the majority of recent daylight operations that the German fighters are shy of the power-operated turrets and stand off at 600-400 yards using their cannon. The result is that if any close formation is adopted by the bombers they present a mass target while adding nothing to their mutual fire support, owing to the extreme difficulty of achieving a correct aim at long range without present sight.

It has therefore been necessary to develop a form of evasive action which will give the bombers a chance to carry out individual evasion while maintaining their track to the target and giving each other assistance. Just before the fighters attack the Lancasters should climb up to about 600ft and Nos 2 and 3 should come well up on the beam of the leader. When the fighters close in the leader of the Vic should undulate violently between 600ft and ground level, while Nos 2 and 3 carry out a modified form of corkscrew on either side of the leader, beginning with a diving turn outwards of about 20m degrees and varying their height between 600 and 100ft. Practice is necessary to ensure that the outside aircraft are never more than 300 to 400 yards from the leader and that they do not mask his guns by sliding in behind him during their inward movement. Nos 2 and 3 should attempt to keep as close as possible to the leader until an attack actually develops so that during their evasion they will not go too far away from him. This evasive manoeuvre enables a formation to continue upon track while it gives the fighters difficult deflection shooting. The fighters found it hard to attack the leader as he was protected by the guns of the outside aircraft, and if they followed the outside aircraft in its corkscrew, they were soon drawn under the leader's guns. A further advantage of this manoeuvre is that the slipstream of the formation is fanned out over a large area and frequently upsets the fighters' aim, being particularly unpleasant near the ground. This evasion has been tried by nearly all the squadrons of heavy bombers and has proved very satisfactory under practice conditions.

R/T and Fighting Control: An advantage of the formation corkscrew movement is that the fighting control by the leader is not essential. It is still necessary so that the leader can warn Nos 2 and 3 when he wishes to change course, but with the present standard of R/T equipment and maintenance, it is not advisable to rely absolutely on TR.9 control.

High-level attacks: Little high-level formation flying has yet been attempted. It is considered that the corkscrew evasion described for low-level attacks will again be effective and would be useful against flak prior to the actual bombing run. It is thought, however, that fighting control from the leader would be essential, so that the formation could have time to settle down preparatory to bombing.

Night flying

A short night flight was carried out with the fighter observing the exhaust flames from the Lancaster; there was no moon and 10/10ths cloud. The flames appear as a very dim glow and can be seen from about 500 yards dead astern. On closing range they appeared rather like eight bright cigarette ends at about 150 to 200 yards. The exhausts are not visible from any position other than dead astern and at long ranges are unlikely to catch the eye of a night-fighter pilot until he is looking directly at them.

(Report dated 30 May 1942.)

APPENDIX V

Order of Battle

The following tables are base on the Bomber Command Order of Battle record held by the Air Historical Branch and, for training units, Form SD161 (Location of Units). By recording the Lancaster units on a monthly basis, starting with January 1942, as this is the first month in which No 5 Group records include the type, the ORBATS show the growth of Lancaster strength (aircraft numbers are those on strength at the time of the record and not simply the Unit Establishment - UE). In the 1942 records the figures given for aircraft strength show those on strength to the squadron plus those on strength to the Conversion Flight e.g. 15+2 means 15 Lancasters on the Squadron strength plus a further two held by the Conversion Flight. No strength figures were recorded for the training units. The location is the airfield at which the Squadron was based for that month's stats return.

BOMBER COMMAND ORDERS OF BATTLE

Squadron	Location	Strength	Remarks
30 Jan 42			
No 5 Gp (AVM J C Slessor wef 12 May 41)			
44 Sqn	Waddington	21	non-op
97 Sqn	Coningsby	4	non-op
27 Mar 42			
No 5 Gp			
44 Sqn	Skellingthorpe	22	
61 Sqn	Woolfox Lodge	2	non-op
97 Sqn	Woodhall Spa	12	
207 Sqn	Bottesford	10	non-op
29 May 42			
No 5 Gp (AVM W A Coryton wef 25 Apr 42)			
44 Sqn	Waddington	9+3	
50 Sqn	Skellingthorpe	0+2	non-op
61 Sqn	Syerston	14+2	
83 Sqn	Scampton	17+2	non-op
97 Sqn	Woodhall Spa	20+2	
106 Sqn	Coningsby	6+3	non-op
207 Sqn	Bottesford	12+3	
No 26 Gp			
109 Sqn	Stradishall	1	
24 Jul 42			
No 5 Gp			
44 Sqn	Waddington	18+2	
49 Sqn	Scampton	8+2	non-op
50 Sqn	Swinderby	17+2	
61 Sqn	Syerston	17+2	
83 Sqn	Scampton	16+3	
97 Sqn	Woodhall Spa	19+2	
106 Sqn	Coningsby	14+1	
207 Sqn	Bottesford	16+3	
1654 CU	Wigsley	5	
No 26 Gp			
109 Sqn	Stradishall	1	
18 Sep 42			
No 3 Gp (AVM J E A Baldwin wef 29 Aug 39) (AVM the Hon R A Cochrane wef 14 Sep 42)			
83 Sqn	Wyton	19+2	
109 Sqn	Wyton	1	
1 BDU	Gransden Lodge	0	(I UE but nil on strength)
No 5 Gp			
9 Sqn	Waddington	15+2	
44 Sqn	Waddington	20+3	
49 Sqn	Scampton	16+3	
50 Sqn	Swinderby	18+3	
57 Sqn	Scampton	6	non-op
61 Sqn	Syerston/St Eval	14+3	
97 Sqn	Woodhall Spa	19+3	
106 Sqn	Coningsby	15+2	
207 Sqn	Syerston	20+3	
1654 CU	Wigsley	8	
26 Nov 42			
No 1 Gp (AVM R D Oxland wef 27 Nov 40)			
12 Sqn	Wickenby	15	non-op
101 Sqn	Holme	10	
103 Sqn	Elsham Wolds	16	
460 Sqn	Breighton	13	
No 3 Gp			
83 Sqn	Wyton	15	
No 5 Gp			
9 Sqn	Waddington	16	
44 Sqn	Waddington	14	
49 Sqn	Scampton	16	
50 Sqn	Skellingthorpe	17	
57 Sqn	Scampton	17	
61 Sqn	Syerston	18	
97 Sqn	Woodhall Spa	19	
106 Sqn	Syerston	20	
207 Sqn	Langar	14	
467 Sqn	Bottesford	7	non-op

<u>7 Jan 43</u>

No 1 Gp			
12 Sqn	Wickenby	19	
100 Sqn	Grimsby	9	non-op
101 Sqn	Holme	19	
103 Sqn	Elsham	18	
460 Sqn	Breighton	18	
1656 CU	Lindholme		
No 3 Gp			
83 Sqn	Wyton	20	
156 Sqn	Warboys	8	non-op
No 5 Gp			
9 Sqn	Waddington	16	
44 Sqn	Waddington	18	
49 Sqn	Fiskerton	18	
50 Sqn	Skellingthorpe	18	
57 Sqn	Scampton	18	
61 Sqn	Syerston	18	
97 Sqn	Woodhall Spa	20	
106 Sqn	Syerston	20	
207 Sqn	Langar	16	
467 Sqn	Bottesford	18	
1660 CU	Swinderby		
1661 CU	Waddington		

<u>18 Mar 43</u>

No 1 Gp (AVM E A B Rice wef 24 Feb 43)
(AVM R Harrison wef 27 Feb 43)
(AVM the Hon R A Cochrane wef 28 Feb 43)
(Air Cdre D C T Bennett wef 13 Jan 43)

12 Sqn	Wick	20	
100 Sqn	Grimsby	19	
101 Sqn	Holme	22	
103 Sqn	Elsham	24	
460 Sqn	Breighton	21	
1656 CU	Lindholme		
	Blyton		
No 3 Gp			
115 Sqn	East Wretham	17	non-op
No 5 Gp			
9 Sqn	Waddington	18	
44 Sqn	Waddington	18	
49 Sqn	Fiskerton	18	
50 Sqn	Skellingthorpe	17	
57 Sqn	Scampton	18	
61 Sqn	Syerston	19	
97 Sqn	Woodhall Spa	21	
106 Sqn	Syerston	19	
207 Sqn	Langar	18	
467 Sqn	Bottesford	20	
1654 CU	Swinderby		
1660 CU	Barkston Heath		
1661 CU	Wigsley		
	Winthorpe		
No 8 Gp			
83 Sqn	Wyton	19	
156 Sqn	Warboys	22	

<u>13 May 43</u>

No 1 Gp			
12 Sqn	Wickenby	26	
100 Sqn	Grimsby	27	
101 Sqn	Holme	28	
103 Sqn	Elsham	29	
460 Sqn	Binbrook	24	
1656 CU	Lindholme		
1662 CU			
No 3 Gp			
115 Sqn	East Wretham	27	
No 5 Gp			
9 Sqn	Bardney	19	
44 Sqn	Waddington	19	
49 Sqn	Fiskerton	18	
50 Sqn	Skellingthorpe	17	
57 Sqn	Scampton	26	
61 Sqn	Syerston	16	
106 Sqn	Syerston	20	
207 Sqn	Langar	17	
467 Sqn	Bottesford	26	
617 Sqn	Scampton	22	
619 Sqn	Woodhall Spa	11	non-op
1654 CU	Swinderby		
1660 CU			
1661 CU			
No 8 Gp			
7 Sqn	Oakington	1	re-equip
83 Sqn	Wyton	21	
97 Sqn	Bourn	27	
156 Sqn	Warboys	33	

<u>22 Jul 43</u>

Most squadrons still have a UE of 16+4, the PFF units plus a few other squadrons now have 24+4.

No 1 Gp			
12 Sqn	Wickenby	23	
100 Sqn	Grimsby	25	
101 Sqn	Ludford Magna	28	
103 Sqn	Elsham	27	
460 Sqn	Binbrook	27	
1656 CU	Lindholme		
1662 CU			
1667 CU			
No 3 Gp			
115 Sqn	East Wretham	21	
1678 CU	Mildenhall		
No 5 Gp			
9 Sqn	Bardney	18	
44 Sqn	Dunholme Lodge	17	
49 Sqn	Fiskerton	20	
50 Sqn	Skellingthorpe	17	
57 Sqn	Scampton	26	
61 Sqn	Syerston	18	
106 Sqn	Syerston	18	
207 Sqn	Langar	18	
467 Sqn	Bottesford	25	
617 Sqn	Scampton	22	non-op
619 Sqn	Woodhall Spa	15	

1654 CU	Swinderby		
1660 CU			
1661 CU			
No 6 Gp (AVM G E Brooks wef 25 Oct 42)			
426 Sqn	Linton on Ouse	24	non-op
1679 CU	Linton on Ouse		
No 8 Gp			
7 Sqn	Oakington	21	non-op
83 Sqn	Wyton	25	
97 Sqn	Bourn	33	
156 Sqn	Warboys	33	
PFF NTU			

<u>16 Sep 43</u>

No 1 Gp			
12 Sqn	Wickenby	25	
100 Sqn	Grimsby	20	
101 Sqn	Ludford Magna	26	
103 Sqn	Elsham	26	
166 Sqn	Kirmington	0	re-eq
460 Sqn	Binbrook	21	
1656 CU	Lindholme		
1662 CU			
1667 CU			
No 3 Gp			
115 Sqn	Little Snoring	21	
514 Sqn	Foulsham	6	non-op
1678 CU	Mildenhall		
No 5 Gp			
9 Sqn	Bardney	14	
44 Sqn	Dunholme Lodge	13	
49 Sqn	Fiskerton	18	
50 Sqn	Skellingthorpe	13	
57 Sqn	East Kirkby	24	
61 Sqn	Syerston	13	
106 Sqn	Syerston	14	
207 Sqn	Langar	14	
467 Sqn	Bottesford	22	
617 Sqn	Coningsby	20	non-op
619 Sqn	Woodhall Spa	13	
1654 CU	Swinderby		
1660 CU			
1661 CU			
1668 CU	Syerston		
No 6 Gp			
408 Sqn	Linton on Ouse	22	non-op
426 Sqn	Linton on Ouse	22	
1679 CU	Linton on Ouse		
No 8 Gp			
7 Sqn	Oakington	28	
83 Sqn	Wyton	21	
97 Sqn	Bourn	34	
156 Sqn	Warboys	29	
405 Sqn	Gransden Lodge	15	
PFF NTU			

<u>31 Dec 43</u>

No 1 Gp			
12 Sqn	Wickenby	16	
100 Sqn	Grimsby	18	
101 Sqn	Ludford Magna	22	
103 Sqn	Elsham	17	
166 Sqn	Kirmington	23	
300 Sqn	Ingham	0	re-equip
460 Sqn	Binbrook	27	
550 Sqn	Grimsby	7	
576 Sqn	Elsham	8	
625 Sqn	Kelstern	17	
626 Sqn	Wickenby	14	
1656 CU	Lindholme		
1662 CU			
1667 CU			
No 3 Gp			
15 Sqn	Mildenhall	17	non-op
115 Sqn	Witchford	30	
514 Sqn	Waterbeach	32	
622 Sqn	Mildenhall	12	non-op
1678 CU	Stradishall		
No 5 Gp			
9 Sqn	Bardney	15	
44 Sqn	Dunholme Lodge	14	
49 Sqn	Fiskerton	15	
50 Sqn	Skellingthorpe	15	
57 Sqn	East Kirkby	17	
61 Sqn	Skellingthorpe	16	
106 Sqn	Metheringham	15	
207 Sqn	Spilsby	12	
463 Sqn	Waddington	14	
467 Sqn	Waddington	14	
617 Sqn	Coningsby	32	non-op
619 Sqn	Woodhall Spa	17	
630 Sqn	East Kirkby	17	
1654 CU	Swinderby		
1660 CU	Wigsley		
1661 CU	Winthorpe		
1668 CU	Balderton		
No 6 Gp			
408 Sqn	Linton on Ouse	21	
426 Sqn	Linton on Ouse	22	
432 Sqn	East Moor	20	
1679 CU	Linton on Ouse		
No 8 Gp			
7 Sqn	Oakington	32	
83 Sqn	Wyton	19	
97 Sqn	Bourn	30	
156 Sqn	Warboys	27	
405 Sqn	Gransden Lodge	17	
PFF NTU			

<u>24 Feb 44</u>

No 1 Gp			
12 Sqn	Wickenby	19	
100 Sqn	Grimsby	19	
101 Sqn	Ludford Magna	29	
103 Sqn	Elsham	19	
166 Sqn	Kirmington	30	
300 Sqn	Ingham	4	non-op
460 Sqn	Binbrook	30	

550 Sqn	North Killingholme	21	
576 Sqn	Elsham	19	
625 Sqn	Kelstern	21	
626 Sqn	Wickenby	19	
1656 CU	Lindholme		
1662 CU	Sandtoft		
1667 CU	Faldingworth		
1 LFS	Blyton		
No 3 Gp			
15 Sqn	Mildenhall	21	
115 Sqn	Witchford	24	
514 Sqn	Waterbeach	26	
622 Sqn	Mildenhall	19	
1678 CU	Waterbeach		
3 LFS	Feltwell		
No 5 Gp			
9 Sqn	Bardney	19	
44 Sqn	Dunholme Lodge	21	
49 Sqn	Fiskerton	16	
50 Sqn	Skellingthorpe	17	
57 Sqn	East Kirkby	19	
61 Sqn	Coningsby	19	
106 Sqn	Metheringham	19	
207 Sqn	Spilsby	18	
463 Sqn	Waddington	19	
467 Sqn	Waddington	17	
617 Sqn	Woodhall Spa	28	
619 Sqn	Coningsby	20	
630 Sqn	East Kirkby	18	
5 LFS	Syerston		
No 6 Gp			
408 Sqn	Linton on Ouse	20	
419 Sqn	Middleton St George	1	re-equip
426 Sqn	Linton on Ouse	22	
431 Sqn	East Moor	1	re-euip
No 8 Gp			
7 Sqn	Oakington	30	
83 Sqn	Wyton	23	
97 Sqn	Bourn	30	
156 Sqn	Warboys	30	
405 Sqn	Gransden Lodge	23	
PFF NTU			

20 Apr 44

No 1 Gp			
12 Sqn	Wickenby	21	
100 Sqn	Grimsby	22	
101 Sqn	Ludford Magna	36	
103 Sqn	Elsham	21	
166 Sqn	Kirmington	30	
300 Sqn	Faldingworth	9	1 Flt op
460 Sqn	Binbrook	33	
550 Sqn	North Killingholme	20	
576 Sqn	Elsham	21	
625 Sqn	Kelstern	21	
626 Sqn	Wickenby	20	
1656 CU	Lindholme		
1662 CU	Sandtoft		
1 LFS	Hemswell		
No 3 Gp			
15 Sqn	Mildenhall	21	
75 Sqn	Mepal	17	1 Flt op
115 Sqn	Witchford	47	
514 Sqn	Waterbeach	26	
622 Sqn	Mildenhall	21	
1678 CU	Waterbeach		
3 LFS	Feltwell		
No 5 Gp			
9 Sqn	Bardney	19	
44 Sqn	Dunholme Lodge	20	
49 Sqn	Fiskerton	21	
50 Sqn	Skellingthorpe	20	
57 Sqn	East Kirkby	19	
61 Sqn	Skellingthorpe	20	
106 Sqn	Metheringham	21	
207 Sqn	Spilsby	20	
463 Sqn	Waddington	21	
467 Sqn	Waddington	21	
617 Sqn	Woodhall Spa	34	
619 Sqn	Dunholme Lodge	19	
630 Sqn	East Kirkby	19	
5 LFS	Syerston		
No 6 Gp			
408 Sqn	Linton on Ouse	19	
419 Sqn	Middleton St George	10	non-op
426 Sqn	Linton on Ouse	12	re-equip Hal
No 8 Gp			
7 Sqn	Oakington	32	
35 Sqn	Graveley	22	
83 Sqn	Coningsby	20	loan to 5 Gp
97 Sqn	Coningsby	22	loan to 5 Gp
156 Sqn	Upwood	21	
405 Sqn	Gransden Lodge	19	
582 Sqn	Little Staughton	18	
635 Sqn	Downham Market	20	

29 Jun 44

No 1 Gp			
12 Sqn	Wickenby	16	
100 Sqn	Grimsby	20	
101 Sqn	Ludford Magna	32	
103 Sqn	Elsham	21	
166 Sqn	Kirmington	29	
300 Sqn	Faldingworth	23	
460 Sqn	Binbrook	36	
550 Sqn	North Killingholme	19	
576 Sqn	Elsham	18	
625 Sqn	Kelstern	21	
626 Sqn	Wickenby	18	
1656 CU	Lindholme		
1662 CU	Sandtoft		
1 LFS	Hemswell		
No 3 Gp			
15 Sqn	Mildenhall	22	
75 Sqn	Mepal	33	
90 Sqn	Tuddenham	31	
115 Sqn	Witchford	32	

514 Sqn	Waterbeach	31	
622 Sqn	Mildenhall	19	
1678 CU	Waterbeach		
3 LFS	Feltwell		
No 5 Gp			
9 Sqn	Bardney	19	
44 Sqn	Dunholme Lodge	20	
49 Sqn	Fiskerton	21	
50 Sqn	Skellingthorpe	20	
57 Sqn	East Kirkby	20	
61 Sqn	Skellingthorpe	20	
106 Sqn	Metheringham	18	
207 Sqn	Spilsby	21	
463 Sqn	Waddington	17	
467 Sqn	Waddington	17	
617 Sqn	Woodhall Spa	29	
619 Sqn	Dunholme Lodge	20	
630 Sqn	East Kirkby	21	
5 LFS	Syerston		
No 6 GP			
408 Sqn	Linton on Ouse	23	
419 Sqn	Middleton St George	20	
428 Sqn	Middleton St George	12	
No 8 Gp			
7 Sqn	Oakington	19	
35 Sqn	Graveley	20	
83 Sqn	Coningsby	19	loan to 5 Gp
97 Sqn	Coningsby	19	loan to 5 Gp
156 Sqn	Upwood	20	
405 Sqn	Gransden Lodge	22	
582 Sqn	Little Staughton	18	
635 Sqn	Downham Market	19	
PFF NTU	Wyton		
24 Aug 44			
No 1 Gp			
12 Sqn	Wickenby	21	
100 Sqn	Grimsby	22	
101 Sqn	Ludford Magna	33	
103 Sqn	Elsham	21	
166 Sqn	Kirmington	30	
300 Sqn	Faldingworth	20	
460 Sqn	Binbrook	32	
550 Sqn	North Killingholme	20	
576 Sqn	Elsham	20	
625 Sqn	Kelstern	21	
626 Sqn	Wickenby	20	
No 3 Gp			
15 Sqn	Mildenhall	20	
75 Sqn	Mepal	30	
90 Sqn	Tuddenham	34	
115 Sqn	Witchford	31	
149 Sqn	Methwold	0	re-equip
218 Sqn	Methwold	19	
514 Sqn	Waterbeach	21	
622 Sqn	Mildenhall	21	
No 5 Gp			
9 Sqn	Bardney	21	
44 Sqn	Dunholme Lodge	21	
49 Sqn	Fiskerton	23	
50 Sqn	Skellingthorpe	20	
57 Sqn	East Kirkby	22	
61 Sqn	Skellingthorpe	20	
106 Sqn	Metheringham	20	
207 Sqn	Spilsby	21	
463 Sqn	Waddington	22	
467Sqn	Waddington	20	
617 Sqn	Woodhall Spa	31	
619 Sqn	Dunholme Lodge	20	
630 Sqn	East Kirkby	21	
No 6 Gp			
408 Sqn	Linton on Ouse	15	
419 Sqn	Middleton St George	23	
428 Sqn	Middleton St George	22	
No 8 Gp			
7 Sqn	Oakington	21	
35 Sqn	Graveley	20	
83 Sqn	Coningsby	17	loan to 5 Gp
97 Sqn	Coningsby	16	loan to 5 Gp
156 Sqn	Upwood	19	
405 Sqn	Gransden Lodge	21	
582 Sqn	Little Staughton	21	
635 Sqn	Downham Market	20	
19 Oct 44			
No 1 Gp			
12 Sqn	Wickenby	22	
100 Sqn	Grimsby	24	
101 Sqn	Ludford Magna	31	
103 Sqn	Elsham	22	
153 Sqn	Scampton	22	
166 Sqn	Kirmington	28	
170 Sqn	Kelstern	22	
300 Sqn	Faldingworth	16	
460 Sqn	Binbrook	35	
550 Sqn	North Killingholme	31	
576 Sqn	Elsham	23	
625 Sqn	Kelstern	26	
626 Sqn	Wickenby	26	
No 3 Gp			
15 sqn	Mildenhall	26	
75 Sqn	Mepal	31	
90 Sqn	Tuddenham	24	
115 Sqn	Witchford	28	
149 Sqn	Methwold	27	
186 Sqn	Tuddenham	25	
195 Sqn	Witchford	19	
218 Sqn	Methwold	22	
514 Sqn	Waterbeach	30	
622 Sqn	Mildenhall	24	
No 5 Gp			
9 Sqn	Bardney	22	
44 Sqn	Spilsby??	22	
49 Sqn	Fulbeck	24	
50 Sqn	Skellingthorpe	23	
57 Sqn	East Kirkby	23	
61 Sqn	Skellingthorpe	23	
106 Sqn	Metheringham	23	

Unit	Station	Aircraft	Notes
189 Sqn	Fulbeck	0	forming
207 Sqn	Spilsby	20	
227 Sqn	Fulbeck	20	
463 Sqn	Waddington	25	
467 Sqn	Waddington	25	
617 Sqn	Woodhall Spa	31	
619 Sqn	Strubby	19	
630 Sqn	East Kirkby	20	
No 6 Gp			
408 Sqn	Linton on Ouse	1	
419 Sqn	Middleton St George	30	
428 Sqn	Middleton St George	28	
431 Sqn	Croft	5	re-equip
No 8 Gp			
7 Sqn	Oakington	23	
35 Sqn	Graveley	26	
83 Sqn	Coningsby	20	loan to 5 Gp
97 Sqn	Coningsby	24	loan to 5 Gp
156 Sqn	Upwood	22	
405 Sqn	Gransden Lodge	22	
582 Sqn	Little Staughton	21	
635 Sqn	Downham Market	21	
<u>25 Jan 45</u>			
No 1 Gp			
12 Sqn	Wickenby	20	
100 Sqn	Grimsby	21	
101 Sqn	Ludford Magna	30	
150 Sqn	Hemswell	22	
153 Sqn	Elsham	23	
166 Sqn	Kirmington	32	
170 Sqn	Hemswell	22	
300 Sqn	Faldingworth	18	
460 Sqn	Binbrook	29	
550 Sqn	North Killingholme	34	
576 Sqn	Fiskerton	18	
625 Sqn	Kelstern	35	
626 Sqn	Wickenby	23	
No 3 Gp			
15 Sqn	Mildenhall	20	
75 Sqn	Mepal	31	
90 Sqn	Tuddenham	25	
115 Sqn	Witchford	30	
149 Sqn	Methwold	30	
186 Sqn	Stradishall	21	
195 Sqn	Wratting Common	32	
218 Sqn	Chedburgh	29	
514 Sqn	Waterbeach	29	
622 Sqn	Mildenhall	21	
3 LFS	Feltwell		
No 5 Gp (AVM H A Constantine wef 16 Jan 45)			
9 Sqn	Bardney	21	
44 Sqn	Spilsby	21	
49 Sqn	Fulbeck	20	
50 Sqn	Skellingthorpe	21	
57 Sqn	East Kirkby	20	
61 Sqn	Skellingthorpe	21	
106 Sqn	Metheringham	20	
189 Sqn	Fulbeck	21	

Unit	Station	Aircraft	Notes
207 Sqn	Spilsby	21	
227 Sqn	Balderton	20	
463 Sqn	Waddington	22	
467 Sqn	Waddington	22	
617 Sqn	Woodhall Spa	31	
619 Sqn	Strubby	21	
630 Sqn	East Kirkby	20	
5 LFS	Syerston		
No 6 Gp			
419 Sqn	Middleton St George	18	
424 Sqn	Skipton on Swale	18	
428 Sqn	Middleton St George	20	
431 Sqn	Croft	19	
433 Sqn	Skipton on Swale	19	
434 Sqn	Croft	18	
No 7 (Training) Gp 1 Jan 45			
1656 CU	Lindholme		
1662 CU	Blyton/Sandtoft		
1667 CU	Sturgate		
1668 CU	Bottesford		
1669 CU	Langar		
1653 CU	North Luffenham		
1651 CU	Woolfox Lodge		
1661 CU	Winthorpe		
1666 CU	Dishforth		
No 8 Gp			
7 Sqn	Oakington	18	
35 Sqn	Graveley	20	
83 Sqn	Coningsby	22	loan to 5 Gp
97 Sqn	Coningsby	21	loan to 5 Gp
156 Sqn	Upwood	18	
405 Sqn	Gransden Lodge	18	
582 Sqn	Little Staughton	15	
635 Sqn	Downham Market	18	
PFF NTU			
<u>22 Mar 45</u>			
No 1 Gp (AVM R S Blucke wef 12 Feb 45)			
12 Sqn	Wickenby	20	
100 Sqn	Grimsby	19	
101 Sqn	Ludford Magna	32	
103 Sqn	Elsham	19	
150 Sqn	Hemswell	16	
153 Sqn	Scampton	21	
166 Sqn	Kirmington	27	
170 Sqn	Hemswell	18	
300 Sqn	Faldingworth	20	
460 Sqn	Binbrook	27	
550 Sqn	North Killingholme	27	
576 Sqn	Fiskerton	19	
625 Sqn	Kelstern	29	
626 Sqn	Wickenby	21	
No 3 Gp			
15 Sqn	Mildenhall	22	
75 Sqn	Mepal	26	
90 Sqn	Tuddenham	21	
115 Sqn	Witchford	32	
138 Sqn	Tuddenham	20	
148 Sqn	Methwold	30	

186 Sqn	Stradishall	31	
195 Sqn	Wratting Common	30	
218 Sqn	Chedburgh	29	
514 Sqn	Waterbeach	32	
622 Sqn	Mildenhall	22	
G-H TF	Feltwell		
No 5 Gp			
9 Sqn	Bardney	22	
44 Sqn	Spilsby	16	
49 Sqn	Fulbeck	19	
50 Sqn	Skellingthorpe	17	
57 Sqn	East Kirkby	16	
61 Sqn	Skellingthorpe	19	
106 Sqn	Metheringham	16	
189 Sqn	Fulbeck	17	
207 Sqn	Spilsby	18	
227 Sqn	Balderton	18	
463 Sqn	Waddington	21	
467 Sqn	Waddington	19	
617 Sqn	Woodhall Spa	41	
619 Sqn	Strubby	17	
630 Sqn	East Kirkby	21	
5 LFS	Syerston		
No 6 Gp (AVM C McEwen wef 21 Mar 45)			
419 Sqn	Middleton St George	23	
424 Sqn	Skipton on Swale	20	
427 Sqn	Leeming	20	
428 sqn	Middleton St George	25	
429 Sqn	Leeming	19	non-op
431 Sqn	Croft	20	
433 Sqn	Skipton on Swale	20	
434 Sqn	Croft	19	
No 7 (Training) Gp			
1656 CU	Lindholme		
1662 CU	Blyton/Sandtoft		
1667 CU	Sturgate		
1668 CU	Bottesford		
1669 CU	Langar		
1653 CU	North Luffenham		
1651 CU	Woolfox Lodge		
1660 CU	Swinderby		
1661 CU	Winthorpe		
1654 CU	Wigsley		
1666 CU	Wombleton		
No 8 Gp			
7 Sqn	Oakington	19	
35 Sqn	Graveley	19	
83 Sqn	Coningsby	22	loan to 5 Gp
97 Sqn	Coningsby	19	loan to 5 Gp
156 Sqn	Upwood	19	
405 Sqn	Gransden Lodge	18	
582 Sqn	Little Staughton	21	
635 Sqn	Downham Market	19	
PFF NTU	Warboys		

<u>19 Apr 45</u>

No 1 Gp			
12 Sqn	Wickenby	23	
100 Sqn	Elsham	21	
101 Sqn	Ludford Magna	45	
103 Sqn	Elsham	21	
150 Sqn	Hemswell	21	
153 Sqn	Scampton	19	
166 Sqn	Kirmington	33	
170 Sqn	Hemswell	20	
300 Sqn	Faldingworth	21	
460 Sqn	Binbrook	37	
550 Sqn	North Killingholme	30	
576 Sqn	Fiskerton	31	
625 Sqn	Scampton	19	
626 Sqn	Wickenby	22	
No 3 Gp			
15 Sqn	Mildenhall	24	
75 Sqn	Mepal	33	
90 Sqn	Tuddenham	26	
115 Sqn	Witchford	33	
138 Sqn	Tuddenham	22	
149 Sqn	Methwold	32	
186 Sqn	Stradishall	34	
195 Sqn	Wratting Common	35	
218 Sqn	Chedburgh	30	
514 Sqn	Waterbeach	39	
622 Sqn	Mildenhall	23	
G-H TF	Feltwell		
No 5 Gp			
9 Sqn	Bardney	19	
44 Sqn	Spilsby	22	
49 Sqn	Fulbeck	20	
50 Sqn	Skellingthorpe	23	
57 Sqn	East Kirkby	15	
61 Sqn	Skellingthorpe	22	
106 Sqn	Metheringham	21	
189 Sqn	Bardney	22	
207 Sqn	Spilsby	21	
227 Sqn	Strubby	21	
463 Sqn	Waddington	19	
467 Sqn	Waddington	21	
617 Sqn	Woodhall Spa	25	
619 Sqn	Strubby	21	
630 Sqn	East Kirkby	21	
5 LFS	Syerston		
No 6 Gp			
415 Sqn	East Moor	1	non-op
419 Sqn	Middleton St George	27	
420 Sqn	Tholthorpe	2	non-op
424 Sqn	Skipton on Swale	23	
427 Sqn	Leeming	21	
428 Sqn	Middleton St George	25	
429 Sqn	Leeming	23	
431 Sqn	Croft	25	
433 Sqn	Skipton on Swale	21	
434 Sqn	Croft	22	
No 7 (Training) Gp			
1656 CU	Lindholme		
1662 CU	Blyton/Sandtoft		
1667 CU	Sturgate		
1668 CU	Bottesford		
1669 CU	Langar		

1653 CU	North Luffenham		
1651 CU	Woolfox Lodge		
1660 CU	Swinderby		
1661 CU	Winthorpe		
1654 CU	Wigsley		
1659 CU	Topcliffe		
No 8 Gp			
7 Sqn	Oakington	21	
35 Sqn	Graveley	25	
83 Sqn	Coningsby	21	loan to 5 Gp
97 Sqn	Coningsby	23	loan to 5 Gp
156 Sqn	Upwood	21	
405 Sqn	Gransden Lodge	22	
582 Sqn	Little Staughton	22	
627 Sqn	Woodhall Spa	1	non-op
635 Sqn	Downham Market	20	
PFF NTU	Warboys		
1323 Flt	Warboys		

N.B. The April SD161 also states that 51 Sqn at Snaith (No 4 Gp) had Lancasters on UE.

The Bomber Command ORBAT for **1 July 1946** demonstrates the phenomenal run-down of units in the space on one year; units marked + are cadre only. Aircraft numbers are UE and not actual strength.

No 1 Gp (all have Lancaster I/III, the Group also has four Lincoln cadre sqns)

9 Sqn+	Binbrook	8	
12 Sqn+	Binbrook	8	
83 Sqn	Coningsby	16	
97 Sqn	Coningsby	16	
101 Sqn+	Binbrook	8	
300 Sqn	Faldingworth	16	not part of RAF
617 Sqn+	Binbrook	8	
No 3 Gp (most with Lancaster B.I (FE))			
7 Sqn+	Mepal	10	
15 Sqn+	Mildenhall	10	
35 Sqn	Graveley	16	
44 Sqn+	Mildenhall	10	
49 Sqn+	Mepal	10	
90 Sqn+	Tuddenham	8	
115 Sqn+	Graveley	10	
138 Sqn+	Tuddenham	8	
149 Sqn+	Tuddenham	8	
207 Sqn	Tuddenham	8	

The total declared Bomber Command strength was:

Lancaster B.I (FE)	7 sqns	72 aircraft UE
Lancaster I/III	10 sqns	106 aircraft UE

In addition the Command had four Lincoln and two Mosquito XVI squadrons (40 and 16 aircraft UE total), a total strength of only 234 aircraft!

APPENDIX VI

Lancaster Units

The major part of the Lancaster's career was with RAF Bomber Command, in particular from 1942 to 1945; in the immediate post war period the type was used by various other squadrons for maritime roles. The following list gives the basic details for each squadron. (Many thanks to Andy Thomas for providing much of the the information in this appendix.)

BOMBER COMMAND

No 7 Sqn

"Per diem per noctem" (By day and by night)

Marks:	I, III, I (FE)
Dates:	May 1943 - Jan 1950
Group:	8 (PFF) Gp
Bases:	Oakington; Mepal; Upwood
First Raid:	Jul 8/9, 1943 (Cologne)
Operational losses:	87
Unit Codes:	MG; XU ('C' Flt)
Previous type:	Stirling

No 9 Sqn

"Per noctum volamus" (Through the night we fly)

Marks:	I, III, VII
Dates:	Aug 1942 - Jul 1946
Group:	5 Gp
Bases:	Waddington, Bardney, Salbani (India), Binbrook
First Raid:	Sep 10/11, 1942 (Düsseldorf)
Operational Losses:	177
Unit Codes:	WS
Previous type:	Wellington
Victoria Cross	Flt Sgt G Thompson (air signaller) [posthumous]

No 12 Sqn

"Leads the field"

Marks:	I, III
Dates:	Nov 1942 - Jul 1946
Group:	1 Gp
Bases:	Wickenby, Binbrook
First Raid:	Dec 11/12, 1942 (Turin)
Operational losses:	111
Unit Codes:	PH; GZ ('C' Flt)
Previous type:	Wellington

No 15 Sqn

"Aim sure"

Marks:	I, I (Special), III
Dates:	Dec 1943 - Mar 1947
Group:	3 Gp
Bases:	Mildenhall, Wyton
First Raid:	Jan 15/16, 1944 (Brunswick)
Operational Losses:	45
Unit Codes:	LS; DJ ('C' Flt)
Previous type:	Stirling

No 35 Sqn

"Uno animo agimus" (We act with one accord)

Marks:	I, III
Dates:	Mar 1944 - Sep 1949
Group:	8 (PFF) Gp
Bases:	Graveley, Stradishall, Mildenhall
First Raid:	Mar 15/16, 1944 (Stuttgart)
Operational Losses:	27
Unit Codes:	TL
Previous type:	Halifax

No 44 (Rhodesia) Sqn

"Fulmina regis justa" (The King's thunderbolts are righteous)

Marks:	I, III
Dates:	Dec 1941 - Sep 1947
Group:	5 Gp
Bases:	Waddington, Dunholme Lodge, Spilsby, Mepal, Wyton
First Raid:	Mar 3/4, 1942 (minelaying)
Operational Losses:	149
Unit Codes:	KM
Victoria Cross:	Sqn Ldr J D Nettleton (pilot), Apr 17, 1942, Augsburg
Previous type:	Hampden

No 49 Sqn

"Cave canem" (Beware of the dog)

Marks:	I, III
Dates:	Jul 1942 - Mar 1950
Group:	5 Gp
Bases:	Scampton, Fiskerton, Syerston, Mepal, Upwood
First Raid:	Jul 31/Aug 1, 1942 (Düsseldorf)
Operational Losses:	102
Unit Codes:	EA
Previous type:	Manchester

No 50 Sqn

"From defence to attack"

Marks:	I, III
Dates:	May 1942 - Oct 1946
Group:	5 Gp

Bases: Skellingthorpe, Swinderby, Sturgate, Waddington
First Raid: May 30/31, 1942 (Cologne)
Operational Losses: 112
Unit Codes: VN
Previous type: Manchester

No 57 Sqn
"Corpus non animum muto" (I change my body not my spirit)
Marks: I, III
Dates: Sep 1942 - May 1946
Group: 5 Gp
Bases: Scampton, East Kirkby, Elsham Wolds
First Raid: Oct 12/13, 1942 (Wismar)
Operational Losses: 108
Unit Codes: DX, QT ('C' Flt)
Previous type: Wellington

No 61 Sqn
"Per purum tonantes" (Thundering through the clear sky)
Marks: I, II, III
Dates: Jun 1942 - May 1946
Group: 5 Gp
Bases: Syerston, Skellingthorpe, Coningsby, Sturgate, Waddington
First Raid: May 5/6, 1942 (Stuttgart)
Operational Losses: 116
Unit Codes: QR
Victoria Cross: Flt Lt W Reid (pilot), Dec 3/4, 1944, Dusseldorf
Previous type: Manchester

No 75 (New Zealand) Sqn
"Ake ake kia kaha" (For ever and be strong)
Marks: I, III
Dates: Mar 1944 - Oct 1945
Group: 3 Gp
Bases: Mepal, Spilsby
First Raid: Apr 9/10, 1944 (Villeneuve St Georges)
Operational Losses: 47
Unit Codes: AA, JN ('C' Flt)
Previous type: Stirling

No 83 Sqn
"Strike to defend"
Marks: I, III
Dates: Apr 1942 - Jul 1946
Group: 5 Gp, 8 (PFF) Gp
Bases: Scampton, Wyton, Coningsby
First Raid: Apr 28/29, 1942 (Trondheim)
Operational Losses: 91
Unit Codes: OL
Previous type: Manchester

No 90 Sqn
"Celer" (Swift)
Marks: I, III
Dates: May 1944 - Dec 1947
Group: 3 Gp
Bases: Tuddenham, Wyton
First Raid: Jun 11/12, 1944 (tactical targets)
Operational Losses: 25
Unit Codes: WP, XY ('C' Flt)
Previous type: Stirling

No 97 Sqn
"Achieve your aim"
Marks: I, III
Dates: Jan 1942 - Jul 1946
Group: 5 Gp, 8 (PFF) Gp
Bases: Coningsby, Woodhall Spa, Bourn
First Raid: Mar 20/21, 1942 (minelaying)
Operational Losses: 101
Unit Codes: OF
Previous type: Manchester

No 100 Sqn
"Sarang tebuan jangan dijolok" (Don't let anyone attack the hornet's nest)
Marks: I, III
Dates: Jan 1943 - May 1946
Group: 1 Gp
Bases: Grimsby, Elsham Wolds, Scampton
First Raid: Mar 4/5, 1943 (minelaying)
Operational Losses: 92
Unit Codes: HW, JA ('C' Flt), FZ ('C' Flt)
Previous type: reformed

No 101 Sqn
"Mens agitat molem" (Mind over matter)
Marks: I, III
Dates: Oct 1942 - Aug 1946
Group: 1 Gp
Bases: Holme on Spalding Moor, Ludford Magna, Binbrook
First Raid: Nov 20/21, 1942 (Turin)
Operational Losses: 113
Unit Codes: SR
Previous type: Wellington

No 103 Sqn
"Noli me tangere" (Touch me not)
Marks: I, III
Dates: Oct 1942 - Nov 1945
Group: 1 Gp
Bases: Elsham Wolds
First Raid: Nov 21/22, 1942 (minelaying)
Operational Losses: 135
Unit Codes: PM
Previous type: Halifax

No 106 Sqn
"Pro libertate" (For freedom)
Marks: I, III
Dates: May 1942 - Feb 1946
Group: 5 Gp
Bases: Coningsby, Syerston, Metheringham
First Raid: May 30/31, 1942 (Cologne)
Operational Losses: 105

Unit Codes: ZN
Victoria Cross: Sgt N C Jackson (air engineer), Apr 26/27, 1944, Schweinfurt
Previous type: Manchester

No 109 Sqn
"Primi hastati" (The first of the legion)
Marks: I
Dates: May - Oct 1942
Group: 8 (PFF) Gp
Base: Wyton
Note: Partial temporary equipment for a primarily Mosquito equipped unit
Victoria Cross: Sqn Ldr R A M Palmer DFC (pilot) [posthumous] (flying a Lancaster of 582 Sqn), Dec 23, 1944, Cologne.

No 115 Sqn
"Despite the elements"
Marks: I, II, III, I (FE)
Dates: Mar 1943 - Jan 1950
Group: 3 Gp
Bases: East Wretham, Little Snoring, Witchford, Graveley, Stradishall, Mildenhall
First Raid: Mar 20/21, 1943 (minelaying)
Operational Losses: 110
Unit Codes: KO, A2 ('C' Flt), IL ('C' Flt)
Previous type: Wellington

No 138 Sqn
"For Freedom"
Marks: I, III
Dates: Mar 1945 - Sep 1947
Group: 3 Gp
Bases: Tuddenham, Wyton
First Raid: Mar 29, 1945 (Salzgetter)
Operational Losses: 1
Unit Codes: AC, NF
Previous type: Stirling

No 148 Sqn
"Trusty"
Marks: I
Dates: Nov 1946 - Jan 1950
Group: 3 Gp
Base: Upwood
Furst Raid:
Unit Codes: AU
Previous type: Liberator

No 149 Sqn
"Fortis nocte" (Strong by night)
Marks: I, III
Dates: Aug 1944 - Nov 1949
Group: 3 Gp
Bases: Methwold, Tuddenham, Stradishall, Mildenhall
First Raid: Sep 17, 1944 (Boulogne)
Operational Losses: 4
Unit Codes: OJ, TK ('C' Flt)
Previous type: Stirling

No 150 Sqn
"Always ahead" (Greek script)
Marks: I, III
Dates: Nov 1944 - Nov 1945
Group: No 1
Bases: Fiskerton, Hemswell
First Raid: Nov 11/12, 1944 (Harburg)
Operational Losses: 6
Unit Codes: IQ
Previous type: Wellington

No 153 Sqn
"Noctivdus" (Seeing by night)
Marks: I, III
Dates: Oct 1944 - Sep 1945
Group: 1 Gp
Bases: Kirmington, Scampton
First Raid: Oct 7, 1944 (Emmerich)
Operational Losses: 22
Unit Codes: P4
Previous type: Hurricane

No 156 Sqn
"We light the way"
Marks: I, III
Dates: Jan 1943 - Sep 1945
Group: 8 (PFF) Gp
Bases: Upwood, Wyton
First Raid: Jan 26/27, 1943 (Lorient)
Operational Losses: 104
Unit Codes: GT
Previous type: Wellington

No 166 Sqn
"Tenacity"
Marks: I, III
Dates: Sep 1943 - Nov 1945
Group: 1 Gp
Base: Kirmington
First Raid: Sep 22/23, 1943
Operational Losses: 114
Unit Codes: AS
Previous type: Wellington

No 170 Sqn
"Vidre non videri" (To see and not to be seen)
Marks: I, III
Dates: Oct 1944 - Nov 1945
Group: 1 Gp
Bases: Kelstern, Dunholme Lodge, Hemswell
First Raid: Oct 19/20, 1944
Operational Losses: 13
Unit Codes: TL
Previous type: nil

No 186 Sqn
(no badge/motto)

Marks: I/III
Dates: Oct 1944 - Jul 1945
Group: 3 Gp
Bases: Tuddenham, Stradishall
First Raid: Oct 18, 1944 (Bonn)
Operational Losses: 8
Unit Codes: XY, AP ('C' Flt)
Previous type: nil

No 189 Sqn
(no badge/motto)
Marks: I, III
Dates: Oct 1944 - Nov 1945
Group: 5 Gp
Bases: Bardney, Fulbeck, Metheringham
First Raid: Nov 1, 1944 (Homburg)
Operational Losses: 16
Unit Codes: CA
Previous type: nil

No 195 Sqn
"Velocitate fortis" (Strong by speed)
Marks: I, III
Dates: Oct 1944 - Aug 1945
Group: 3 Gp
Bases: Witchford, Wratting Common
First Raid: Oct 26, 1944 (Leverkusen)
Operational Losses: 14
Unit Codes: A4, JE ('C' Flt)
Previous type: nil

No 207 Sqn
"Semper paratus" (Always prepared)
Marks: I, III, I (FE)
Dates: Mar 1942 - Aug 1949
Group: 5 Gp
Bases: Bottesford, Langar, Spilsby, Methwold, Tuddenham, Stradishall, Mildenhall
First Raid: Apr 24/25, 1942 (Rostock)
Operational Losses: 131
Unit Codes: EM
Previous type: Manchester

No 214 Sqn"Ulter in Umbris" (Avenging in the shadows)
Mark: B I (FE)
Dates: Nov 1945 - Apr 1946 & Nov 1946 - Feb 1950
Group: 3 Gp
Bases: Fayid (Egypt), Upwood
Unit Codes: QN
Previous type: Liberator

No 218 Sqn
"In time"
Marks: I, III
Dates: Aug 1944 - Aug 1945
Group: 3 Gp
Bases: Methwold, Chedburgh
First Raid: Sep 8, 1944 (Le Havre)
Operational Losses: 16
Unit Codes: HA, XH ('C' Flt)
Previous type: Stirling

No 227 Sqn
no badge/motto
Marks: I, III
Dates: Oct 1944 - Sep 1945
Group: 5 Gp
Bases: Bardney, Balderton, Strubby, Graveley
First Raid: Oct 11, 1944 (Walcheren)
Operational Losses: 15
Unit Codes: 9J
Previous type: Beaufighter

No 300 (Polish) Sqn
no motto
Marks: I, III
Dates: Apr 1944 - Oct 1945
Group: 1 Gp
Bases: Faldingworth
First Raid: Apr 18/19, 1944 (Rouen)
Operational Losses: 30
Unit Codes: BH
Previous type: Wellington

No 405 (Vancouver) Sqn RCAF
"Ducimus" (We lead)
Marks: I, III, X
Dates: Aug 1943 - Sep 1945
Group: 6 Gp, 8 (PFF) Gp
Bases: Gransden Lodge, Linton-on-Ouse, Greenwood (Canada)
First Raid: Aug 17/18, 1943 (Peenemünde)
Operational Losses: 50
Unit Codes: LQ
Previous type: Halifax

No 408 (Goose) Sqn RCAF
"For freedom"
Marks: II, X
Dates: Oct 1943 - Jul 1944 (Mk II) & May - Sep 1945 (Mk X)
Group: 6 Gp
Bases: Linton-on-Ouse, Greenwood (Canada)
First Raid: Oct 7/8, 1943 (Stuttgart) [Mk II]
Operational Losses: 41
Unit Codes: EQ
Previous type: Halifax

No 419 (Moose) Sqn RCAF
"Moose aswayita" (Beware of the moose)
Mark: X
Dates: Mar 1944 - Sep 1945
Group: 6 Gp
Bases: Middleton St George, Yarmouth (Canada)
First Raid: Apr 27/28, 1944 (Friedrichshafen)
Operational Losses: 39
Unit Codes: VR
Victoria Cross: Plt Off A C Mynarski RCAF (air gunner)

[posthumous], Jun 12, 1944, Cambrai.
Previous type: Halifax

No 420 (Snowy Owl) Sqn RCAF
"Pugnamus finitum" (We fight to a finish)
Mark: X
Dates: Apr - Sep 1945
Group: 6 Gp
Bases: Tholthorpe, Debert (Canada)
Operational Losses: nil - not used on operations
Unit Codes: PT
Previous type: Halifax

No 424 (Tiger) Sqn RCAF
"Castigandos castigamus" (We chastise those who deserve to be chastised)
Marks: I, III
Dates: Jan - Oct 1945
Group: 6 Gp
Bases: Skipton-on-Swale
First Raid: Feb 1/2, 1945 (Ludwigshafen)
Operational Losses: 5
Unit Codes: QB
Previous type: Halifax

No 425 (Alouette) Sqn RCAF
"Je te plumerai" (I shall pluck you)
Mark: X
Dates: May - Sep 1945
Group: 6 Gp
Bases: Tholthorpe, Debert (Canada)
Operational Losses: nil - not used on operations
Unit Codes: KW
Previous type: Halifax

No 426 (Thunderbird) Sqn RCAF
"On wings of fire"
Mark: II
Dates: Jun 1943 - May 1944
Group: 6 Gp
Base: Linton-on-Ouse
First Raid: Aug 17/18, 1943 (Peenemünde)
Operational Losses: 28
Unit Codes: OW
Previous type: Wellington

No 427 (Lion) Sqn RCAF
"Ferte manus certas" (Strike sure)
Marks: I, III
Dates: Feb 1945 - May 1946
Group: 6 Gp
Base: Leeming
First Raid: Mar 11, 1945 (Essen)
Operational Losses: nil
Unit Codes: ZL
Previous type: Halifax

No 428 (Ghost) Sqn RCAF
"Usque ad finem" (To the very end)
Mark: X
Dates: Jun 1944 - Sep 1945
Group: 6 Gp
Bases: Middleton St George, Yarmouth (Canada)
First Raid: Jul 7, 1944 (Normandy)
Operational Losses: 18
Unit Codes: NA
Previous type: Halifax

No 429 (Bison) Sqn RCAF
"Fortunae nihil" (Nothing to chance)
Marks: I, III
Dates: Mar 1945 - May 1946
Group: 6 Gp
Base: Leeming
First Raid: Apr 4/5, 1945 (Leuna)
Operational Losses: 1
Unit Codes: AL
Previous type: Halifax

No 431 (Iroquois) Sqn RCAF
"The hatiten ronteriios" (Warrior of the air)
Mark: X
Dates: Oct 1944 - Sep 1945
Group: 6 Gp
Bases: Croft, Dartmouth (Canada)
First Raid: Dec 17/18, 1944 (Duisberg)
Operational Losses: 11
Unit Codes: SE
Previous type: Halifax

No 432 (Leaside) Sqn RCAF
"Saeviter ad lucem" (Ferociously towards the light)
Mark: II
Dates: Oct 1943 - Feb 1944
Group: 6 Gp
Bases: Skipton-on-Swale, East Moor
First Raid: Nov 26/27, 1943 (Berlin)
Operational Losses: 8
Unit Codes: QO
Previous type: Wellington

No 433 (Porcupine) Sqn RCAF
"Qui s'y frotte s'y pique" (Who opposes it gets hurt)
Marks: I, III
Dates: Jan - Oct 1945
Group: 6 Gp
Base: Skipton-on-Swale
First Raid: Feb 1/2, 1945 (Ludwigshafen)
Operational Losses: 3
Unit Codes: BM
Previous type: Halifax

No 434 (Bluenose) Sqn RCAF
"In exelsis vincimus" (We conquer the heights)
Marks: I, III, X
Dates: Dec 1944 - Sep 1945
Group: 6 Gp
Bases: Croft, Dartmouth (Canada)

First Raid: Jan 2/3, 1945 (Nuremberg)
Operational Losses: 5
Unit Codes: WL
Previous type: Halifax

No 460 Sqn RAAF
"Strike and return"
Marks: I, III
Dates: Oct 1942 - Oct 1945
Group: 1 Gp
Bases: Breighton, Binbrook, East Kirkby
First Raid: Nov 22/23, 1942 (Stuttgart)
Operational Losses: 140
Unit Codes: UV, AR
Previous type: Halifax

No 463 Sqn RAAF
"Press on regardless"
Marks: I, III
Dates: Nov 1943 - Sep 1945
Group: 5 Gp
Bases: Waddington, Skellingthorpe
First Raid: Nov 26/27, 1943 (Berlin)
Operational Losses: 69
Unit Codes: JO
Previous type: nil

No 467 Sqn RAAF
"Recidite adversarius atque ferocitea" (To rain down with hostility and ferocity)
Marks: I, III
Dates: Nov 1942 - Sep 1945
Group: 5 Gp
Bases: Scampton, Bottesford, Waddington, Metheringham
First Raid: Jan 2/3, 1943 (minelaying)
Operational Losses: 104
Unit Codes: PO
Previous type: nil

No 514 Sqn
"Nil obstare potest" (Nothing can withstand)
Marks: I, II, III
Dates: Sep 1943 - Aug 1945
Group: 3 Gp
Bases: Foulsham, Waterbeach
First Raid: Sep 3/4, 1943 (Düsseldorf)
Operational Losses: 66
Unit Codes: JI, A2 ('C' Flt)
Previous type: nil

No 550 Sqn
"Per ignem vincimus" (Through fire we conquer)
Marks: I, III
Dates: Oct 1943 - Oct 1945
Group: 1 Gp
Bases: Waltham, North Killingholme
First Raid: Nov 26/27, 1943
Operational Losses: 59
Unit Codes: BQ
Previous type: nil

No 576 Sqn
"Carpe diem" (Seize the opportunity)
Marks: I, III
Dates: Nov 1943 - Sep 1945
Group: 1 Gp
Bases: Elsham Wolds, Fiskerton
First Raid: Nov 26/27, 1943 (Berlin)
Operational Losses: 66
Unit Codes: UL
Previous type: nil

No 582 Sqn
"Praecolamus designantes" (We fly before marking)
Marks: I, III
Dates: Apr 1944 - Sep 1945
Group: 8 (PFF) Gp
Base: Little Staughton
First Raid: Apr 9/10, 1944 (Lille)
Operational Losses: 28
Unit Codes: 60 (as in letter)
Victoria Cross: Capt E E Swales DFC SAAF (pilot) [posthumous], Feb 23, 1945, Pforzheim.
Previous type: nil

No 617 Sqn
"Apres moi le deluge" (After me the flood)
Marks: I, I (Special), III, VII
Dates: Mar 1943 - Sep 1946
Group: 5 Gp
Bases: Scampton, Coningsby, Woodhall Spa, Waddington, Digri (India), Binbrook
First Raid: May 16/17, 1943 (Mohne, Eder & Sorpe Dams)
Operational Losses: 32
Unit Codes: AJ, KC, YZ (Mk I [Specials])
Victoria Crosses: Wg Cdr G P Gibson DSO, DFC (pilot), May 16/17, 1943, Dams raid.
Wg Cdr G L Cheshire DSO, DFC (pilot), Sep 9, 1944.
Previous type: nil

No 619 Sqn
no badge or motto
Marks: I, III
Dates: Apr 1943 - Jul 1945
Group: 5 Gp
Bases: Woodhall Spa, Coningsby, Dunholme Lodge, Strubby, Skellingthorpe
First Raid: Jun 11/12, 1943 (Düsseldorf)
Operational Losses: 77
Unit Codes: PG
Previous type: nil

No 622 Sqn
"Bellamus noctu" (We make war by night)
Marks: I, III

Dates: Dec 1943 - Aug 1945
Group: 3 Gp
Bases: Mildenhall
First Raid: Jan 14/15, 1944
Operational Losses: 44
Unit Codes: GI
Previous type: Stirling

No 625 Sqn
"We avenge"
Marks: I, III
Dates: Oct 1943 - Oct 1945
Group: 1 Gp
Bases: Kelstern, Scampton
First Raid: Oct 18/19, 1945
Operational Losses: 66
Unit Codes: CF
Previous type: nil

No 626 Sqn
"To strive and not to yield"
Marks: I, III
Dates: Nov 43-Oct 45
Group: No 1 Gp
Bases: Wickenby
First Raid:
First op loss:
Operational Losses:
Unit codes: UM
Previous type: nil

No 630 Sqn
"Nocturna mors" (Death by night)
Marks: I, III
Dates: Nov 1943 - Jul 1945
Group: 5 Gp
Base: East Kirkby
First Raid: Nov 18/19, 1943 (Berlin)
Operational Losses: 59
Unit Codes: LE
Previous type: nil

No 635 Sqn
"Nos ducimus ceteri secunter" (We lead others follow)
Marks: I, III, VI
Dates: Mar 1944 - Sep 1945
Group: 8 (PFF) Gp
Base: Downham Market
First Raid: Mar 22/23, 1944 (Frankfurt)
Operational Losses: 34
Unit Codes: F2
Victoria Cross: Sqn Ldr I W Bazalgette DFC (pilot) [posthumous], Aug 4, 1944, Trossy St Maxim.
Previous type: nil
Coastal Command and Overseas units

No 18 Sqn
"Animo et fide" (With courage and faith)
Marks: GR 3
Dates: Sep 1946 only
Command/Area: Middle East
Role: Maritime Reconnaissance
Base: Ein Shemer (Palestine)
Unit Codes: none
Previous type: Boston

No 37 Sqn
"Wise without eyes"
Marks: III; VII; GR 3
Dates: Apr 1946 - Aug 1953
Command/Area: Mediterranean, Middle East
Role: Maritime Reconnaissance
Bases: Fayid (Egypt), Shallufa (Egypt), Ein Shemer (Palestine), Luqa (Malta)
Unit Codes: none
Previous type: Liberator

No 38 Sqn
"Ante lucem" (Before the dawn)
Marks: ASR 3, GR 3
Dates: Jul 1946 - Dec 1953
Command/Area: Mediterranean, Middle East
Role: Maritime Reconnaissance
Bases: Luqa (Malta), Ein Shemer (Palestine), Shallufa (Egypt), Ramat David (Palestine)
Unit Codes: RL
Previous type: Warwick

No 40 Sqn
"Hostem coelo expellere" (To drive the enemy from the sky)
Mark: B VII
Dates: Jan 1946 - Apr 1947
Command/Area: Middle East
Role: Heavy bomber
Bases: Abu Sueir (Egypt), Shallufa (Egypt)
Unit Codes: BL
Previous type: Liberator

No 70 Sqn
"Usquam" (Anywhere)
Mark: I
Dates: Apr 1946 - Apr 1947
Command/Area: Middle East
Role: Heavy Bomber
Bases: Fayid (Egypt), Kabrit (Egypt), Shallufa (Egypt)
Unit Codes: none
Previous type: Liberator

No 82 Sqn
"Super omnia ubique" (Over all things everywhere)
Mark: PR 1

Dates: Oct 1946 - Dec 1953
Command/Area: Bomber
Role: Photo-survey
Bases: Benson, Leuchars, Eastleigh (Kenya), Takoradi (Gold Coast), Wyton
Unit Code: none

Previous type: Mosquito

No 104 Sqn
"Strike hard"
Mark: B VII
Dates: Nov 1945 - Apr 1947
Command/Area: Middle East
Role: Heavy Bomber
Bases: Abu Sueir (Egypt), Shallufa (Egypt)
Previous type: Liberator

No 120 Sqn
"Endurance"
Mark: GR 3
Dates: Nov 1946 - Apr 1951
Command/Area: Coastal
Role: Maritime Reconnaissance
Bases: Leuchars, Kinloss
Unit Codes: BS
Previous type: Liberator

No 160 Sqn
"Api soya paragasamu" (We seek and strike)
Mark: GR III
Dates: Aug - Sep 1946
Command/Area: Coastal
Role: Maritime Reconnaissance
Base: Leuchars
Unit Codes: BS
Previous type: Liberator

No 178 Sqn
"Irae emissarii" (Emissaries of wrath)
Mark: III
Dates: Nov 1945 - Apr 1946
Command/Area: Middle East
Role: Heavy Bomber
Base: Fayid (Egypt)
Unit Codes: nil
Previous type: Liberator

No 179 Sqn
"Delentem deleo" (I destroy the destroyer)
Mark: ASR III
Dates: Feb - Sep 1946
Command/Area: Coastal:
Role: Maritime Reconnaissance
Base: St Eval
Unit Codes: OZ
Previous type: Warwick

No 203 Sqn
"Occidens oriensque" (West and East)
Marks: GR 3, ASR 3
Dates: Aug 1946 - Mar 1953
Command/Area: Coastal
Role: Maritime Reconnaissance
Bases: Leuchars, St Eval, St Mawgan, Topcliffe
Unit Codes: CJ
Previous type: Liberator

No 210 Sqn
"Yn y nwyfre yn hedfan" (Hovering in the heavens)
Marks: GR 3, ASR 3
Dates: Jun 1946 - Oct 1952
Command/Area: Coastal
Role: Maritime Reconnaissance
Bases: St Eval, St Mawgan, Topcliffe
Unit Codes: OZ
Previous type: nil

No 224 Sqn
"Fedele all'amico" (Faithful to a friend)
Marks: GR 3
Dates: Oct 1946 - Nov 1947
Command/Area: Coastal
Role: Maritime Reconnaissance
Base: St Eval
Unit Codes: XB
Previous type: Liberator

No 231 Sqn
no badge/motto
Mark: III
Dates: Dec 1945 - Jan 1946
Command/Area: Transport
Role: Transport
Base: Full Sutton
Unit Codes: nil
Previous type: various

No 279 Sqn
"To see and be seen"
Mark: ASR III
Dates: Sep 1945 - Mar 1946
Command/Area: Coastal
Role: Air-Sea Rescue
Base: Beccles
Unit Codes: RL
Previous type: various

No 541 Sqn
"Alone above all"
Mark: PR 1
Dates: Jun - Sep 1946
Command/Area: Bomber
Role: Photo-survey
Base: Benson
Unit Codes: nil on Lancasters
Previous type: nil

No 621 Sqn
"Ever ready to strike"
Mark: ASR III
Dates: Apr - Sep 1946
Command/Area: Middle East
Role: Maritime Reconnaissance
Bases: Aqir (Palestine), Ein Shemer (Palestine)
Unit Codes: nil
Previous type: Warwick

No 683 Sqn
"Nihil nos later" (Nothing remains concealed)

Mark:	PR 1
Dates:	Nov 1950 - Nov 1953
Command/Area:	Middle East
Role:	Photo-survey
Bases:	Fayid (Egypt), Kabrit (Egypt), Eastleigh (Kenya), Khormaksar (Aden), Habbaniya (Iraq)
Unit Codes:	nil
Previous type:	nil

POST WAR RCAF

No 404 Sqn

Mark	10MR
Dates:	Apr 1951 - Sep 1955
Base:	Greenwood (Nova Scotia)
Role:	Maritime Patrol
Unit Codes:	AF, SP

No 405 Sqn

Mark:	10MR
Dates:	Apr 1950 - Nov 1955
Base:	Greenwood (Nova Scotia)
Role:	Maritime Patrol
Unit Codes:	AG

No 407 Sqn

Mark:	10MR
Dates:	Jul 1952 - May 1959
Base:	Comox (British Columbia)
Role:	Maritime Patrol
Unit Codes:	RX

No 408 Sqn

Mark:	10P
Dates:	Jan 1949 - Mar 1964
Base:	Rockcliffe (Ontario)
Role:	Photo-survey
Unit Codes:	AK, MN

No 413 Sqn

Mark:	10P
Dates:	Jan - Apr 1949
Base:	Rockcliffe (Ontario)
Role:	Photo-survey
Unit Codes:	AP

MISCELLANEOUS RAF UNITS

Lancaster Finishing Schools:

No 1 LFS	Dec 43-Jul 45	Lindholme, Hemswell
Code 3C		
No 3 LFS	Nov 43-Jan 45	Feltwell
Code AS		
No 5 LFS	Nov 43-Mar 45	Syerston
Code RC, CE		
No 6 LFS	Dec 44-Nov 45	

HEAVY CONVERSION UNITS (HCU)

1651	Dec 44-Jul 45	Woolfox Lodge
Code BS, QQ		
1653	Nov 44-Feb 48	Nth Luffenham,
Lindholme		
Code A3		
1654	Jan-Aug 45	Swinderby, Wigsley
Code UG, JF		
1656	Nov 42-Nov 43,	Lindholme
Code EK	Nov 44-Nov 45	
1657	Nov 44-Dec 44	Stradishall
Code AK		
1659	Nov 44-Sep 45	Topcliffe
Code FD, RV		
1660	Oct 42-Nov 43	Swinderby
Code TV, YW	Jan 45-Nov 46	
1661	Jan 43-Nov 43	Winthorpe
Code GP, KB	Dec 44-Aug 45	
1662	Feb 43-Nov 43	Blyton
Code KF, PE		
1664	May 43-Apr 45	Croft
Code DH, ZU		
1666	Dec 44-Aug 45	Wombleton
Code ND, OY		
1667	Jul 43-Nov 43	Lindholme, Sandtoft
Code GG	Nov 44-Nov 45	Faldingworth
Code LR		
1668	Aug 43-Nov 43	Balderton, Bottesford
Code J9, ZK, QY	Jul 44-Mar 46	
1669	Nov 44-Mar 45	Langar, Full Sutton
Code JP, 2K	Jan 46-Apr 46	
1678	May 43-Jun 44	Little Snoring, East Wretham, Foulsham, Waterbeach, Code SW
1679	May 43-Jan 44	East Moor, Wombleton

OPERATIONAL CONVERSION UNITS (OCU)

230 OCU	Mar 47-Feb 55	Lindholme, Code A3
236 OCU	Jul 47-?	Kinloss
	Code K7	

OTHER UNITS

1323 AGLT Flight
1348 (ASR) Flight
1384 Flight
1577 (SD) Flight
1689 Flight
6 (C) OTU (became 236 OCU)
1 Ferry Unit
16 Ferry Unit
Airborne Forces Experimental Establishment (AFEE)
Aircraft & Armament Experimental Establishment (A&AEE)
Air Photography Development Unit (APDU)
Anti-Submarine Warfare Development Unit (ASWDU)
Blind Landing Experimental Unit (BLEU)
Bomber Command Instrcutors School (BCIS)
Bomber Command Film Unit (BCFU)
Bomber Development Unit (BDU)
Central Bomber Establishment (CBE)
Central Gunnery School (CGS)
Central Navigation School (CNS)
Central Signals Establishment (CSE)
Central Photographic Establishment (CPE)
Empire Air Armament School (EAAS)
Empire Air Navigation School (EANS)
Empire Central Flying School (ECFS)
Empire Test Pilots School (ETPS)
Gee-H Training Flight (GHTF)
Joint Anti-Submarine Scholl (JASS)
National Gas Turbine Establishment (NGTE)
Pathfinder Force Navigation Training Unit (PFF NTU)
Radar warfare Establishment (RWE)
Royal Aircraft Establishment (RAE)
RAF College
School of Maritime Reconnaissance
Transport Command Development Unit (TCDU)
Telecommunications Flying Unit (TFU)
Torpedo Development Unit (TDU)

MISCELLANEOUS RCAF UNITS:

No 2 (M) OTU - Mk 10MR for maritime training. **Code XV**.

No 107 Rescue Unit (RU) - Mk 10ASR for air sea rescue duties. **Code CX.**

No 121 Composite Unit (KU) - Mk 10ASR for transport & rescue duties. **Code QT**.

No 123 Rescue Flight - Mk 10ASR for air sea rescue duties. **Code CJ**.

Central Flying School (CFS) - Mk 10T for multi-engine training. **Code GS**.

Central Experimental & Proving Establishment (CEPE) - Mk 10 for trials and evaluation duties. **Code PX**.

APPENDIX VII

Lancaster Ops

The following list gives details of Lancaster operations. The first column gives date, the second shows total number of bombers and the third shows number of Lancasters. The fourth column gives target details (g= gardening/minelaying, v= V-weapon targets, loc = lines of communication), the final column shows Lancaster losses – this does not include aircraft which crashed in the UK.

1942				
3/4.3		4	g	
10/11.3	126	2	Essen	
20.36		g		
24/25.3	35		g	
25/26.3	254	7	Essen	
8/9.4	272	7	Hamburg	
10/11.4	254	8	Essen	
17.4	12	12	Augsburg	7
23/24.4	161	1	Rostock	
(3 further raids on Rostock but no details)				
27/28.4	43	12	Tirpitz	1
28/29.4	34	11	Tirpitz	
4/5.5	121	14	Stuttgart	
5/6,5	77	4	Stuttgart	
6/7.5	97	10	Stuttgart	
8/9.5	193	21	Warnemunde	4
16/17.5	14	7	g	
19/20.5	197	13	Mannheim	
26/27.5	4	4	g	
29/30.5	77	14	Paris/Gennevilliers	
30/31.5	1047	73	Cologne	1
1/2.6	956	74	Essen	4
2/3.6	195	27	Essen	2
3/4.6	170		Bremen	2
5/6.6	180	13	Essen	1
6/7.6	233	20	Emden	
8/9.6	170	13	Essen	3
16/17.6	106	15	Essen	
19/20.6	194	9	Emden	
20/21.6	185		Emden	1
22/23.6	227	11	Emden	1
25/26.6	960	96	Bremen	
27/28.6	144	24	Bremen	2
28/29.6	4		g	
29/30.6	253	64	Bremen	
2/3.7	325	53	Bremen	
3 /4 .7	6		g	2
8/9.7	258	52	Wilhelmshaven	1
11.7	44	44	Danzig	2
13/14.7	194	13	Duisburg	1
18.7	10	10	Essen	
19/20.7	99	28	Vegsack	
21/22.7	291	29	Duisburg	
23/24.7	215	45	Duisburg	2
25/26.7	313	33	Duisburg	2
26/27.7	403	77	Hamburg	2
29/30.7	291		Saarbrucken	2
31/1.8	630	113	Dusseldorf	2
3 /4.8	8	8	g	
4/5.8	38		Essen	1
5/6.8	50		Ruhr	1
8/9.8	12	12	g	
9/10.8	192	42	Osnabruck	
10/11.8	52		g	
11/12.8	154	33	Mainz	1
Leaflet				
?			Le Havre	1
12/13.8	138		Mainz	2
15/16.8	131		Dusseldorf	2
17/18.8	139		Osnabruck	1
?18/19.8	118		Flensburg	
24/25.8	226	61	Frankfurt	6
27/28.8	306		Kassel	3
Gdynia				
28/29.8	159	71	Nuremburg	4
31/.9	5	5	g	
1 /2.9	231		Saarbrucken	1
2/3.9	200		Karlsruche	2
4/5.9	251	76	Bremen	3
? 6/7.9	207		Duisburg	
8/9.9	249		Frankfurt	
10/11.9	479	89	Dusseldorf	5
13/14.9	446		Bremen	2
14/15.9	202		Wilhelmshaven	
16/17.9	369		Essen	9
18/19.9	115		g	2
19/20.9	89	68	Munich	3
23/24.9	83	83	Wismar	2
24/25.9	51		g	1
29/30.9	14	14	g	1
1 /2.10	78	78	Wismar	2
2/3.10	188	31	Krefeld	1
5/6.10	257	74	Aachen	1
6/7.10	237	68	Osnabruck	2
12/13.10	59	59	Wismar	2
13/14.10	288	82	Kiel	1
15/16.10	289	62	Cologne	5
17.10	94	94	Le Creusot	1

22/23.10	112	112	Genoa	
24.10	88	88	Milan	3
6.11	19	5	Var.	
6/7.11	72	72	Genoa	2
7/8.11	175	85	Genoa	1
9/10.11	213	72	Hamburg	5
13/14.11	76	67	Genoa	
15/16.11	78	27	Genoa	
18/19.11			Turin	
20/21.11	232	86	Turin	
22/23.11	222	97	Stuttgart	5
25.11	11	5	Var.	1
27/28.11	32		Stettin	
28/29.11	228	117	Turin	
29/30.11	36	7	Turin	
2/3.12	112	27	Frankfurt	1
6/7.12	272	101	Mannheim	1
	14		g	
8/9.12	133	108	Turin	1
	80		g	1
9/10.12	227	115	Turin	1
11/12.12	82	20	Turin	
14/15.12	68	23	g	
17/18.12	104	27	Var.	1
20/21.12	232	111	Duisburg	6
21/22.12	137	119	Munich	8
31/1.1	10	8	Dusseldorf	1
(Oboe trial)				
1943				
2/3.1	42	18	g	
3 /4.1	22	19	Essen	3
	45	6	g	
4/5.1	33	29	Essen	2
7/8.1	22	19	Essen	
8/9.1	42	38	Duisburg	3
	73		g	2
9/10.1	52	50	Essen	3
11/12.1	76	72	Essen	1
12/13.1	59	55	Essen	1
13/14.1	69	66	Essen	4
14/15.1	122	6	Lorient	
15/16.1	157	4	Lorient	
16/17.1	201	190	Berlin	1
17/18.1	187	170	Berlin	19
21/22.1	82	79	Essen	4
23/24.1	121	8	Lorient	
	83	80	Dusseldorf	2
26/27.1	157	11	Lorient	1
27/28.1	162	124	Dusseldorf	3
30/31.1	148	135	Hamburg	5
2 /3.2	161	116	Cologne	3
3 /4.2	263	62	Hamburg	1
4/5.2	188	77	Turin	3
	4	4	La Spezia	
	128	9	Lorient	
7/8.2	323	80	Lorient	3
8/9.2	6	6	g	
11/12.2	177	129	Wilhelmshaven	3

13/14.2	466	164	Lorient	2
14/15.2	142	142	Milan	2
	4	4	La Spezia	
16/17.2	377	131	Lorient	1
18/19.2	195	127	Wilhelmhaven	4
19/20.2	338	52	Wilhelmshaven	4
21/22.2	143	130	Bremen	
24/25.2	115	8	Wilhelmshaven	
25/26.2	337	169	Nuremberg	6
26/27.2	427	145	Cologne	3
28/1.3	437	152	St. Nazaire	2
1/2.3	302	156	Berlin	7
3/4.3	417	149	Hamburg	4
5/6.3				
8/9.3	335	170	Nuremberg	2
9/10.3	264	142	Munich	5
10/11.3	37	20	g	2
11/12.3	314	152	Stuttgart	2
	14	3	g	
12/13.3	457	156	Essen	8
13/14.3	68	17	g	1
20/21.3	16	4	g	
22/23.3	357	189	St Nazaire	1
26/27.3	455	157	Duisburg	1
27/28.3	396	191	Berlin	3
28/29.3	323	50	St Nazaire	1
19/30.3	329	162	Berlin	11
2 /3.4	102		St Nazaire /Lorient	1
	33		g	1
3 /4.4	348	225	Essen	9
4/5.4	577	203	Kiel	5
8/9.4	392	156	Duisburg	6
9/10.4	109	104	Dusiburg	8
10/11.4	502	136	Frankfurt	5
13/14.4	211	208	La Spezia	4
			g	
14/15.4	462	98	Stuttgart	3
16/17.4	327	197	Pilsen	18
18/19.4	178	173	La Spezia	1
			v g	
20/21.4	339	194	Stettin	13
22/23.4	32		g	1
26/27.4	561	215	Duisburg	3
27/28.4	160	46	g	1
28/29.4	207	68	g	7
30/1.5	305	190	Essen	6
4/5.5	596	255	Dortmund	6
12/13.5	572	238	Duisburg	10
13/14.5	442	98	Bochum	1
	168	156	Pilsen	9?
16/17.5	19	19	Dams Raid	8
18/19.5	17	13	g	
21/22.5	104	4	g	
23/24.5	826	343	Dortmund	8
25/26.5	759	323	Dusseldorf	9
27/28.5	518	274	Essen	6
29/30.5	719	292	Wuppertal	7
11/12.6	783	326	Dusseldorf	14
	72	29	Munster	

12/13.6	503	323	Bochum	14
14/15.6	203	197	Oberhausen	17
16/17.6 212	202		Cologne	14
19/20.6	316	28	Le Creusot	1
			/ Montchanin	
20/21.6	60	60	Friedrichshafen	
21/22.6	705	262	Krefeld	9
22/23.6	557	242	Mulheim	8
23/24.6	52	52	La Spezia	
24/45.6	630	251	Wuppertal	8
25/26.6	473	214	Gelsenkirchen	13
27/28.6	30	15	g	1
28/29.6	608	267	Cologne	8
1 /2.7	12	12	g	
3 /4.7	653	293	Cologne	8
6/7.7	43		g	1
8/9.7	288	282	Cologne	7
9/10.7	418	218	Gelsenkirchen	5
12/13.7	295	295	Turin	13
	374	18	Aachen	2
15/16.7	24	24	N.Itlay	2
16/17.7	18	18	N.Italy	1
24/25.7	791	347	Hamburg	4
25/26.7	705	294	Essen	5
27/28.7	787	353	Hamburg	11
29/30.7	777	340	Hamburg	9
			leaflets, Italy	
30/31.7	273	82	Remscheid	2
2 /3.8	740	329	Hamburg	13
7/8.8	197	197	N.Itlay	
9/10.8	457	286	Mannheim	3
10/11.8	653	318	Nuremberg	6
12/13.8	504	321	Milan	1
	152	6	Turin	
14/15.8	140	140	Milan	1
15/16.8	199	199	v	7
16/17.8	154	14	v	1
17/18.8	596	324	Peenemunde	23
22/23.8	462	257	Leverkusen	3
23/24.8	727	335	Berlin	17
27/28.8	674	349	Nuremberg	11
30/31.8	660	297	Monchengladbach	7
31/1.9	622	331	Berlin	16
2 /3.9	41	5	Foret de Mormal	
3 /4.9	320	316	Berlin	22
5/6.9	605	299	Mannheim	13
6/7.9	404	257	Munich	3
14/15.9	8	8	Dortmund-Ems	1
15/16.9	369	40	Montlucon	
	8	8	D-Ems	5
16/17.9	340	43	Modane	
	12	12	Antheor	1
22/23.9	711	322	Hannover	7
	29	21	Oldenburg	
23/24.9	628	312	Mannheim	18
	29	21	Darmstalt	
27/28.9	678	312	Hannover	10
	29	21	Brumswick	1
29/30.9	352	213	Bochum	4

	14	14	g	
1 /2.10	251	243	Hagen	2
2 /3.10	296	294	Munich	8
3 /4.10	547	204	Rassel	4
4 /5.10	406	162	Frankfurt	3
	66	66	Ludwigshafen	
7/8.10	343	343	Stuttgart	4
	16	16	Frierichshafen	
8/9.10	504	282	Hannover	14
	119	7	Bremen	
18/19.10	360	360	Hannover	18
20/21.10	358	358	Leipzig	16
22/23.10	569	322	Kassel	78
	36	28	Frankfurt	1
3 /4.11	589	344	Dusseldorf	11
	62	52	Cologne	
10/11.11	313	313	Modane	
11/12.11	134	10	Cannes	
	10	10	Antheor	
17/18.11	83	66	Ludwigshafen	1
18/19.11	444	440	Berlin	9
	395	33	Mannheim	2
22/23.11	764	469	Berlin	11
23/24.11	383	365	Berlin	20
25/26.11	262	26	Frankfurt	1
26/27.11	450	443	Berlin	28
	178	21	Stuttgart	
2 /3.12	458	425	Berlin	37
3 /4.12	527	307	Leipzig	9
16/17.12	493	483	Berlin	25
	47	9	v	
20/21.12	650	390	Frankfurt	14
	54	44	Mannheim	
22/23.12	51	11	v	
23/24.12	379	364	Berlin	16
29/30.12	712	457	v	11
30/31.12	16	10	v	
1944				
1/ 2.1	421	421	Berlin	28
2 /3.1	383	362	Berlin	27
4 /5.1	80	11	v	
5/6.1	358	348	Steltt	14
	6	6	g	
14/15.1	498	496	Brunswick	38
20/21.1	769	495	Berlin	13
21/22.1	648	421	Magdeburg	22
	34	22	Berlin	1
	111	12	v	
25/26.1	76	12	v	
27/28.1	530	515	Berlin	33
28/29.1	677	432	Berlin	20
30/31.1	534	440	Berlin	32
8/9.2	12	12	Limoges	
12/13.2	10	10	Antheor	
15/16.2	891	561	Berlin	26
	24	24	Frankfurt	
19/20.2	823	561	Leipzig	44
20/21.2	598	460	Stuttgart	7

24/25.2	734	554	Schweinfurt	26
25/26.2	594	461	Augsburg	16
1 /2.3	557	415	Stuttgart	3
7/8.3	304	56	Le Mans	
9/10.3	44	44	Marignane	
10/11.3	102	102	France	1
15/16.3	863	617	Stuttgart	26
	22	22	Woippy	
16/17.3	21	21	Clermont-Ferrand	
18/19.3	846	620	Frankfurt	10
	19	19	Bergerac	
20/21.3	20	20	Angouleme	
22/23.3	816	620	Frankfurt	26
23/24.3	20	20	Lyons	
24/25.3	811	577	Berlin	44
25/26.3	192	47	Aulnoye	
	22	22	Lyons	
26/27.3	705	476	Essen	6
9/30.3	19	19	Lyons	
30/31.3	795	572	Nuremberg	64
5/6.4	145	144	Toulouse	1
9/10.4	239	40	Lille	1
	225	166	Villeneuve-St-Georges	
	103	103	g	9
10/11.4	180	180	Tours	1
	163	148	Laon	1
	147	132	Aulnoye	7
11/12.4	352	341	Aachen	9
18/19.4	289	273	Rouen	
	206	202	Juvisy	1
	181	61	Noisy-le-See	
	171	24	Tergnier	
	168	36	g	
20/21.4	379	357	Cologne	4
	269	247	La Chapelle	6
	196	14	Ottignies	
	175	14	Lens	
22/23.4	596	323	Dusseldorf	13
	255	238	Brunswick	2?
	181	52	Laon	4
23/24.4	114	14	g	
24/25.4	637	369	Karlsruhe	11
	260	244	Munich	9
	6	6	Milan	
26/27.4	493	342	Essen	6
	226	215	Schweinfurt	21
	217	20	Villeneuve-St-Georges	
27/28.4	323	322	Friedrichshafen	18
	223	16	Montzen	1
28/29.4	92	88	St-medard-en-Jalles	
	55	51	Oslo	
29/30.4	73	68	St-Medard	
	59	54	Clermont-Ferrand	
30/1.5	143	20	Somain	
	128	13	Acheres	
	116	116	Maintenon	
1 /2.5	139	131	Toulouse	
	137	40	St-Ghislain	1
	132	14	Malines	
	120	96	Chambly	3
	75	75	Lyons	
	50	46	Tours	
3/ 4.5	362	346	Mailly-le-Camp	42
	92	84	Montdidier	4
6/7.5	149	64	Mantes-la-Jolie	2
	68	64	Sable-sur-Sarthe	
	52	52	Aubigne	1
7/8.5	99	93	Nantes	1
	62	58	Salbis	7
	61	53	Tours	1
	55	55	Rennes	
8/9.5	123	53	Haine-st-Pierre	3
	64	58	Brest	1
	38	30	Cap Griz Nez	
9/10.5	414	180	Coastal Batteries	1
	64	56	Gennevilliers	5
	43	39	Annecy	
10/11.5	506	291	Railway	1
11/12.5	201	190	Bourg-Leopold	5
	135	47	Boulogne	
	132	126	Hasselt	5
	110	105	Louvain	4
12/13.5	120	20	Louvain	2
	111	7	Hasselt	1
15/16.5	?	g		3
19/20.5	143	32	Boulogne	
	122	118	Orleans	1
	121	112	Amiens	1
	117	113	Tours	
	116	112	Le Mans	3
	63	15	Merville	
	44	39	Mont Couple	1
21/22.5	523	510	Duisburg	29
	107	70	g	3
22/23.5	375	361	Dortmund	18
	235	225	Brunswick	13
22/23.5	133	13	Le Mans	
	128	12	Orleans	
24/25.5	442	264	Aachen	7
	63	59	Eindhoven	
	224	102	Coastal Batteries	
	51	44	Antwerp	
27/28.5	331	56	Bourg-Leopold	
	170	162	Aachen	12
	104	100	Nantes	1
	83	78	Rennes	
	272	208	Coastal Batteries	1
28/29.5	126	118	Angers	1
	201	181	Coatsal Batteries	1
30/31.5	54	50	Boulogne Coastal Batts	
31/1.6	219	125	Trappes	4
	129	16	Au Fevre	
	115	60	Mont Couple	
	115	111	Tergnier	2
	86	82	Saumur	
	68	68	Maisy	
1 /2.6	58	58	Saumur	
2/3.6	128	19	Trappes	1

	107	103	Berneval	
	271	136	Coastal Batteries	1
3 /4.6	100	96	Ferme Díurville	
	135	127	Coastal Batteries	1
4/5.6	259	125	Coastal Batteries	
			g	
5/6.6	1012	551	Coastal Batteries	1
	110	24	RCM	1
	58	?	Spec ops	
6/7.6	1065	589	LoC	10
7/8.6	337	122	LoC	17
	122	112	Foret de Cerisy	2
8/9.6	483	286	Loc (1st Tallboy)	3
9/10.6	401	206	Airfields	
	112	108	Etampes	6
10/11.6	432	323	Rail	15
11/12.6	329	225	Rail	3
12/13.6	671	285	LoC	6
	303	286	Gelsenkirchen	
13/14.6	4	g		
14.6	234	221	Le Havre (1st daylight)	1
14/15.6	337	223	Caen area	
	330	61	Rail	1
15.6	297	155	Boulogne	
15/16.6	227	119	Fouillard + Chatellerault	
	224	184	Rail	11
16/17.6	405	236	v	
	321	147	Sterkrade/Hotten ?	
17/18.6	317	196	Rail	1
	114	19	v	
19.6	30	19	Watten v	
20.6	20	17	Wizernes v	
21.6	322	142	v	
21/22.6	139	133	Wesseling	37
21/22.6	132	123	Scholven/Buer	8
22.6	234	119	v	
22/23.6	221	111	Rail	4
23/24.6	412	226	v	5
	207	203	Rail	2
24.6	321	166	v	
	18	16	Wizernes v	1
24/25.6	739	535	v	22
25.6	323	106	v	
	20	17	Siracourt v	
27.6	111	2	Mimoyecques v	
27/28.6	721	477	v	3
	223	214	Rail	4
28.6	111	2	Wizernes	
28/29.6	230	28	Rail	2
29.6	305	286	v	3
30.6	266	151	Villen-Bocage	1
	107	102	Oisemont	
30/1.7	118	118	Vierzon	14
1.7	328	6	v	
1 /2.7	6	6	g	
2.7	384	374	v	
4.7	328	6	v	
	19	17	v St-Leu-d' Esserent	
4/5.7 246	231		v	13

	287	282	Rail	14
5/6.7	542	321	v	4
	154	154	Dijon	
6.7	551	210	v	
7.7	467	283	Caen area	1
7/8.7	212	208	St-Leu-d'Esserent	29
	128	123	Vaires	
9.7	347	120	v	1
10.7	223	213	Nucort	
10/11.7	6	6	g	
11.7	32	26	Gapennes v	
12.7	222	46	v	18
	159	153	Vaires	
12/13.7	385	378	Rail	10
	230	17	v	
13.7	13	13	v	
14.7	19	19	v, St-Philibert-Ferme	
14/15.7	253	242	Rail	7
	115	4	v	
15.7	53	47	Nucort v	
15/16.7	234	58	v	
	229	222	Rail	3
	6	6	g	1
16.7	33	30	St-Philibert-Ferme v	
17.7	132	20	v	
18.7	942	667	Caen (Op Goodwood)	1
	110	6	Vaires	
18/19.7	194	77	Wesseling	
	170	157	Scholven/Buer	4
	263	253	Rail	26
	62	2	Acquet	
19.7	144	132	v	
20.7	369	174	v	1
20/21.7	317	302	Courtrai	9
	166	4	Bottrop	1
	158	147	Homberg	20
	87	23	v	
21.7	52	2	Anderbeck v	
21/22.7	6	6	g	
22.7	60	48	v	
22/23.7	6	6	g	
23.7	60	48	v	
23/24.7	629	519	Kiel	4
	119	14	Donges	
	2	v		
	6	6	g	1
24.7	36	28	v	
24/25.7	614	461	Stuttgart	17
	113	104	Donges	3
	112	2	Ferfay v	
25.7	100	94	St-Cyr	1
	93	81	v	
25/26.7	550	412	Stuttgart	8
	135	11	Wanne-Eickel	
	51	36	v	
26/27.7	187	178	Givors	4
	6	6	g	
27.7	72	36	v	

28/29.7	496	494	Stuttgart	39
	307	106	Hamburg	4
	119	?	Fore de Nieppe	
30.7	692	462	Villers Bocage-Caumont	4
31.7	131	127	Joigny-La-Roche	1
	103	97	Rilly-La-Montage	2
	57	52	Le Havre	1
31/1.8	202	104	v	1
1.8	777	385	v	
2.8	394	234	v	2
	54	54	Le Havre	1
3.8	114	601	v	6
4.8	291	112	v	2
	288	288	Bec-d'Ambes +Pauillac	
	30	27	Etaples	
5.8	742	257	v	
	39	31	v	
	306	306	Oil storage	1
	17	15	Brest	1
	14	14	Etaples	
6.8	222	107	v	3
	62	6	Hazelbrouck	
	15	12	Lorient	
6/7.8	10	10	Spec Op	
7.8	27	25	Lorient	
7/8.8	1019	614	Normandy Battle	10
8.8	202	49	Foret de Chantilly	
8/9.8	180	170	Oil storage	1
9.8	172	23	v	
9.8	16	8	Foret De Mormal	
	31	29	La Pallice	
9/10.8	311	171	v	
	190	176	Foert De Challerault	2
	10	10	g	
10.8	103	98	Dugny	
	80	60	Ferme-Du-Forestal	
10/11.8	215	109	Oil storage	
	124	20	Dijon	
	12	12	g	
	3	3	Bremen	
11.8	459	270	Rail storage	
	56	53	Bordeaux, La Pallice	
1/12.8	189	179	Givors	
	6	6	g	
12.8	117	16	Foret de Montrichard	
	68	68	U-boat pens	
12/13.8	379	242	Brunswick	17
	297	191	Russelheim	13
	144	91	Falaise	
	14	10	g	
13.8	29	28	U-boat pens	1
	15	15	Bordeaux	1
14.8	805	411	Normandy Battle/Falaise	2
	159	155	Brest	2
14/15.8	6	6	g	
15.8	1004	599	Nt Ftr airfields	3
16.8	26	25	La Pallice	
16/17.8	46	461	Stettin	5
	348	195	Kiel	2

	?	?	g	2
18.8	169	158	L'Isle-Adam	1
	69	64	Bordeaux	
	32	16	v	2
	23	23	La Pallice	
18/19.8	288	216	Bremen	1
	234	10	Sterkrade	1
	144	18	Connantre	
	113	108	Ertvelde Rieme	
19.8	52	52	La Pallice	
24.8	23	22	Ijmuiden	
25.8	161	16	v	1
25/26.8	412	412	Russelheim	15
	196	190	Darmstadt	7
	334	32	Brest	1
26/27.8	382	372	Kiel	17
	174	17	Konigsberg	4
	?	?	g	5
27.8	243	13	Hamburg	
	226	40	Mimoyecques	
	25	24	Brest	
28.8	150	48	v	1
29/30.8	403	402	Stettin	23
	189	189	Konigsberg	15
	31	31	g	1
31.8	601	418	v	6
1.9	121	9	v	
2.9	67	67	Brest	
3.9	675	348	Airfields	
5.9	348	313	Le Havre	
	66	60	Brest	
6.9	344	311	Le Havre	
	181	76	Emden	1
8.9	333	304	Le Havre	2
9.9	272	22	v	
9/10.9	137	113	Monchengladbach	
10.9	992	521	Le Havre	
10/11.9	2	2	g	
11.9	218	103	Le Havre	
	379	154	Oil plants	2
11/12.9	240	226	Darmstadt	12
	76	?	g	3
12.9	412	75	Oil plants	4
	124	5	Munster	
12/13.9	387	378	Frankfurt	17
	217	204	Stuttgart	4
13.9	140	28	Gelsenkirchen	
	118	20	Osnabruck	
14.9	184	51	Willhelmshaven	
	45	35	Wassenar	
15.9	38	38	Tirpitz	
15/16.9	490	310	Kiel	2
	68	?	g	
16/17.9	282	254	Op Market Garden	2
17.9	762	370	Boulogne	1
	132	112	Op Market Garden	
	32	27	Eikenhorst	
17/18.9	243	?	Op Market Garden	
18.9	74	34	Walcheren	

18/19.9	213	206	Bremerhaven	1
	4	4	g	
19.9	56	28	Walcheren	
19/20.9	237	227	Monchengladbach	4
20.9	646	437	Calais	1
23.9	50	6	Walcheren	
23/24.9	549	378	Neuss	5
	141	136	Dortmund-Ems Canal	14
	113	107	Munster/Handorf	1
24.9	188	101	Calais	7
25.9	872	430	Calais	
26.9	722	388	Calais	2
26/27.9	237	226	Karlsruhe	2
27.9	341	222	Calais	1
	175	71	Bottrop	
	171	21	Sterkrade	
27/28.9	227	217	Kaiserslauten	1
28.9	494	230	Calais area	
29/30.9	15	15	g	
30.9	139	21	Sterkrade	
	136	25	Bottrop	
3.10	259	252	Walcheren	
4.10	140	47	Bergen	1
4/5.10	47	47	g	2
5.10	228	227	Wilhelmshaven	1
5/6.10	551	531	Saarbrucken	3
6.10	320	46	Oil plants	2
6/7.10	523	247	Dortmund	2
	253	246	Bremen	5
7.10	351	90	Kleve	
	350	340	Emmerich	3
	123	121	Walcheren	
	13	13	Kembs dam	2
9/10.10	435	40	Bochum	1
11.10	18	160	Ft Frederick Hendrik	
	115	115	Breskens	1
	63	61	Walcheren	
12.10	137	111	Wanne-Eickel	
	96	86	Breskens	
14.10	1013	519	Duisburg	13
14/15.10	1005	498	v	5
	24	233	Brunswick	1
15.10	18	18	Sorpe Dam	
15/16.10	506	241	Willhelmshaven	
	15	15	g	2
17.10	49	47	Walcheren	
18.10	128	128	Bonn	1
19/20.10	583	565	Stuttgart	6
	270	263	Nuremberg	2
21.10	75	75	Walcheren	1
21/22.10	263	21	Hannover	
22.10	100	100	Neuss	
22/23.10	20	20	g	
23.10	112	112	Walcheren	4
23/24.10	1055	561	Essen	5
24/25.10	25	25	g	
25.10	771	508	Essen	2
	243	32	Homberg	
26.10	105	105	Leverkusen	
26/17.10	10	10	g	1
28.10	723	428	Cologne	3
	277	86	Walcheren	1
28/29.10	244	237	Bergen	3
	14	14	g	
29.10	358	194	Walcheren	1
	37	37	Tirpitz	1
30.10	110	102	Walcheren	
	102	102	Wesseling	
30/31.10	90	435	Cologne	
31.10	101	101	Bottrop	1
31/1.11	493	331	Cologne	2
1.11	242	226	Homberg	1
1/2.11	288	74	Oberhausen	1
2.11	184	184	Homberg	5
2/3.11	992	561	Dusseldorf	8
4.11	176	176	Solingen	4
4/5.11	749	336	Bochum	5
	176	174	D-Ems canal	3
5.11	173	173	Solingen	1
6.11	738	324	Gelsenkirchen	3
6/7.11	242	235	Mitteland canal	10
	128	128	Koblenz	2
	12	12	g	
8.11	136	136	Homberg	1
9.11	277	256	Wanne-Eickel	2
11.11	122	122	Castrop-Rauxel	
11/12.11	245	23	Harburg	7
	228	209	Dortmund	
	26	26	g	
12.11	31	31	Tirpitz	1
15.11	177	177	Dortmund	2
16.11	498	485	Duren	3
	508	413	Julich	
	182	182	Heinsberg	1
18.11	479	94	Munster	
18/19.11	309	285	Wanne-Eickel	1
20.11	183	183	Homberg	5
20/21.11	43	43	Koblenz	
21.11	160	160	Homberg	3
21/22.11	283	274	Aschaffenburg	2
	273	79	Castrop-Rauxel	
	270	18	Sterkrade	
	144	13	Mitteland canel	2
	128	123	D-Ems canal	
	18	18	g	1
22/23.11	178	171	Trondheim	2
23.11	168	168	Gelsenkirchen	1
26.11	75	75	Fulda	
26/27.11	278	270	Munich	1
27.11	169	169	Cologne	1
27/28.11	351	341	Freiburg	1
	290	102	Neuss	
	12	12	g	
28/29.11	316	32	Essen	
	153	153	Neuss	
29.11	311	294	Dortmund	6
30.11	60	60	Bottrop	
	60	60	Osterfeld	2

30/1.12	576	126	Duisburg	
2.12	93	93	Dortmund	
2/3.12	504	87	Hagen	1
3.12	187	183	Heimbach	
4.12	160	160	Oberhausen	1
	30	27	Urft dam	
4/5.12	535	369	Karlsruhe	1
	292	282	Heilbronn	12
5.12	94	94	Hamm	
	56	56	Schwammenauldam	
5/6.12	497	100	Soest	
6/7.12	487	475	Leuna	5
	453	72	Osnabruck	1
	265	255	Giessen	8
8.12	205	205	Urft dam	1
	163	163	Duisburg	
11.12	238	233	Urft dam	1
11.12	150	150	Osterfeld	1
12.12	140	140	Witten	8
12/13.12	540	349	Essen	6
13/14.12	59	52	Oslo fjord	
	10	10	g	
15.12	138	138	Siegen	
	17	17	Ijmuiden	
15/16.12	341	327	Ludwigshafen	1
	15	15	g	1
16.12	108	108	Siegen	1
17/18.12	523	81	Duisburg	
	330	317	Ulm	2
	288	280	Munich	4
18/19.12	236	23	Gdynia	4
	14	14	g	
19.12	32	32	Trier	
19/20.12	12	12	g	
21.12	113	113	Trier	
21/22.12	208	207	Politz	8
	136	67	Cologne	
	114	97	Bonn	
	30	30	g	
22/23.12	168	166	Koblenz	
	106	14	Bingen	1
23.12	153	153	Trier	1
	30	27	Cologne	6
24.12	338	79	Airfields	2
24/25.12	104	104	Hangelar	1
	102	97	Cologne	5
26.12	294	146	St Vith	
27.12	211	200	Rheydt	1
27/28.12	28	66	Opladen	2
28.12	167	167	Cologne	
28/29.12	186	129	Monchengladbach	
	178	162	Bonn	1
	68	67	Oslo Fjord	
	11	11	g	
29.12	277	107	Koblenz	
	16	16	Rotterdam	
29/30.12	346	324	Scholven	4
	197	24	Troisdorf	
30.12	13	13	Ijmuiden	
30/31.12	470	93	Cologne	1
	166	154	Houffalize	1
	11	11	g	
31.12	155	155	Vohwinkel	2
31/1.1.45	166	149	Osterfeld	2
	28	28	Oslo Fjord	1
	10	10	g	1
1945				
1.1	104	102	D-Ems canal	2
*VC				
1/2.1	157	152	Mitteland canal	
	146	146	Vohwinkel	1
	139	18	Dortmund	
2/3.1	524	514	Nuremberg	4
	389	22	Ludwigshafen	
3.1	99	99	Dortmund + Castrop-Rauxel	1
4/5.1	354	347	Royan	4
5.1	160	160	Ludwigshafen	2
5/6.1	664	310	Hannover	8
	140	131	Houffalize	2
6/7.1	482	154	Hanan	2
	147	147	Neuss	1
	49	49	g	2
7/8.1	654	645	Munich	11
11.1	152	152	Krefeld	
12.1	33	32	Bergen	4
13.1	158	158	Saarbrucken	1
13/14.1	274	20	v	
	225	218	Politz	2
	10	10	g	
14.1	134	134	Saarbrucken	
14/15.1	587	573	Leuna	10
	151	3	Grevenbroich	
	115	3	Dulmen	
	10	10	g	
15.1	82	82	Recklinghausen	
	63	53	Bochum	
16/17.1	371	44	Magdeburg	
	328	328	Zeitz	10
	237	231	Brux	1
	138	138	Wanne-Eickel	1
	31	8	g	
22/23.1	302	286	Duisburg	2
	152	29	Gelsenkirchen	
28.1	153	153	Cologne	4
28/29.2	602	258	Stuttgart	6
	6	6	g	
29.1	148	148	Krefeld	
1.2	160	160	Monchengladbach	
1/2.2	396	382	Ludwigshaven	6
	340	40	Mainz	
	282	271	Siegen	3
2/3.2	507	495	Wiesbaden	3
	323	27	Wanne-Eickel	
	261	250	Karlsruhe	14
3.2	36	36	Ijmuiden	

3/4.2	210	192	Bottrop	8
	149	149	Dortmund	4
4/5.2	238	20	Bonn	3
	123	11	Osterfeld	
	120	12	Gesenkirchen	
	27	15	g	
5/6.2	35	35	Rail	
7.2	100	100	Wanne - Eickel	1
7/8.	464	156	Goch	
	305	295	Kleve	1
	188	177	Dortmund - Ems	3
	45	30	g	
8.2	15	1	Ijmuiden	
8/9.2.	482	475	Pölitz	12
	228	8	Wanne - Eickel	
	151	151	Krefeld	2
	10	10	g	
13/14.2	805	796	Dresden	8
	368	34	Böhlen	
14.2	36	36	Rail	1
14/15.2	717	499	Chemnitz	8
	232	224	Rositz	4
	95	95	Heligoland	
	54	30	g	1
15/16.2	55	37	g	
16.2	100	100	Wesel	
17.2	298	27	Wesel	
18.2	160	160	Wesel	
18/19.2	25	21	g	2
19/20.2	260	254	Böhlen	
20/21.2	528	514	Dortmund	14
	173	6	Düsseldorf	1
	128	6	Monheim	
	165	154	Mitteland Canal	
21/22.2	373	362	Duisburg	7
	349	36	Worms	1
	177	165	Mitteland Canal	9
22.2	167	167	Oil	1
22/23.2	35	3	Rail	
23.2	342	27	Essen	
	133	133	Gelsenkirchen	
23/24.2	380	367	Pforzheim	12
	83	73	Horten	1
	22	22	g	
24.2	340	26	Kamen	
	170	166	Dortmund - Ems	
24/25.2	35	3	g	
25.2	153	153	Kamen	1
26.2	149	149	Dortmund	
27.2	458	131	Mainz	
	149	149	Gelsenkirchen	1
28.2	156	156	Gelsenkirchen	
1.3	478	372	Mannheim	3
	151	151	Kamen	
2.3	858	531	Cologne	6
2/3.3	10	?	g	
3/4.3	234	21	Kamen	
	222	212	Dortmund - Ems	7
	31	31	g	1

4.3	128	128	Wanne - Eickel	
5.3	170	170	Gelsenkirchen	1
5/6.3	760	498	Chemnitz	14
	258	248	Böhlen	4
6.3	119	119	Salzbergen	1
6/7.3	198	191	Sassnitz	1
	138	87	Wesel	
	15	15	g	
718.3	531	526	Dessau	18
	281	25	Hemmingstedt	1
	241	234	Harburg	14
	20	5	g	
8/9.3	312	62	Hamburg	
	276	262	Kassel	
	37	14	g	
9.3	159	159	Datteln	1
	23	21	Bielefeld	
10.3	155	155	Scholuen/Buer	
11.3	1079	750	Essen	3
11/12.3	22	22	g	
12.3	1108	748	Dortmund	2
12/13.3	19	16	g	3
13.3	354	24	Wuppertal	
	38	38	Rail	
13/14.3	227	195	Oil	1
14.3	169	169	Oil	1
	33	32	Rail	
14/15.3	255	244	Lützkendorf	18
	230	121	Zweibrucken	
	161	23	Homberg	
15.3	188	14	Oil	
	16	16	Rail	
15/16.3	267	134	Hagen	6
	265	257	Misburg	4
16/17.3	293	277	Nuremburg	24
	236	225	Würzburg	6
	24	12	g	
17.3	167	167	Oil	
17/18.3	95	66	N.France	
18.3	100	100	Oil	
18/19.3	324	45	Witten	1
	285	277	Hanau	1
19.3	79	79	Gelsenkirchen	
	37	37	Rail	
20.3	153	16	Recklinghausen	
	113	113	Rail	
20/21.3	235	224	Böhlen	9
	166	166	Hemmingstedt	1
	12	12	Halle	1
21.3	178			16
			Rheine	1
	160	160	Münster	3
	139	133	Bremen	
	20	20	Rail	1
21/22.3	159	151	Hamburg	4
	143	131	Bochum	1
22.3	235	227	Hildesheim	4
	130	12	Dülmen	
	124	12	Dorsten	

	100	100	Bocholt		9.4	57	57	Hamburg	2
	102	102	Rail		9/10.4	599	591	Kiel	3
22/23.3	29	21	g			98	70	g	
23.3	128	128	Rail	2	10.4	230	134	Leipzig	1
	80	80	Wesel		10/11.4	315	307	Plauen	
23/24.3	218	195	Wesel			95	76	Leipzig	7
24/3	177	16	Sterkrade		11.4	143	14	Nuremberg	
	175	16	Gladbeck			114	14	Bayreuth	
	185	173	Oil	3	13.4	34	34	Swinemüde	
25.3	175	14	Münster		13/14.4	482	37	Kiel	2
	156	14	Osnabruck			109	82	g	
	275	267	Hannover	1	15.4	20	20	Swinemunde	
25/26.3	9	1	Hague		14/15.4	512	500	Potsdam	1
27.3	276	268	Paderborn			28	24	Cuxhaven	
	150	150	Hamm		16.4	18	18	Swinemunde	1
	115	115	Farge		16/17.4	233	222	Pilsen	1
29.3	130	130	Salzgitter		17/18.4	101	90	Cham	
31.3	469	361	Hamburg	8	18.4	969	617	Heligoland	
3.4	255	247	Nordhausen	2	18/19.4	123	114	Komotau	
314.4	9	9	g		19.4	49	49	Munich	
4.4	244	243	Nordhausen	1		36	36	Heligoland	
4/5.4	341	327	Leuna	2	20.4	100	100	Regensburg	1
	327	36	Harburg	2	21/22.4	20	20	g	
	272	258	Lützkendorf	6	22.4	767	651	Bremen	2
	30	30	g	3	23.4	148	148	Flensburg	
6.4	55	54	Ijmuiden		24.4	110	110	Bad Oldesloe	
7.4	17	15	Ijmuiden		24/25.4	37	7	Pow camps	
718.4	186	175	Molbis		25.4	482	158	Wangerooge	2
8/9.4	440	160	Hamburg	3		375	359	Berchtesgaten	2
	242	231	Lützkendorf	6	25/26.4	119	107	Tonsberg	1

Index